Classics In
Child Development

Classics In
Child Development

Advisory Editors

JUDITH KRIEGER GARDNER
HOWARD GARDNER

Editorial Board

Wayne Dennis
Jerome Kagan
Sheldon White

BIOGRAPHIES OF CHILD DEVELOPMENT

THE MENTAL GROWTH CAREERS OF EIGHTY-FOUR INFANTS AND CHILDREN

Part One by
ARNOLD GESELL

Part Two by
CATHERINE S. AMATRUDA
BURTON M. CASTNER
HELEN THOMPSON

ARNO PRESS

A New York Times Company

New York — 1975

Reprint Edition 1975 by Arno Press Inc.

Reprinted from a copy in
    The Newark Public Library

Classics in Child Development
ISBN for complete set: 0-405-06450-0
See last pages of this volume for titles.

Manufactured in the United States of America

Library of Congress Cataloging in Publication Data

Gesell, Arnold Lucius, 1880-1961.
    Biographies of child development.

    (Classics in child development)
    Reprint of the ed. published by P. B. Hoeber, New
York.
    Includes index.
    1. Child study. 2. Intellect. I. Title.
II. Series.
BF431.G45 1975   155.4'13   74-21409
    ISBN 0-405-06461-6

BIOGRAPHIES OF
CHILD DEVELOPMENT

BIOGRAPHIES OF
CHILD DEVELOPMENT

*THE MENTAL GROWTH CAREERS OF
EIGHTY-FOUR INFANTS AND CHILDREN*

A Ten-Year Study from the Clinic of Child
Development at Yale University

Part One by
ARNOLD GESELL, PH.D., M.D.

Part Two by
CATHERINE S. AMATRUDA, M.D.
BURTON M. CASTNER, PH.D.
HELEN THOMPSON, PH.D.

PAUL B. HOEBER, INC
MEDICAL BOOK DEPARTMENT OF HARPER & BROTHERS
NEW YORK   LONDON

FOREWORD

THE mind grows. To understand the individuality of patterns of mental growth we must have a psycho-biographic interest in the growth careers of individual children. This book assembles concrete studies of individual differences in the patterning of early behavior development.

These studies are presented as a joint product of the members of the staff of the Yale Clinic of Child Development. Each report carries the name of the examiner chiefly concerned with the original examinations or final interpretations. A series of thirty cases published ten years ago is reviewed in Part One to determine the consistency of the after careers with the early estimates of developmental status.

Occasionally more than one examiner contributed to the series of developmental examinations of a given case. For some of the early examinations we are indebted to Miss Elizabeth Evans Lord, Ph.D., Miss Ruth W. Washburn, Ph.D., and Dr. M. C. Putnam, formerly on the staff of the Clinic. We are also especially indebted to Mrs. Louise B. Ames, Assistant in Research, for her help in the editorial organization of the case reports.

The growth graphs in Part One are continuations of graphs which were first published in 1928 in a volume entitled *Infancy and Human Growth.** These graphs depict, in terms of maturity levels, the early mental growth and the growth which has taken place in the subsequent decade. A broken vertical line separates the first series of reported examinations, from the later follow-up series.

The reports in the present volume deal with a wide diversity of children, presenting many different varieties of be-

* Macmillan Company.

v

havior development. Each case is discussed in terms of its implications for a scientific, diagnostic understanding of the growth process. Major attention is given to objective and demonstrable tokens of growth, which can be normatively appraised. But emotional and personality factors which influence behavior are also stressed.

The individual reports are based upon voluminous data, but they are not presented with the comprehensiveness of complete case studies. The confidence in which the original clinical records are held is fully protected; and the identity of the children is entirely concealed.

Each individual report aims at succinctness and is directed toward specific conclusions and queries. We believe the reader will welcome this brevity in spite of recognized shortcomings. It is well known that much case-study literature remains unread and ineffective because the significance of individual cases is obscured by a mass of detail, undifferentiated in emphasis.

At the end of the book will be found an Addendum which includes references to publications detailing the methods and materials used in the developmental examinations of infants and young children. Readers who wish to become more concretely acquainted with the diagnostic procedures may consult these references.

The arrangement and general plan of the present volume are discussed in the Introductory Chapter. In selecting eighty-four cases from the thousands in our files, we have chosen those which have been most instructive to us as examiners. These "cases" represent individual young persons, with whose careers we have had a cumulative contact which has yielded biographic, developmental data. In reviewing these data, we have subjected ourselves to self-criticism, so that the reader may have some benefit from our experience and from our unusual opportunity to study the early stages of mental growth careers.

This opportunity has depended upon the facilities of a

university clinic which has worked in close association with other medical and community agencies. The underlying re-searches were supported by generous grants of The Laura Spelman Rockefeller Memorial and The Rockefeller Foun-dation.

CONTENTS

PART ONE

by

Arnold Gesell

ix

PART TWO

by

Catherine S. Amatruda, Burton M. Castner, and Helen Thompson

CONTENTS

LIST OF ILLUSTRATIONS

GROWTH GRAPHS

PART ONE

CHAPTER I

INTRODUCTION: A RETROSPECTIVE SURVEY
OF GROWTH CAREERS

WITHIN the last twenty-five years some 10,000 infants and children have been examined by the staff of the Yale Clinic of Child Development. A large proportion of these children were studied at repeated intervals, and the records of examinations and interviews now in our files number many thousands. The present volume represents an effort to share some of the teachings of these clinical records with others who are interested in the practical and theoretical problems of child management.

The tide of young humanity which has flowed through the Clinic has been unique in several respects: in the large number of infants and pre-school children; in the variety and the appealing nature of the conditions presented. All types and degrees of development have come for diagnosis, observation, guidance, or treatment, ranging from profound disability and defect to exceptional giftedness and sure promise of eminence in maturity. The children have come from every walk of life—from the squalor of poverty to superior homes. A large proportion have come from no homes at all, for we have given special attention to dependent, neglected, and uncared-for children, prior to foster home placement and adoption.

Infants and children have been referred by over a score of social agencies, parents, physicians, and teachers, by hospitals, schools, and child-caring institutions. The reasons for referral are too numerous to list; a few of them as formulated by parents and teachers are picturesque; others are little

3

short of tragic; still others are not depressing at all, and simply express a desire to bring about the best possible social and educational adjustment of relatively normal (or superior) children in home or community situations. Many of the diagnostic and advisory problems, however, have had a distinctly medical aspect; they were concerned with the developmental status of children suffering from sensory and motor handicaps and various forms of physical defect and disease. Some of the children presented no specific problem but came at periodic intervals on a basis of developmental supervision, or for normative studies of their behavior development.

The Clinic has always operated entirely under university auspices, so that service and research have been maintained in intimate and interacting relationships. Frequently the investigatory interest has been shared with and even stimulated by the parents themselves. And as for the children, including the infants, they have built up an enormous mass of evidence testifying to their readiness to respond to any reasonable demand that we might make of them, whether they were bright or dull, timid or aggressive, speechless or communicative, twelve weeks old or twelve years old.

One capacity all of these varied children had in common: the capacity of growth. Even the least endowed retained some growth potentialities. Whether the potentialities were great or small, symmetric or impaired, it was our clinical task and our scientific interest to appraise the growth capacity of each child. It is a fortunate circumstance that the bulk of our clinical records were made by a small, continuous group of examiners who have acquired a cumulative familiarity with many of the children and have maintained follow-up contacts over a period of years. As a result, each of us on the staff has a sizeable collection of "cases" which bristle with special interest, by reason of numerous personal associations, growing out of repeated follow-up contacts. Often the Clinic file folder has expanded to the dimensions of a thick volume—a well-thumbed volume, and even the file number takes on a halo of personal identity.

It has seemed to us impractical and even unprofitable to subject all these varied clinical records to statistical analysis. The variables are too numerous and diversified to be crowded into homogeneous categories. It is not the purpose of the present volume to summarize the totality of records; but rather, to select from the entire array some of those which have had special significance from the standpoint of clinical application or of developmental psychology.

The basis of selection has been the instructiveness of the record. The examiners have selected cases which have thrown light on the trends and variabilities of behavior development, or which have exposed the difficulties of diagnosis.

This method of selection has resulted in an uneven distribution which tends to exaggerate the frequency of cases with irregular or atypical development. The reader will please understand that we have presented these cases in a desire to call attention to diagnostic pitfalls and hazards. We have had to exercise self criticism in order to select the most significant cases, and to profit from their instruction. But overemphasis of exceptional cases will also lead to error. The serious student need not be misled by apparent contradictions, and he will not convert exceptions into general rules.

Run-of-the-mine cases do not figure strongly in this volume. Our aim is to present a wide diversity of specimens of growth careers. Among these specimens we have included several which are quite unusual and which are not encountered in ordinary clinical work. They are, however, especially instructive because, as Goethe remarked, Nature reveals her secrets in rare moments of abnormality. In such unusual and yet not altogether aberrant anomalies as hemihypertrophy and *pubertas praecox,* Nature has virtually set up experiments in the physiology of development—experiments which afford glimpses into the mechanics of development. Through these experiments we also gain an appreciation of the ma-

turational factors which confer stability and characteristicness upon growth careers. In cerebral palsies and in cretinism
we get a deepened understanding of the modifiable and non-
modifiable aspects of growth. A few cases of idiocy are included, because they disclose significant integrating and stabilizing forces which operate even in extreme reductions of
growth potentiality. The emphasis throughout is not on
abilities as such, but on the underlying growth process. The
developmental diagnosis of infant behavior becomes a worse
than worthless enterprize if the dynamics of that process are
overlooked.

The present volume divides itself naturally into two parts.
Part One deals with a group of cases which were first reported in a previous volume some ten years ago. These same
cases are reviewed on the basis of subsequent developmental
examinations and follow-up contacts. Bringing the earlier
summaries and the later findings into comparison enables us
to make comments concerning possibilities and limitations of
the developmental diagnosis of infant behavior. These possibilities are further discussed in a brief chapter dealing with
the general problems of appraisal of growth trends (Chapter
IV).

These chapters will serve as an introduction to the more
extended series of individual studies of growth careers assembled in Part Two. The latter series embraces both typical
and atypical forms of mental growth. Many of the cases are
concerned with social and guidance problems such as adoption, foster home care, reading disabilities, and school adjustments. A final chapter (Chapter VI) deals with The Individuality of Growth Careers and considers the significance
of personality factors in the patterning of behavior growth.

Throughout the text repeated reference is made to practical problems of diagnosis and prognosis. It is hoped that the
volume will therefore have value for those who are directly
engaged in clinical and guidance work. The subject-matter,

however, is also addressed to those who have a general inter-est in the psychology of development, and who may find in the concrete accounts of growth careers problems which in-vite reflection and further study. The teaching of human psychology has suffered from over-conventionalized textbook abstractions. If teachers in training and in service, if nurses and physicians are to acquire a vivid realization of the mind as a growing organism, they must become more concretely acquainted with the life histories of individual infants and children.

CHAPTER II

MENTAL GROWTH TRENDS

IN INFANCY AND TEN YEARS LATER

TEN years ago the senior author (A.G.) reported a summary of mental-growth studies of over one-hundred infants. All told, these studies were based on more than five-hundred developmental examinations made by him and his associates. Ninety of these studies were analyzed statistically as a group. Thirty-three additional cases, representing a wide range of variation, were individually summarized by means of growth graphs, and were discussed from the standpoint of both diagnosis and prognosis.[1]

Not without a sense of adventure (and of risk!) we recently assembled all of these individual case studies for further review, to determine to what extent the findings and predictions formulated during the period of infancy were consistent with the diagnoses of a decade later. Fortunately, in nearly all of these cases we have been able to secure sufficient follow-up data to establish a comparison. Some of the cases are more fully documented than others. One case dropped completely out of sight; in two instances death intervened; but data are available for a total of thirty cases.

These cases will now be discussed informally as a separate series and serve as an introduction to the major series of new studies presented in Part Two of this volume. Growth graphs and excerpts from the case summaries of ten years ago are reproduced to bring into clearer evidence the follow-up find-

[1] Gesell, Arnold: *Infancy and Human Growth*. N. Y., Macmillan, 1928, pp. xvii + 418. (See especially Chapters VII-XVI.)

ings. To facilitate comparisons, the denomination of the cases and the order of presentation correspond to the original 1928 eport.

Since in this series of cases we are dealing with a long reach of years, chief emphasis will be placed upon the general trend and tempo of development. Here as elsewhere we shall use the developmental quotient (D.Q.) as a convenient index of current developmental rate, rather than as a designation of the actual or latent caliber of the individual. This caliber and the ultimate developmental outlook must always be subject to clinical appraisal and interpretive qualifications. Furthermore, it will be understood that the index of current developmental rate (D.Q.) is a conventional derivation based upon a determination of maturity level by the Yale norms up to the age of 6 years, as the I.Q. at later ages is based upon a measurement of mental age by the Stanford-Binet scale.

With such qualifications, we use the concept of the constancy of the developmental rate not as a law which is established, but as an *assumption which is made for expository convenience*, one which needs critical correction at every turn when practical clinical responsibilities are involved. When examined in detail, the developmental complex proves to be very intricate. In the very nature of things, individuality makes it impossible for all the components of behavior (postural, perceptual, adaptive, language and social) to mature in lock step along an unbroken front. At any given moment the margin of advance is an irregular rather than a smooth line. Furthermore, over a long series of moments the margin shows fluctuations, possibly rhythmic in character. The tide of behavior development does not move erratically, but it moves unevenly. In vague analogy we may picture surface currents, under currents, apparent back flows, eddies, pools, in the ceaseless streaming of morphogenetic events, which we call mental growth.

With such admissions, the concept of constancy of developmental rate seems utterly naïve and unsophisticated. Nevertheless, in the present stage of methodology it is serv-iceable. It has expository value. Our normative criteria are based upon a hypothetical normative infant who passes through the ascending stages of development at a hypo-thetically constant rate. The very intricacy and integrative-ness of the growth complex, imparts to these criteria a high degree of indicativeness, because the deviations are self-limited in scope and frequency.

Each growth complex, to be sure, has its characteristic trend and tempo. We use the normative determinations to define and to direct a clinical judgment of status. A series of such determinations enables us to discern and to appraise a trend of development. Even a single determination clinically interpreted may have heavy prognostic import as to the prospective rate of development.

We are not, therefore, undertaking a critical discussion of the constancy of the intelligence quotient. Our clinical judg-ments of the cases reported were never based solely on de-velopmental quotients or intelligence quotients. We are sim-ply reviewing our own clinical appraisals in retrospect, and incidentally we shall expose the limitations as well as the positive aids of normative determinations. We are keenly aware that every child has a distinctive growth pattern; and in a recent publication[1] have gone to great lengths to affirm the importance of a genetic *analysis* of the growth status in terms of the various components of the growth complex. However, in the present primitive stage of our knowledge, undue insistence upon detailed analysis and upon the uni-versal tendency toward deviation would lead to pedantic and futile perfectionism. In the presence of clinical problems we are called upon to give reasonably brief characterizations of developmental *status,* and frequently for urgent practical

[1] Gesell, A., and Thompson, H., assisted by Amatruda, C. S.: *The Psychology of Early Growth, including norms of infant behavior and a method of genetic analysis.* N. Y., Macmillan, 1938, pp. ix + 290.

reasons, we are called upon to frame a judgment of developmental *outlook*. In some instances prognosis should be completely withheld; in other instances it must be cautiously
built up through successive examinations with increasing precision of formulation. In still other instances, a fairly precise
prognosis can be made with confidence on the basis of one
examination.

The present volume will give special weight to those cases
which reveal the hazards of prognosis. This emphasis should
not, however, conceal the fact that in actual clinical practice
the possibilities of constructive prediction, even with our
present diagnostic tools, are extremely wide and diversified.
The very complexity of the growth process is offset by a
stabilizing, integrating factor. It is this factor which creates
the opportunities for diagnosis and relatively accurate prognosis. In the rudimentary state of our methods and knowledge we must give relentless recognition to the pitfalls and
errors of diagnosis. In the following chapter, however, we
shall also insist upon the positive and less fallible aspects of
the developmental diagnosis of infant behavior. Ten years
of experience[1] with improved methods have sharpened our
caution, but have not dulled our faith in the possibilities of
clinical prediction. We would not greatly alter the faith as
expressed (and qualified) when we first reported, in 1928,
the series of cases reassembled in the following chapter:

. . . Atypical cases are not, of course, in any sense lawless or accidental; they simply are less familiar and do not yield as readily to
accustomed standards and procedures.

If we were in possession of a biometric diagnostic scale which
worked with automatic precision, a discussion of clinical prediction
would be superfluous; for then each individual measurement and each
group of measurements would denote a future as well as present behavior value. It is because we are so far removed from such Utopian

[1] It should be stated that some of the early developmental diagnoses reported
in the present volume were made before our monthly increment developmental
schedule had been completed. The present developmental schedules, based on
lunar months, were put into use in the Clinic in 1927.

perfection that emphasis must be placed on the importance of clinical experience and clinical method. There is no occasion, however, for complete diagnostic agnosticism! In spite of its obscurities and its ambiguities, infancy is prophetic. The child is not a creature of circumstance. He is part and parcel of the great stream of life. He is biologically father of the man. And the infant is father of the child. Adulthood is not added unto infancy; it inheres in infancy. Because of this inherent continuity in the life cycle, there is ample scope for progressive prediction in the consecutive study of infant behavior.

CHAPTER III

COMPARATIVE STUDIES OF EARLY AND LATER DEVELOPMENT IN THIRTY INFANTS AND CHILDREN

THIS chapter undertakes a re-survey of the growth ca-reers of thirty infants and children whose early behavior development was reported in a previous volume (1928). Our developmental studies were then in a more primitive stage, but in order to define the problems and the data, we attempted a quantitative presentation of the growth trends, by means of tables and growth graphs.

Ten years have elapsed since the original report. Numer-ous re-examinations and follow-up contacts have been made in the interval. To what extent did the early trends and tempos foreshadow those of subsequent years?

In order to facilitate comparison and to preserve the con-tinuity of the data, we shall review our thirty infants and children in the same order in which they were first presented, and we shall call them by the same names.

These names are initials seriated in alphabetic sequence. The growth studies are grouped as follows:

A. Normal and Retarded Development
   § 1. Child A.B.; § 2. Child B.C.; § 3. Child C.D.; § 4. Child D.E., E.F., F.G., G.H., H.I., I.J.
B. Acceleration and Superiority of Equipment
   § 5. Child J.K.; § 6. Child K.L.; § 7. Child L.M.; § 8. Child M.N.; § 9. Child N.O.; § 10. Child O.P.
C. Atypical and Pseudo-atypical Growth Complexes
   § 11. Child P.Q.; § 12. Child Q.R.; § 13. Child R.S.; § 14. Child S.T.; § 15. Child T.U.; § 16. Child V.W.

A. NORMAL AND RETARDED DEVELOPMENT

§ 1. A.B.
A Median Course of Mental Growth
(4 months—13 years)

This boy was presented in the first clinical series as representative of the most numerous group of infants, namely
those whose course of early development plots close to a
normative median curve. Excerpts from the original reports
which follow summarize his early status. Nine examinations
were made in the period from 4 months to 24 months.

Early status:

A.B. was first examined when he was 4 months old. He
made an excellent showing on the developmental schedule for
that age, scoring success on twenty-four out of a possible
twenty-six items. The notation made on the clinical record
at that time is interesting in the light of the eight subsequent
examinations: "Impression is very definitely one of fully
average endowment. Responses have not the quality of vividness or immediacy noted in certain cases where superiority
is suggested, though the quality of the attention is good and
the baby is normally reactive." This impression has been
steadily sustained by eight periodic examinations. He is now
2 years of age.

On the basis of these impressions a qualified forecast was ventured and formulated as follows: "Too little is known about the problem of mental growth to permit unqualified prediction; but it may be urged that from the developmental point of view this boy has had a great deal of chance to display either superior or inferior deviation in his growth characteristics. He has not done so. In a relative sense, he has undergone a very important part of his fundamental growth. The best general index of future development is attained development. His attainment has been consistently high average in quality and scope. And though he is but 2 years old, the eight examinations already made cover as much developmental ground as will an equal number of annual examinations in the next decade. It is certain that under ordinary circumstances this infant will not, as a youth, prove inferior in his general capacities."

Subsequent development:

The foregoing paragaph definitely poses questions of prognosis which have been partially answered by the lapse of time. A.B. was re-examined at the age of 31 months. At the age of 4 years he moved to a distant state. In spite of a prolonged illness he is now, at the age of 13 years, able to do satisfactory work in a public-school seventh grade. The trend of his development has definitely been toward a high average rather than an inferior level. He is an avid reader, and has shown skill in carving objects out of soap. The case is typical of many run-of-the-mine cases in which the developmental outlook can be safely forecast in broad and general terms. He also illustrates the limitations of forecast. We saw nothing in his behavior in infancy to suggest that he would be an adept sculptor of soap at the age of 13! This is not to say that methods will not some day be available for discovering sculpture-aptitude in the pre-school years. With improvements of technique, developmental diagnosis will become increasingly analytic; but the present series of case sketches will be chiefly confined to the general trends and tempo of mental growth. A.B. may be taken as an example of a numerous group who tend to cling near a median course of growth, with a tendency to exceed rather than to disappoint the implications of the developmental ratings made in infancy. He is now crossing the brink of the teens. To what extent his adolescence will introduce new tempos and trends into his growth remains in obscurity. The data of the present volume are for the most part limited to the periods of infancy, early childhood, and pre-adolescence.

§ 2. B.C.

Low Average Trend in Infancy; High Average Trend
in Later Childhood
(3 months—12 years)

This boy shows the most striking reversal of trend to be reported in the present series. Although he stands in bold relief as an exception, he clearly illustrates the importance of caution when the early genetic conditions are complicated. He was born out of wedlock by a mother who was less than 15 years of age, and who missed only two weeks of high-school attendance when the child was born. He was never seen by his mother and spent the whole first year in an institution. An excessive proportion of this year was spent in a supine position in a crib. In addition to institutionalization, he suffered from rickets and possibly from megacolon, a condition discovered several years later. There also was a probable but indeterminable factor of prematurity of birth. An eager young couple were anxious to adopt him and to give him every advantage, including a college education.

Early status:

Seven developmental examinations were made during the first year. The quotients fluctuated in the 80 to 85 zone. The following excerpts from the original records summarize our impressions at that time.

"Fortunately he is a 'normal' child. . . . But with regard to the question of college educability, the outlook has become increasingly dubious. He has maintained a steady pace of development, but it has been pitched consistently on a low-average level. The whole complex of mental growth has now assumed an import away from college educability rather than toward it. This statement is made for its descriptive value and not, of course, to suggest any rigid classification or procedure which would in any way prejudice his opportunities in life. It must, however, be recalled that the prospective adoptive parents did themselves formulate the criterion of college educability."

Our clinical records show that even in the early examinations we were impressed with the child's sociability and winning temperament. One note states, "Impossible to make a definite prognosis of development in the case of this baby after four examinations, because the clinical impression is so much obscured by physical conditions and by atypical environment. Quality of child's social response at the time of the fourth examination (as evidenced by response to mirror) so relatively mature as to make one unwilling to take too gloomy a view."

At the age of 1 year we found that B.C.'s behavior was consistently at a 10-month level and the following entry was made:

"Again we would say that the educational outlook is somewhat below the average and that he should not be adopted on the assumption that he will outgrow his retardation completely. We are unwilling, however, to venture an absolute prognosis because of certain social and attention qualities which are quite normal, and because he has lived for almost all of his life in an institutional environment and also because his mother apparently was of full average intelligence. Our

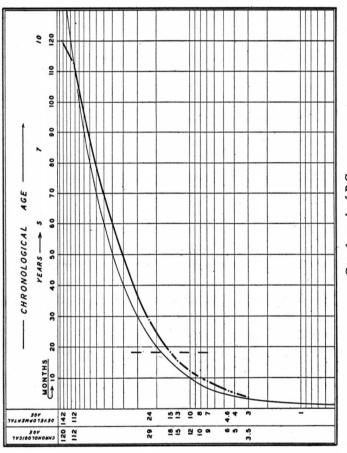

Growth graph of B.C.

record does not state whether he was prematurely born, and this would also influence to some extent the developmental outlook."

At the age of 1 year he was transferred to a good foster home. He was examined again at 15 months and at 18 months. Although he retained his attractive, responsive personality, there was no definite improvement in the behavior picture. He was not a full average, alert, perceptive, exploring 18-month run-about.

Subsequent development:

At the age of 29 months he still presented a picture of low average intelligence. His development was apparently proceeding at the former slightly retarded rate. The clinical note on the examination at 29 months of age summarizes as follows.

"The present level cannot, with all possible allowance, be considered as being above 24 months and the developmental quotient appears again between 80 and 85. The successes above 24 months are in the fields of language and personality; and there is, therefore, ground for assuming that they have been largely influenced by environmental factors. The failures at and below the 24-month level, while possibly one or two may have been due to inadequate attention and obedience to directions, are practically all in the field of adaptive behavior, and this fact may be significant in considering the question of prognosis. Personality is still fairly attractive."

At the age of 9 years and 3 months the picture has decisively changed. It now appears that the slight relative acceleration in the fields of language and personal-social behavior were symptoms of a general acceleration which has now brought him to at least a high average level of performance in all fields of behavior. He has a 10-year vocabulary and earns an intelligence quotient over 100.

At the age of 12 years he maintains this gain. His Stanford-Binet mental age is 13 years 10 months; his I.Q., 115. He now gives evidence of a mental level at the highest average range or better. He is in the eighth grade at school. His reading is of eighth-grade quality and spelling satisfactory for his age and grade. His "college educability" is much less in doubt, although he has shown some weaknesses in making adjustments with other boys. At the Clinic he was courteous, cooperative, poised, his behavior suggesting the type of child who is more at home with adults than with other children.

Comment:

In retrospect, this case suggests the presence of deep-seated retarding factors which remained obscure in infancy and which even now are none too clear. It seems probable that an undiagnosed intestinal condition, combined with an institutional environment and the juvenility of his mother, had a depressing effect on the early rate of mental growth. Ordinarily such retarding conditions come to light before the second year and due allowance can be made for them. Not so in the present instance. The potentially normal rate did not assert itself until about the age of 3 years.

It is noteworthy, however, that we were repeatedly led to formulate reservations, even though the rate of development was shown to be consistently slow on successive examinations. We recognized behavior symptoms which were definitely "normal" and promising; although we did not expect such a complete reversal of trend. The engaging and reactive personality was discovered on the early examinations.

At 4.5 months special note was made of a high degree of responsiveness. He laughed readily and his attention was recorded as excellent. At 5 months he was again responsive, but displayed an abnormally preoccupied inspection of his hand. At 18 months he showed moderately persistent attention in the performance-box situations; he had a vocabulary of seven words and talked in jargon. It appears now that we should have weighted more heavily these favorable expressions of adaptive, language, and social behavior. They were indicators of potentialities which had not yet come completely to the surface. When the retarding forces—probably principally somatic—were lessened, these potentialities were realized. Mental growth tends toward such optimal realization.

This does not mean, however, that winning personality traits in childhood insure a full average level of development. The case of C.D. which follows next resembles superficially that of B.C. For a while we thought that the course of intellectual development would be similar in these two children. But time has revealed no reversals in C.D. Rather it has shown a significant consistency of trend over a period of fifteen years.

§ 3. C.D.
Consistent Mild Retardation, with Early Manifestation of Individuality
(9 months—15 years)

In contrast to the case of B.C. just summarized, this girl, C.D., presents a remarkably consistent mental growth trend at a borderline or low average level. In resemblance to B.C., she gave predictive indications of her individuality at a very early age.

This case is one of the most completely documented in our files. C.D. came to our attention at the age of 9 months, when our clinical procedures were first being applied to prospective adoption infants. We regarded her then as an excellent test case to determine the prognostic value of our developmental estimates. We followed her development with special interest. Six developmental examinations were made prior to the age of 4 years. The results of these have already been plotted and reported. Since then, we have made seven more follow-up examinations, the last at the age of 15 years. The developmental story briefly summarized below has proved to be highly consistent.

Early status:

At the age of 9 months, C.D. had every outward appearance of being a normal infant, in countenance, in responsiveness, and general reactiveness. Indeed, her amiable personality cast a spell and consistently exhibited traits which tended to conceal her fundamental limitations. On the developmental examination, however, these limitations were revealed. She rated coherently at the 6-month level.

Was this retardation of only three months a negligible lag which would soon be made up and lost in a few years? It has not proved so. The personality characteristics which were first noted when she was not able even to sit up have persisted, but so has the relative retardation. The lag of three months lengthened into four months at 1 year of age, into six months at 2 years, into twelve months at 3 years, and into about fifteen months at 4 years of age. The developmental quotient of this child has gravitated between 70 and 80.

On the very first examination the attractiveness of C.D.'s personality was felt. She was benign, good-natured, socially responsive. There was no timidity, no irritability, and an untiring amenability. The developmental examination and the photographing were accomplished with ease; and as far as readiness of rapport was concerned, the examination might have gone on indefinitely. There was much smiling and a genial out-going attentiveness to the persons in the examining-room.

All this was at the early age of 9 months. In spite of a checkered career in institutions and boarding-homes, these qualities have persisted.

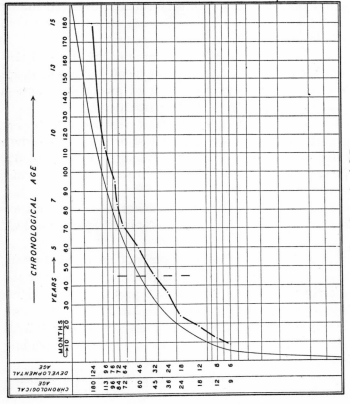

Growth graph of C.D.

Subsequent development:

Eleven years have elapsed since the above summary was written. An almost identical summary would serve for the ages between 5 and 15 years. Brief excerpts from the clinical records indicate the consistency of the developmental trend.

5 years. Succeeds best on performance tests, including block building and drawing, but weak in comprehension. Cannot add one penny and another penny.

6 years. Ties shoestrings, but counts uncritically and fails on comprehension questions. Developmental quotient is approximately 80. Displays good-natured amenability and is almost amusingly pliable in the test situations.

7 years. Quietly responsive and extremely coöperative. No amount of repetition of one type of test brings any let-down in a desire to do what is asked for. Intelligence quotient 85. Will probably have difficulty with abstract and academic aspects of school work.

8 years. Has been in two foster homes since previous examination, but displays the usual outgoing friendliness. I.Q. 80.

9.5 years. I.Q. 85. Responses are more delayed than usual, particularly on verbal tests. Tests of laterality show that she is completely sinistral, though she was presumed to be right-handed in infancy. Reading rates at Grade 1.6; spelling, both oral and written, at Grade 1.7. Reading shows some reversals and is slow. The errors are characteristic of a specific reading disability.

15 years. I.Q. 75. Reading rates at Grade 4.4; written spelling, at Grade 4.2; and oral spelling at Grade 3.8.

The personality picture has scarcely changed at all during the long period in which we have been acquainted with C.D. She was today, as always, friendly and pleasantly coöperative. The somewhat inferior quality of her intelligence and judgment make it necessary to provide good supervision and training through adolescence. If she is adequately protected, there is an excellent prospect of her making satisfactory social and vocational adjustments in adult life.

Comment:

The outstanding feature of this case is the consistency of the mental growth trend, particularly in the fields of adaptive behavior requiring judgment and abstraction. Possibly even more significant is the consistency of the temperamental traits which were apparently not affected by a succession of social and environmental changes in varied foster homes. It will be recalled that B.C.'s temperamental traits remain highly consistent in spite of the reversal in the trend of his mental growth. Numerous other case studies show that the individuality of the child declares itself strongly even in the first year of life. When methods of identifying specific personality traits become more refined, these traits will doubtless prove to have a high degree of predictiveness.

§ 4. D.E., E.F., F.G., G.H., H.I., I.J.
Six Siblings: Three Normal; Three Retarded
(4 months—21 years)

Graph 3 assembles the mental-growth trends of six children who are brothers and sisters. The solid lines on the early sections of the graph plot the curves for the first developmental examinations made in infancy and childhood; the broken lines show extensions of these curves on the basis of subsequent examinations. Here is a strange juxtaposition. These children were born from the same father and mother, and bear a family resemblance. They were reared in the same home. In physique and countenance, all six siblings superficially appear normal. In mentality, three fall definitely within the zone of average and low-average mentality; the remaining three fall far below this zone.

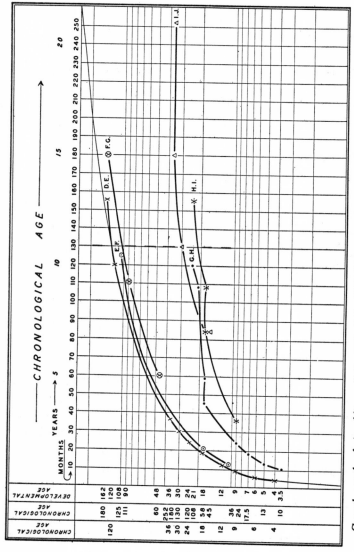

Growth graph of six siblings: D.E., E.F. F.G., G.H.,H.I., I.J. The two columns for Chronological Age in this graph carry the ages at the time of the examinations. The first column lists the ages of the normal siblings; the second column, the ages of the defective siblings.

Early status:

Detailed discussion of the individual cases is not necessary for the present purpose. The graph adequately indicates that three of the children began their pre-school careers with average or near-average promise, with developmental ratios of approximately 100, 95, and 80. The defective siblings on their early examinations earned ratios of 35, 30, and 25.

Subsequent development:

D.E. (F). Eight examinations between the ages of 4 months and 3 years yielded almost full average ratings. At 10 years she was making normal progress through the grades, and rated at average age in reading comprehension and in arithmetic reasoning. At 13 years of age she was in the seventh grade and doing passable work with an "educational age" of 12 years, a school grade ability of 6.2, an educational quotient of 92. Her school progress has been consistent with the import of the pre-school ratings. Noteworthy is the persistence of an extremely shy disposition which was evident in infancy.

E.F. (M). This boy likewise is making moderately good progress through the elementary grades. At 12 months and at 20 months of age he was classified as at a low average developmental level. At the age of 10.5 years on educational tests he shows a rating of 10 years in reading, 7.5 years in spelling, 9 years in language, 10 years in arithmetic. He was assigned an educational quotient of 88 by a school examiner. He was given average ratings in coöperation, industry, dependability, and social control by most of his teachers. With respect to initiative, the rating was somewhat lower.

F.G. (F). This girl was rated at a dull normal level of intelligence at the ages of 5.5 and 9 years. She graduated from the elementary school at the age of 15 years and has been employed as a domestic. Her career has been in general consistent with the early indications.

G.H. (M). When 10 months of age this boy rated near the 4-month level. At the age of 45 months, he rated near the 18-month level. At the age of 6 years he was not yet walking. He had made very slight progress and still rated near the 18-month level (D.Q. 30). At the age of 9 years he rated at the 21-month level and at the age of 10 years he was still unable to walk without assistance and was residing in an institution. His developmental level was approximately at the 2-year level, and his D.Q., 25.

H.I. (M). This boy was also admitted to an institution where he creeps around on the floor. He is unable to walk and articulates only a few words. At the age of 3 years he rated near the 9-month level. At 9 years he rated at the 18-month level. At 13 years he rates at the 2-year level, from the standpoint of developmental levels, an advance of little more than a year in ten years of time. This advance has been so slow that his developmental quotient has declined from approximately 30 to 15.

I.J. (F). This child's developmental progress likewise has been very slow. When 7 years of age she rated at about the 21-month level; at 15 years, at less than 3 years. At the age of 21 years she may still be rated at less than 3 years. If we make a comparative inventory of her performance at 14 years and at 21 years, we find no losses or regressions and only one or two meager increments such as the ability to place five blocks in a row in imitation of a train. Parenthetically it should be said that, from the standpoint of environment, she has had excellent care and ample stimulation. But she cannot make a verbal distinction between one and two blocks, and she cannot combine a vertical and horizontal stroke to make a cross. She cannot fold a piece of paper twice at right angles. She cannot combine three blocks to build a bridge. She cannot copy a circle.

Although in her mental growth she reached a virtual plateau at the age of 14.5 years, her mental organization has maintained its integrity and we find no evidences of deterioration. She may be compared to the girl P.Q. who was likewise arrested at a low level of intelligence but showed a comparable stability in her behavior equipment.

Comment:

The decisively bimodal distribution of normal and subnormal types of development in this one family has some general significance. The six developmental curves suggest that the growth potentiality is not determined by a compromise or quantitative blend of two strains, but is rather the expression of the dominance of one ancestral strain. This is also suggested by the mother's anxious questioning when we made examinations of her infants, "Does the baby take after me, or after the father?"

That there is a neuropathological hereditary factor can scarcely be doubted, even though the mother is competent enough to manage her household and the father able to find more or less regular employment. The high degree of similarity between the three retarded siblings indicates a comparable genetic factor, since there is no history of illness or injury to account for the mental deficiency. The three normal children likewise have had much in common in the general ratings of their development. There are no ascertainable environmental factors to account for the individual differences in these six siblings.

B. ACCELERATION AND SUPERIORITY OF EQUIPMENT

§ 5. J.K.
Sustained Acceleration Throughout Infancy and Childhood
(2 months—12 years)

In 1926 a tiny baby boy, J.K., only 2 months of age, impressed the examiner with his alertness and responsiveness.

At the age of 3 months this impression was intensified. The following entries went into the clinical research record at that early age: "*Personality and Ability Forecast:* Strong, vigorous baby, well handled. Personality should be forceful and well equilibrated. *Suggestive Data:* Baby not only exhibits strength, but maturity of motor development. (The mother early began a daily program of muscular exercises for the baby.) *Research Query:* What will be the ultimate effect on total development of special training in motor control?"

Partly to answer this query, eight more examinations were made prior to his second birthday. Each examination revealed a definite acceleration on the developmental schedule and confirmed our impression that he was a well-constituted infant. But would these symptoms of acceleration and superiority extend into later years?

We formulated four alternative possibilities: (A) This acceleration is an untimely ripening; it is essentially abnormal and therefore will lead to premature arrest or curtailment of development. The precocity bodes ill. (B) This acceleration is simply a freak in the ordinary time-growth relationship, neither wholesome nor unwholesome. It is an accidental nonconsequential variation and will not in any way interefere with the child's future. He will realize his endowment, large or small, irrespective of his developmental tempo. The road is independent of the rate of travel. (C) The precocity is largely motor and not fundamental. It presages an energetic, executive, motor-minded individual who will make a success in certain practical fields, but will otherwise classify as an ordinary or average person. (D) The precocity is part of the child's biological endowment and not an incident. It represents a positive growth potency, as well as an accelerated rate of function and is a dynamic factor in the creation of drive and in the maturation of a relatively superior order of abilities. What retardation is to inferiority, this acceleration is to superiority.

We listed these possibilities in an ascending order of probability when J.K. was 21 months old. We saw him again at the age of 12 years. Fortunately he did not disappoint us. He satisfied the best expectations. He was an alert, responsive, attractive boy, poised in manner, with a steady, penetrating gaze that bespoke superior intelligence. Although not a prodigy in school, he has shown strong drives and inventiveness in engineering fields. He handles with ease such polysyllabic words as inapplicability; he rates near the 18-year mental level, with a Stanford-Binet I.Q. of 150.

The consistency of his accelerated development can be more briefly shown by a condensed recapitulation of the results of fifteen examinations made between the ages of 2 months and 12 years.

Early status:

First examination (age 2 months). Alert, responsive, ready social smiling.

Second examination (age 3 months). Motor development advanced, attention vivid, strong drive.

Third examination (age 4 months). Advanced in both adaptive and motor abilities. Normatively rates at 5-month level.

Fourth examination (age 9 months). Rates near 12-month level, articulates three words—mama, dada, bye-bye. Stands a moment without support. Lowers himself from standing to sitting.

Fifth examination (age 10 months). Rates at the 14-month level. Impression of superiority strengthened and reinforced. Reacts quickly. Quality of attention good.

Sixth examination (age 12 months). Vocabulary of six words. Builds tower of three blocks. Points to hands, hair, eyes. Fills cup with blocks in spontaneous play.

Seventh examination (age 16 months). Vocabulary of twelve words or more.

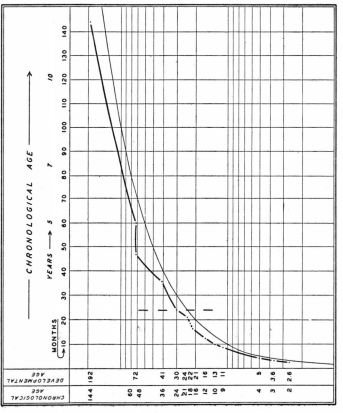

Growth graph of J.K.

Eighth examination (age 17 months). Vocabulary of twenty-five words.

Ninth examination (age 18 months). Fifteen additional phrases and words. Similar gains in other fields of behavior. Amazing feats in climbing.

Tenth examination (age 21 months). Rates at 2-year level. Highly resourceful, active, investigatory.

Subsequent examinations:

Eleventh examination (age 2 years). Superior reactions in form-board situation and color matching; rates at the 30 month-level.

Twelfth examination (age 3 years). Developmental level of 3.5 years. Interest, attention, and social adaptations excellent.

Thirteenth examination (age 4 years). Mental level of 6 years. Superiority indicated by comprehension and quality of conversation.

Fourteenth examination (age 5 years). Developmental level 6 years. Stanford-Binet mental age 6 years and 4 months.

Fifteenth examination (age 12 years). Vocabulary average adult level. Mental age at superior adult level. I.Q. 150.

Comment:

During infancy the motor abilities of this boy were conspicuous. So conspicuous, in fact, that we were led to ask whether they did not give a false impression of general precocity. At the conclusion of the fourth examination, age 9 months, he even entertained us with a wheelbarrow stunt and somersaults. At that time, if asked to prophesy, we should probably have predicted a youth with marked athletic interests at the age of 12 years. Such a prediction would have miscarried, because the boy's intellectual interests are now so prominent that they have obscured the motor traits which were formerly so conspicuous. General predictions are naturally safer than specific prognostications; because as a child grows older the precise sphere and mode of his activities are variably influenced by cultural factors. General alertness and intellectual power are based upon biological factors and the general prognosis in this sphere was justified. When we know more about the developmental aspects of adolescence we shall be able to predict with increasing confidence whether the present behavior picture foretells an equivalent grade of adult ability.

§ 6. K.L.
Sustained Acceleration and Strong Drives
(7 months—10.5 years)

This boy presents a case of early sustained acceleration, similar to that of J.K. and will have only brief consideration. In both instances, evidences of advanced development were detected early; but in K.L. the high degree of motor activity was associated with malnutrition and a wiry physique. The question posed was this: "Is the strong drive a compensation for the faulty physical condition?"

The events indicated that it was not. The drive continued strong after physical improvement and has manifested its strength not only in bodily activity but in facility and directness of manipulation and in an eager, searching responsiveness to his environment. Keenness of perception and sensitiveness to social stimuli have been characteristic throughout the entire series of eleven examinations.

The quality of general liveliness in his behavior makeup has been more constant than his psychometric quotients which have ranged from 120 at the age of 10.5 years to the peak of 140 at 3 years of age, when he rated near a 4.5 year level. In imitative and spontaneous drawings his performance has been mediocre; in language it has been advanced. He had a vocabulary of twenty-five words at 13 months;

a 12-year vocabulary at 10.5 years of age. The clinical estimate of superior equipment remained high in spite of an
apparent drop in the ratings on one or two examinations.

Persistence of attention showed itself unmistakably on
the first examination when he strove continuously for a
minute to gain a cube out of reach. Similar persistence
showed itself in the performance-box situation at 21 months.
Whether his high-strung qualities are an asset or liability
cannot be determined without a more careful study of his
personality makeup. That they were derived from his milieu
is doubtful because he displayed them at a very early age.

§ 7. L.M.
Superior Dynamic Qualities from Infancy
(9 months—16 years)

Throughout the pre-school period of development this girl
displayed a vivid, vigorous, well-constituted personality. On
six successive examinations from 9 months to 4 years, these
favorable personality traits were noted, once even after a
long period of debilitating illness. Good attentional qualities
were recorded on the very first examination (age 9 months).

At the age of 1 year our comment on the clinical record
was as follows:

"Bright, eager, well-constituted. Very dominant energetic
assertion of healthy kind, constantly accompanied by *äh-äh*.
Hand-to-mouth reaction more prominent than usual for 1
year old child. Interfered a little with tests. Superior personality traits with high average intelligence. Attention and
adaptability superior."

Language development was definitely advanced at 1 year
(with a seven-word vocabulary and a grunt); and also at 3
years when her use of words was rated at a 4-year level and
her comprehension of sentences, at a 6-year level. At the age
of 4 years there was marked spontaneity and facility in
speech. At 7 years, autocriticism was so great that the vo-

cabulary rating was barely at the 8-year level. A similar inhibition and unwillingness to hazard a guess or a try was observed as a personality trait at the age of 16 years. Even so, L.M. came within one word of the vocabulary norm for 18 years. Her word definitions were clear and discriminative, rather than mechanical or verbalistic. Expressive inflection was frequently used for emphasis.

The superiority in language performance at the age of 1 year has proved to be prophetic. She excels in languages as a high-school student and reading is her favorite occupation. The favorable dynamic qualities noted in infancy persist. Her ability is by no means limited to the language field. On the short-scale Stanford-Binet her quotient rates 130, if 14 years is used as the calculation age.

At the age of 1 year her height was average. At 16 years, she is tall. Her physical stature in infancy was less predictive than her mental stature!

§ 8. M.N.
Early Evidence of Musical Talent and Superior Dynamic Qualities Associated with an Ordinary Rate of Development in Infancy
(3 months—15 years)

This report concerns a sunny-tempered, junior-high-school girl with a keen sense of humor; a voracious reader, a friendly popular companion; a natural leader. She is independent in her thinking, not too readily swayed. Although she shows occasional adolescent "inertia" she is constantly expressing herself artistically in painting, modeling, creative writing, costume designing, and music. She has also shown a fine critical sense in music. By standard achievement tests her percentile rating in educational subjects has been 100 and 99. (Mathematics, in which she was once poor, is now one of her best subjects.) Her intelligence quotient has pretty consistently rated at 135. She is evidently a girl of parts.

Did she show her mental superiority in infancy? Yes, but chiefly in emotional traits and personality makeup. Here we have another instance in which superior promise was not reflected in the early psychometric ratings. There was not generalized acceleration (by our method of measurement) in infancy.

Even in the field of language at the age of 18 months we could not give her a 21-month rating, for she was unable to join two words. However, we placed a high clinical estimate on her language ability because of her bilingual comprehension, and still more because of the exceptionally high quality of her conversational jargon. Developmentally, jargon may be regarded as the forerunner, the matrix, or the *Anlage* of articulate speech. Normatively we assign expressive jargon to the 15-month level and a more elaborate conversational jargon to the 18-month level. So on this normative item, M.N. at the age of 18 months was rated at the 18-month level.

This offers us a good example of both the limitations and the usefulness of a normative rating. An unqualified 18-month rating does not do justice to the language ability of this child. But an interpreted rating becomes accurate and informing. When we say that her jargon is of unusually high quality, we get a behavior picture of a girl whose chatter may still be quite unintelligible but who is already well beyond the gesture level and is really uttering inarticulate sentences with her modulations, phrasings, and dramatic inflections. This is a positive, promising, developmental matrix. It contains paradigms and embryonic syntax. So we were duly impressed by her excellent jargon. Even at the age of 4 months, and again at 6 months, we had been impressed with the extraordinary amount and variety of her vocalizations. At 18 months her jargon was beguiling. She would "talk" confidentially for minutes at a single stretch, uttering not a single enunciated word but conveying much emotional content!

Nature's sequence of development is (1) vocalization, (2) single words, (3) jargon, (4) joined words, (5) articulate speech. There were good individual reasons why M.N. was biding her time in the use of articulate words. There were other fields of behavior, perceptual and expressive, in the total complex of growth which were undergoing complicated and even rapid organization. These contextual fields of behavior also had language components, inarticulate but highly patterned.

We refer especially to M.N.'s musical capacities. The morphogenetic basis for these capacities which are now so apparent were unquestionably laid in the period of infancy. The early records supply convincing evidences:

Age 3 months. Child appears very sensitive to sounds. Turns head to voice instantaneously and seeks the sound of persons walking in the room. "Sensitively attuned" describes the reaction type. Activity inhibited by noise or musical sound in environment.

Age 18 months. Very sensitive to sounds. Paused and listened to the slightest sound in the photographic dome. When a continuous sound ceased she said "humph" with a slowly falling inflection. Listened most intently to a music-box and then said ha! ha! ha! ha! with the musical quality of a scale, from high to low, each *ha* on a separate note.

Age 30 months. Already shows special interest in the piano and marked ability to remember and to carry airs.

Age 38 months. She now knows and sings about seventy-five little songs, each with its proper tune. Just before the holidays she twice heard the girls in an adjoining school sing a Christmas carol. Her father was amazed to hear her sing it correctly after only two hearings.

Age 42 months. Musical ability was now so definitely established that a mild caution against over-emphasis was indicated.

Age 15 years. Musical talent well above the average. Piano lessons discontinued at present for lack of an inner urge toward the instrument. Musical appreciation and critical sense in music, however, are superior.

Comment:

The foregoing constitutes a consistent record of at least retrospective prophecy. It is natural that musical giftedness should declare itself in the pre-school years and even in infancy. Music is a universal language which contains stimuli and patterns to which even the infant is responsive. Not all infants are as responsive as Menuhin was when he was carried in his father's arms to his first concerts. But from the standpoint of developmental mechanics it seems to be almost a rule that musical geniuses are prodigies of musical execution and appreciation in early life. Mozart was not the first nor the last musician able to play a minuet with perfect precision before the kindergarten age. Oliver Goldsmith was a very dull boy at the age of 3, but not Mozart.

What is true of music is in a measure true of other fields of artistic expression. We are not as likely to find prodigious performance in the pre-school years, but we are likely to find those prophetic attitudes and flares out of which superior performance later on develops. So it is and was with M.N. who is naturally talented, though not to genius degree. She now expresses herself constantly and quite naturally in painting, modeling, costume designing, and displays discriminating feeling in her work; but at the age of 3.5 years she drew the accompanying drawing of a man (page 40).

There is no alarming precocity in this drawing, but the concentrated zeal and dramatic *Einfuhlung* which entered into the execution were doubtless weighted with prognostic import.

Again we are confronted with the importance of dynamic personality factors in the early detection and appraisal of superiority. During the first two years this child earned only average ratings on the normative schedules. Advance in language was noted at 18 months and her mother remarked, "Her mind is so keen, her physical coördinations so sure that I feel there are many possibilities in her growth."

At 3.5 years she earned a developmental quotient of 135. Her intelligence quotient throughout the school years has

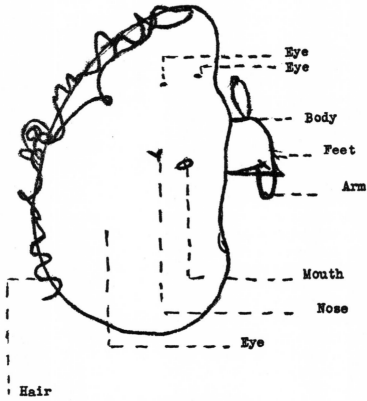

Fig. 1. Drawing of man, by M.N.

been consistently 135 or better. But before she achieved these higher psychometric ratings she had already earned high clinical ratings on the basis of the qualitative excellence of her adjustments and reactions. We are not overfond of the term "qualitative." It tends to imply a mystic added essence.

Actually it refers to quantities and configurations which are too subtle or too involved for numerical expression with present techniques. But, fortunately, such qualities are discernible and not altogether beyond cautious appraisal by the clinician.

Supplementary note on Child Y.Z.:

This child may be briefly mentioned in the present context. We do not attempt a full report because our pre-school contact with Y.Z. was limited to a few specimens of drawing which are pictured on page 224 of *Infancy and Human Growth.*

These precocious drawings have proved to be predictive of artistic talent in a girl now a high-school sophomore, age 15 years. Throughout school life she has been interested in drawing and is rated among the first ranking pupils in the field. In music she is also credited with an excellent ear and a deft touch. A short essay, written for a high-school magazine, shows maturity, sensitiveness of insight, and superior diction. She has a lively sense of humor which sometimes expresses itself in her drawing. At present she is especially fond of elaborate "doodling" designs. She delineates costumes with delicate and somewhat exotic strokes. These drawings show a predilection for slender lines and compositions. This accentuation of the vertical dimension, resulting in elongated forms, was present in the pre-school drawings. It was a method of execution which apparently had predictive significance.

§ 9. N.O.

Extraordinary Command of Words and Ideas, Associated with Marked Spontaneity and Vivacity
(3 years—17 years)

This sketch concerns again a girl who displayed unusually pleasing and well-constituted personality traits in early childhood. At the age of 17 years she is a highly individual, vivid, alert girl, ready for college. Her language was more acceler-ated than that of M.N. She was freely joining words at 18 months, comprehended and framed innumerable questions at 3 years, and always had a vocabulary well in advance of her age.

Her facility with words was in no sense merely verbalistic, but was closely correlated with powers of discrimination and abstraction. She used words maturely as a child; not prig-gishly, but as carriers of ideas, as scalpels for analysis, and also as puppets for playful humor.

At 3 years. "But crosses don't have rounds." (Uses de-scriptive words at 5-year level.)

At 4 years. "A magnet is a thing that catches up things." (Vocabulary at 8-year level.)

At 5 years. "A snake, cow, and sparrow are all alive. A rose, potato, and tree are vegetables." (Statement of simi-larities at 12-year Binet level.)

At this age, having visited Peabody Museum with all its wonders, she said with a sweeping dramatic gesture, "I can't understand it. It's just like magic."

At 6 years. "What is life?"

At 7 years. "Hysterics is when you get afraid and all ex-cited that you can't do something." "The examination was awfully easy this year." (Vocabulary at 10-year-level.)

At 8 years. "I suppose you are going to tell me about the boy that fell off the bicycle and they brought him to the hospital and thought he could not get well. Of course he could not get well; since he got killed." As remarked at the time, all this saves time for the examiner. (Made a superior adult score on fable interpretation.)

Her intelligence quotients on these six annual examinations fluctuated as follows: (a) 150, (b) 150, (c) 150, (d) 145, (e) 135, (f) 135. Our clinical impressions were not much influenced by these fluctuations, because of the uniformly high level of performance in the intellectual fields.

The fundamental neuromotor system did not share in this acceleration. On performance tests like block building and drawing, she rated near normatively average levels. At the age of 5 years she gained 8-year credit on comprehension questions and resolved one of the 10-year absurdities and one of the 12-year similarities; but she was unable to bring two lines of a triangle together in our drawing test.

Her "failure," however, was ameliorated by delightful running comments which she made and by the autocriticism which she displayed. She also had the significant capacity of inventing problems of her own, better suited to her abilities. There was a striking similarity in the types of developmental tests in which N.O. and O.P. (the next case to be reported) succeeded and failed during the pre-school period. Both children showed comparable ineptitude and insight in the drawing tests. But N.O. perhaps displayed greater ability in dealing with the verbal situations, and a more mature power of analysis and deduction.

§ 10. O.P.
High and Fluctuating Intelligence Ratings, Associated with an Ordinary Rate of Motor Development
(3 years—17 years)

Having given somewhat extended consideration to the two superior girls, M.N. and N.O., who were and are his contemporaries, we may dismiss this boy with briefer characterization. As already pointed out, he showed many psychological patterns similar to those of N.O. Like her he showed advanced powers of abstraction and generalization at 3 and 4 years of age. He used ideas with much greater relative skill than he used his hands. At 5 years he showed much the same inability to bring two lines to a junction in drawing the triangle.

Despite the conservatism of his motor capacities, he showed unmistakable powers in intellectual tasks. This suggests some degree of independence in the development of the fundamental and the accessory portions of the neuromuscular system. But at this same examination (age 5 years) when he failed to bring the triangle lines to a point, he was able to reply to my question, "*What is the property of a magnet?*" "The property of the magnet is for lifting iron."

At the age of 6 years, he made written reply to a questionnaire as follows: (1) *Of all the persons in the world, who would you most like to be?* Answer: "God." (2) *If you were this person, where would you like to go?* Answer: "To Yale College." His pre-school desire is about to be fulfilled. At the age of 16 years he passed his college entrance boards and naturally will go to Yale!

His intelligence quotients on the annual examinations between the ages of 3 and 8 years were successively 115, 135 140, 130, 165, 160. The reason for the abrupt jump of 35 points at the age of 7 years is not clear. Again it may be noted that our estimates of his ability were consistently favorable and did not undergo corresponding fluctuations.

C. ATYPICAL AND PSEUDO-ATYPICAL GROWTH COMPLEXES

§ 11. P.Q.
Progressive Retardation of Developmental Rate
(5 months—13 years)

This girl presents a behavior picture and a developmental career in somber contrast to the children we have just been considering. She has reached her teens of life age, but her best behavior patterns scarcely rise above the levels of infancy. She presents a progressive retardation of the rate of mental growth in rather paradoxical combination with a slow but steady advance in mental maturity.

The rate and trend of mental growth are reflected by a series of developmental quotients at ages of 5 months, 7, 8.5,

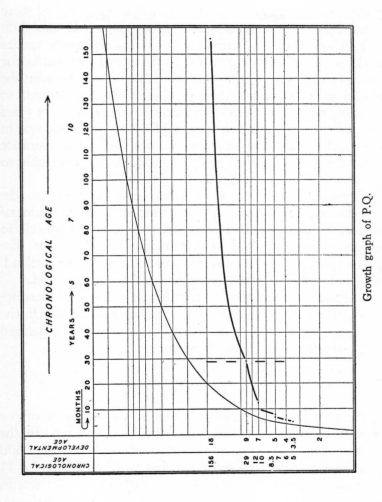

Growth graph of P.Q.

10, 12 and 29 months, and 13 years: 70, 70, 60, 70, 60, 30, 10.

The irregularity of the early course of development is partly due to the fact that the developmental ratings were based upon maximum behavior achievements. It was difficult to assign a single level because of bizarre inconsistencies in the general behavior picture. At the age of 29 months, for example, she was given a 9-month rating chiefly because she placed an index finger upon a pellet, and pulled herself to standing position at the side of the crib. At the age of 4 years she had not yet learned to stand without support. She was in the toddling stage for years and did not walk with assurance until the age of 7 years. Only recently has she been able to go up and down stairs alone.

Approximately nine years intervened between the developmental examination at 29 months and the last examination at 13 years. On this last examination it was possible to assign a maturity level of approximately 18 months. Expressed arithmetically, this reduces to a developmental advance of only one month per year for this entire period.

In spite of progressive retardation in the rate of development, there are no evidences of actual deterioration. On the contrary, the behavior picture appears much more organized and integrated than it did in infancy.

Comment:

Here again we have an example of the tendency of the growth complex to attain an optimal organization. In the present instance this tendency was manifested even in a child of idiot mentality who spoke her first word at the age of 11 years and who at the age of 13 years articulates two words, *shoe* and *bye*. There are certain areas in which virtually no improvement can be detected. As early as the age of 5 months we noted abnormal preoccupation with her hands. She put her fingers in bizarre postures and fixated on her hands for long periods. A similar pattern persists to this day. She contorts and moves her fingers, snapping the joints almost continuously.

This behavior has an intrusive, stereotyped character and imparts an aspect of distraction to her attention. However, she is able to turn the pages of a book adaptively. She responds to a simple commission. She unwraps candy pellets and returns the paper. She squeals ecstatically as she did at an early age in several test situations. She reacts to the picture card by handing it back in typical 18-month manner. As a behavior pattern this particular response was perfect in its "eighteen-monthishness."

The emotional values and references of her social attitude also simulated the 18-month level of maturity. In emotional complexion and maturity she was not incomparable to W.X., age 23 years, who as an adult idiot rates at the 18-month level.[1]

We conclude, therefore, that this steady decline in developmental quotient does not necessarily mean a neuropathological deterioration. On the contrary, this child has made a remarkably satisfactory adjustment in a well-ordered foster home. But this excellent foster home has not been able to overcome to any significant extent the limitations of a defective inheritance (her mother was both psychotic and mentally deficient). The acculturation of nine domestic years has had an apparently negligible effect upon the tempo and trend of her development. There has been an advance of nine months in nine years.

§ 12. Q.R.
Progressive Acceleration of Developmental Rate
(28 months—6 years)

This child deserves brief report because she is the sister of P.Q. and presents a striking contrast in the trend of mental

[1] See Fig. 52 on page 221, "Infancy and Human Growth."

growth. She was born of the same mentally deficient and psychotic mother, but apparently carried the potentialities of normal and even of high average intellectual development. Such development was realized even though at the age of 28 months she could scarcely walk and could say only a few words. She had been handicapped by extreme early neglect and by a succession of infectious diseases and a major surgical operation. In spite of the retardation of her development at 28 months, she was able at the age of 3 years—only eight months later—to walk and to talk and to tell the story of Peter Rabbit.

Her developmental history in contrast to that of her sister strongly suggests the importance of intrinsic determiners of growth potentiality.

By the age of 6 years the developmental outlook had become entirely normal in spite of the severe adversities of her early experiences. She had acquired a responsive, pleasant maturity and generally favorable personality makeup.

Death intervened and we are unable to supply any further developmental data.

§ 13. R.S.
Early Pseudo-normality in Mongolism with Decline in the Developmental Ratio
(6 weeks—6 years)

Although the cause of mongolism is unknown, it probably represents an imperfect growth regulation by the endocrine system. Mongols as a group present a rather wide range of individual differences with respect to the ratio of general development. It is possible that the subcortical divisions of the central nervous system are less affected than the higher centers. In any event, there may be a spurious approximation to the normal behavior picture in the newborn mongol.

R.S. (M) at the age of 6 weeks made a fair approximation

to the 1-month level of behavior. But as he grew older, the developmental quotient shows a diminishing trend. He was examined at the age of 5 years and was rated at the 2-year level. He was re-examined three months later, shortly before his death, and rated at 27-month level. In this very brief interval he had made a slight but perceptible gain.

If we give full psychometric credit to the rating of 1 month level assigned at the age of 6 weeks, his developmental quotient in the space of six years declined from a value of approximately 70 to that of 40. The trend and tempo of development of mongols will receive further attention in a later section.

§ 14. S.T.
Motor Retardation with Subsequent Compensatory Development
(1 year—14 years)

This boy was examined five times in the interval between his first and fourth birthdays. The developmental ratings as a series show a marked acceleration after the first examination when he was 1 year of age. He was re-examined at the age of 9 years and earned a developmental quotient of 85.

At the age of 14 years he is in the seventh grade but doing subaverage work which is consistent with this intelligence status.

At the age of 1 year his motor development was barely at the 6-month level. He needed firm support in the sitting position. He made only pushing reactions with his feet. His maximum motor achievement was the securing of a pellet with whole-hand reaction. Language likewise was near the 6-month level. The picture was complicated by head-rolling. In spite of this extreme retardation, the symptoms did not definitely suggest mental deficiency and the prognosis was carefully safeguarded.

In less than a 6-month interval the motor development progressed from an habitual dorsal position (he had been content to lie on his back in his crib at the age of 8 months) to walking with help. In the language field he progressed from vocalizations to articulating "mama" and "dada." In the adaptive behavior field he progressed from the simple manipulation of objects to the insertion of a block in the performance-box and to the building of a tower of three blocks. At 12 months he had acquired no nursery tricks. At 17 months he was waving bye-bye. This surprising improvement made the prognosis more favorable, although the clouds were by no means all removed.

This improvement has been maintained during succeeding examinations. At the age of 4 years his intelligence is rated at a dull normal level.

Ten years later the rating is similar.

Comment:

In retrospect it seems that the picture of extreme motor retardation at the age of 1 year can be ascribed to prematurity of birth, in combination with wretched care during the neonatal period. Heavy clinical allowance must be made for such a combination. In spite of this adversity, a tendency toward a developmental optimum has been evident.

Born out of wedlock, born prematurely, secreted in an attic during the first few weeks after his birth, handicapped by feeding difficulties, reared in a shifting succession of institutions and foster homes, in one of which he suffered most injudicious and inhumane treatment—the personality problems of this boy now far outweigh considerations of maturity level. The steady continuance of his intellectual growth and the slow amelioration of his motor incoördination indicate developmental reserves which may continue to operate and favorably influence his personality adjustment. He has made remarkable progress in the light of the behavior picture at 1 year of age, when he could not even sit up alone.

§ 15. T.U.
Temporary Developmental Arrest in Infancy Followed by Sustained Average Trend
(3 months—14 years)

This case is unusually instructive because of the definite reversal in developmental trend which was revealed by the first three examinations. When first seen at the age of 3 months, the developmental status of this boy appeared to be entirely normal. We were, however, prepared to find evidences of retardation on the next examination, which was made at the age of 5 months. Indeed, we suspected that such retardation would manifest itself, because at 3 months the posterior fontanelle and the anterior fontanelle were almost closed and the child exhibited marked nystagmus. This combination of physical signs suggested a developmental defect. At the age of 5 months, on twenty eight diagnostic items T.U. rated precisely as he had done on the previous examination. Rarely does one find such an apparently decisive arrest of development at this particular period of the life cycle. On the basis of evidence before us at that time, we definitely suspected the possibility of mental deficiency.

But we were careful to check this possibility by an examination at the age of 7 months. The developmental trend was now decisively reversed. His behavior maturity at this age was approximately at the 5-month level, where he normally should have been on the previous examination.

This progressive upward trend has become permanent. The downward trend noted between the ages of 3 and 5 months was evidently spurious and concealed a developmental readjustment which must have occurred about this time, under a deceptive surface.

Comment:

This decisive sequence of developmental events between 3 and 7 months is instructive from the clinical standpoint. In appraising the developmental status of infants and children there is a temptation to give undue weight to physical stigmata. Physical stigmata have variable importance. Growth potency is more crucial. The trend and tempo of development depend upon deep-seated biochemical factors which in turn are largely dependent upon hereditary determinations. In spite of the premature closure of his fontanelles, this child evidently had insurance factors in his biological equipment. These factors have come to the rescue, and since the age of 7 months he has maintained an average trend of development. It is probable that we underestimated the sensory significance of the nystagmus at the age of 5 months. Subsequent eye examination has shown that the nystagmus did not have a central origin. A diagnosis of a low-grade permanent chorio-retinitis of unknown etiology was made. The child has an albinic fundus, and vision with glasses at present is 20/200 in either eye.

He entered a sight conservation class at the age of 9.5 years, when his mental age was almost 9 years and his intelligence quotient approximately 95. He has made regular progress through the grades and is rated at a high average level in Grade VII both in curriculum subjects and in personality traits, such as coöperation, industry, dependability, initiative, social control, and health habits.

If the outlook at 3 months was doubtful because of the pseudo-arrest in the developmental trend, the prognostic import of the upward trend at 7 months was favorable, because this trend bespoke the presence and prompt release of insurance factors. These insurance factors have preserved the normality of development in spite of a serious congenital handicap.

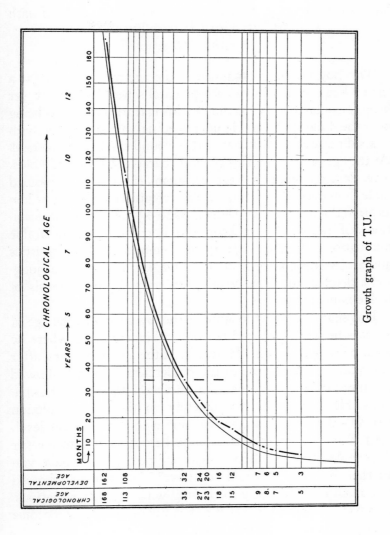

Growth graph of T.U.

§ 16. V.W.
Subnormal, Irregular Developmental Trend, Associated with Consistently Good Personality Traits
(6 months—16 years)

This boy was first examined at the age of 6 months (at a time when our monthly developmental schedules had not yet been formulated). We estimated his maturity status as being near the 4-month level. He impressed us even at this age with a good-natured sociability and a round-eyed attentiveness. At the age of 16 years this general characterization still holds. The developmental ratings as summarized in a subjoined table, however, show considerable irregularity, falling as low as 50 in the period from 18 months to 4 years. The manifestations of personality makeup did not show a comparable fluctuation. On the contrary, the emotional characteristics and a consistent ingredient of native wit and practical judgment deterred us from making an unqualified diagnosis of feeble-mindedness.

It is significant that in spite of the low rating at the age of 4 years he was permitted to enter a kindergarten, where he made a fair adjustment. However, at the age of 6 years, after two years of experience in the kindergarten, he still showed a marked lack of discrimination in verbal and abstract situations. He failed almost completely on the man-completion test. His drawing of a man was not even at the 4-year level. He had not learned the colors and he was unable to answer the simple question, "If you had one penny and I gave you another, how many would you have?" His response showed a fundamental difficulty in dealing with abstract situations. We were prepared to believe that his defect might become more apparent at later age levels.

At the age of 7 years his good-natured affability revealed itself in a characteristic manner. He had been in school long

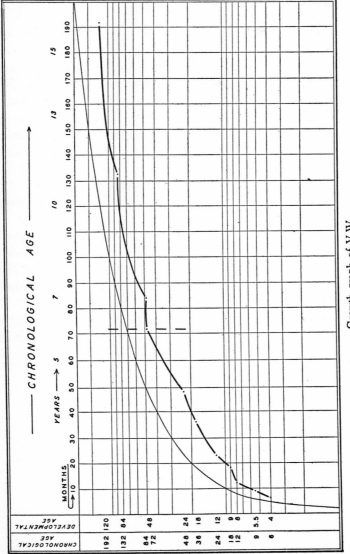

Growth graph of V.W.

enough to learn to "read" a few stories in the primer. His reading consisted in sheer memory recall. Therefore when presented with the book even with the print upside down, he fluently enunciated his well-learned primer sentences and, when memory failed, he resorted to no-matter-what-isms, constructing sentences such as "The apple flew in the air." But in general configuration, the response wore an impressive resemblance to his schoolroom reading. Such mentation would seem to be not too promising. But even at this age when confronted with practical problem-solving situations in the nursery and when confronted with simple social situations, he made significantly good adjustments. Stable personality traits combined with a simple spirit of coöperation and amenability have prevented him from becoming a burden to the school or in his home. After "graduating" from a special class he has been able to secure and to hold a simple, low-salaried job. He still has difficulty with the more abstract situations in formal intelligence tests, but he is able to achieve almost a 12-year vocabulary rating and makes good adjustments where his practical judgment can come into play.

His developmental career and the present behavior picture illustrate the barrenness of a simple categorical classification. On the basis of I.Q. alone, he would have been classified as

TABLE I

V.W.

Examination number	Age	Maturity level	D.Q
1	6 months	4 months	65
2	9 months	5.5 months	60
3	12 months	8 months	70
4	18 months	9 months	50
5	24 months	12 months	50
6	36 months	18 months	50
7	48 months	24 months	50
8	60 months	36 months	60
9	72 months	48 months	70
10	84 months	48 months	60
11	11 years	7 years	65
12	16 years	10 years	70

definitely feeble-minded, particularly between the ages of 4 and 8 years. He has, however, shown so much stability and character that it is advisable to keep him in the borderline category and to emphasize the features of normality rather than the intellectual deficiencies. Even in children of inferior endowment the developmental complex may show a tendency toward improvement rather than deterioration.

D. THE TENDENCY TOWARD OPTIMUM IN GROWTH

§ 17. A.C.
Extreme Cerebral Palsy from Birth Injury, with Significant Approximations to Normal Mentality
(4 years—14 years)

For medical reasons all cases of birth injury should have a thorough neurological examination, as a first essential. But the proper treatment and understanding of the child demands in addition a careful investigation of the total behavior equip- ment and of personality reactions. This becomes doubly im- portant when the motor disabilities are so extreme that the behavior picture bears a deceptive semblance to idiocy.

It must be recognized that no two cases of birth injury are precisely alike. Every injury creates its own peculiar lesion. The injury frequently is brought about by a temporary as- phyxiation of the brain cells, due to a diminution of blood supply during parturition. Injuries are selective. Certain areas and functions of the nervous system may be spared. Moreover, the consequences of any given lesion seem to depend not only on the lesion itself, but upon inherited endowment and stamina.

Double athetosis of severe grade, arising out of a birth in- jury to the basal ganglia and associated with cerebral palsy, constitutes one of the most disabling handicaps to which the human nervous system can be subjected. The present case of A.C. is detailed to indicate the type of problems which demand clinical appraisal and interpretation.[1]

Over a period of ten years the writer followed the developmental career of this boy who was stricken with cerebral palsy as a result of obstructed cerebral blood supply at the time of birth. The patient first came to our notice at the age of 4 years. In body length and weight he was slightly in advance of the average for his age. He had suffered only a few minor illnesses, slept well, and was not markedly fatigable. His features and torso were well formed. His countenance was normal, attractive, and expressive for brief intervals when not in the throes of involuntary activity. He could not hold up his head, sit up, creep, reach, or manipulate. At times he was quiescent, but under the least excitement, arms, head, fingers, face, mouth, tongue—and to a lesser degree legs and toes—went into apparently aimless extensions, flexions, and rotations, with antagonistic muscles shifting their ascendancy. Occasionally the double athetosis became extreme, the movements on the right side being most pronounced and abrupt. There was recurrent spasticity. Crossing of the legs disappeared on relaxation and was not associated with marked contracture. Right and left abdominal, cremasteric and Babinski reflexes were present; eye grounds and pupillary reflexes were normal; knee jerks were variably moderate or hyperactive. Spasms of the pharyngeal, lingual, and associated muscles made swallowing, mastication, and phonation difficult. There was frequent salivation. These latter characteristics, combined with the motor disability, had led a previous physician to a diagnosis of mental deficiency.

This boy was never committed to an institution. He received devoted and intelligent care from his family, and special educational measures were taken in his behalf. He died a few months before the age of 14 years, of appendicitis.

[1] An excellent and concrete discussion of the psychological and diagnostic aspects of cerebral birth injuries will be found in Lord, E. E.: Children Handicapped by Cerebral Palsy. N. Y., Commonwealth Fund, 1937, pp. x + 105.

Necropsy showed an uncomplicated lesion of the basal ganglia of the classic *status marmoratus* type. A detailed report of the findings has been published in a joint study from the Clinic of Child Development and the Department of Pathology of the Yale School of Medicine.[1]

The present summary limits itself to an account of the mental development which took place between the fourth and the fourteenth year.[2]

Early behavior status:

A developmental survey of A.C. at the age of 56 months yielded the following ratings, on some thirty items. The assigned developmental levels represented clinical judgments based upon close observation, but unassisted by language, for even a clear-cut distinction between a *no* or *yes* gesture was beyond his motor capacity. The ratings in the field of motor control must not be taken too literally, because the disorganization of movement was so great as to permit only crude comparison with normal abilities.

The tabulation (p. 60) gives indication of a most unusual complex of abilities and disabilities. The total behavior picture could not be construed as one of feeble-mindedness in any true clinical sense. Although the motor performance was at an infantile level, A.C. never gave an impression of infantilism. His general somatic development, and particularly his personality traits, indicated that he was potentially of normal or even superior capacity and that the birth injury had inflicted a selective rather than a pervasive damage to

[1] Gesell, A., and Zimmerman, H. M.: Correlations of Behavior and Neuropathology in a Case of Cerebral Palsy from Birth Injury. *Am. J. Psychiat.* 94 (3): 505-535 (Nov.) 1937.

[2] Several members of the staff of the Yale Clinic of Child Development participated in the study and the training of A.C. We are particularly indebted to the observations and assistance of Drs. Elizabeth Evans Lord, Burton M. Castner, and Ruth W. Washburn. Mrs. Mary McGrath had immediate charge of the intensive educational program when A.C. was 10 years of age.

Table II

Developmental Survey of A.C. at Age 56 Months

DEVELOPMENTAL ITEMS	ASSIGNED LEVEL
Physique	
1. Chronological age	54 months
2. Height	60 months
3. Weight	60 months
4. Dentition	60 months
Motor Control	
5. Swallowing	5 months
6. Head posture	1–3 months
7. Arm postures	1–3 months
8. Body control	6 months
9. Locomotion	9 months
10. Grasping	3 months
11. Reaching	3 months
12. Holding	12 months
13. "Crayon control"	12 months
Language	
14. Vocalization	4 months
15. Vocabulary	18 months
16. Gesture	18 months
17. Comprehension	48–60 months
Adaptive Behavior	
18. Form and size	48–60 months
19. Color	48–60 months
20. Number	36 months
21. Autocriticism	48–60 months
22. Attention span	60 months
Personal-Social Behavior	
23. Bowel control	36 months
24. Bladder control	36 months
25. Emotional control	56–60 months
26. Affection	56–60 months
27. Sociability	56–60 months
28. Humor sense	48–60 months
29. Social insight	48–60 months
30. Play interests	36–48 months
31. Story interests	36–48 months
32. Educational attitude	60 months

his behavior equipment. In spite of the extreme motor dis-coördinations, his personality remained relatively well integrated, with well-sustained and discriminating emotional attitudes toward his social environment. He won for himself a circle of friends among children of his own age, who visited him and managed to play with him on their own level of social maturity.

These personality characteristics must be given important weight, if we are to arrive at a just correlation of the behavior picture and the neuropathological picture. He was able with great efforts to express *yes* and *no* by crude head gestures which were so ungoverned that they resembled each other, but which his family could sometimes differentiate. He was practically unable to combine a consonant and a vowel, but he managed to make a few slightly distinctive vowel sounds associated with different meanings. A single brief incident must suffice to convey an impression of the most normal aspects of his behavior.

He liked to be propped up at the window so that he could participate in the life about him. On one occasion (age 4 years) he was watching some construction work on the street. He saw the neighbor's children having great fun crawling through the big drain pipes lying by the side of the road. He became greatly interested. Though unable to articulate, he ejaculated "I—I" in no uncertain terms. This was his most vivid utterance, used whenever he was able to muster it, in all situations in which he wished to call attention to his own stake in any event or plan. It was his unmistakable way of indicating that *he* wished to crawl through those pipes, too. Doubtless he had enough "autocriticism" to know that he could not crawl; but he also had enough imagination and drive to desire all possible experience, from sliding down a banister to riding horseback. With the aid of his sisters, he was brought to the entrance of the pipe, and by their combined efforts and his struggling coöperation, he was propelled through the big drain pipe tunnel, to his great delight.

His personality sense was so robust that he wished to have the same school-going status as his playmates. Partly for this reason and also to determine his learning capacities, we devised from time to time lessons in "reading," "drawing," and "number work." There was little difficulty in enlisting the pupil attitude. By the age of 7 years he gave sustained attention for 30 minutes in a reading lesson.

A normal infant, 4 months old, lying on his back can hold his head in the midposition, watch intently a rattle dangled above his chest; and can, moreover, bring both arms to the midline, close in on the rattle, and grasp it. A.C. was never able to execute this most elementary act of prehension; and yet he used his oculomotor muscles with alertness and perceived incongruities in a caricature drawing of a man. The limitations of his experience in manipulation and locomotion did not inflict a drastic arrest of his perception and appreciation of spatial relations.

Likewise in the field of language. His actual utterance was at a meager, infantile level, but his comprehension of words and even verbal nuances was at a normal level. In number comprehension he distinguished between two and three telephone rings and probably had a concept of four. His humor sense, his amusement at accidental absurdities in the home life, his story and play interests, all suggested a considerable approximation to normality in the perception and appreciation of social relations.

Later behavior development:

On the basis of the behavior picture at 56 months of age, it was not easy to predict the subsequent course of development. To what extent were the foregoing indications of normal though atypical behavior characteristics borne out in the subsequent nine years of life?

Even before the age of 5 years, as already suggested, Λ.C. showed a certain eagerness to be going to school. For this reason his early contacts with the Clinic had been converted into blackboard lesson periods which served him as a substitute for school, and gave us an opportunity to observe his response to the teaching of words and numbers. Ordinary methods could not be used. We had to rely on his rather ambiguous *yes-no* head gestures, on crudely differentiated phonations, on facial expression, to establish communication. With the aid of the blackboard, it was possible to present words, incomplete sentences, incomplete drawings, numbers, and sums. By devising games it was possible to test with varying degrees of certainty his powers of recognition and memory.

In a few sessions he learned to distinguish simple words like *ball, cat, hat, man*. By the age of 7 years he had learned to recognize with variable success perhaps thirty-five words. In listening to stories his interest had advanced from *Black Sambo* and *Three Bears* to Grimm's *Fairy Tales*. There was hope that with greater maturity he might learn to read. He had even made some progress in holding a large crayon thrust in his hand, but had made no gain in directing it. His attention span and his social maturity showed a slight, steady increase. His "lessons" at home and at the Clinic were irregular and occurred about once a week. At the age of 8.5 years his attainments were reviewed and it was concluded that he showed essentially the same ability to deal with printed words and numbers which he had shown at the age of 5 years. He gave no convincing evidence that in power of abstraction or true ability to read he was equal to the intellectual level of a normal 6-year-old.

For another year his "schooling" continued in a rather desultory manner. His articulation improved slightly. At favorable periods of relative relaxation he could "pronounce" numbers up to ten, with crude phonetic discrimination of the vowel values. He had scarcely any command over consonants. At the age of 9.5 years he had a recognition reading vocabulary of about fifty words.

In spite of the limitations revealed by this rate of progress, it was decided that the potentialities of intellectual development could only be determined by a more systematic teaching program. It might well be that A.C.'s training thus far had been too incidental and irregular to overcome his pro-found handicap. A skillful teacher was engaged over a period of six months to give training five times a week in two-hour sessions. As a stimulus and to satisfy his ambition to attend a real school, the lessons were conducted in a separate room of an elementary school. A reading-frame was placed athwart his perambulator; interest-provoking devices were used, but the earlier playful approach gave way to a more serious at-tack. He made a good adjustment to the new regime. He soon was scanning with his eyes seven successive pages of the book supported in the reading-frame. The eye movements, accompanied by vocalization, inflections, and tongue move-ments gave the appearance of silent reading.

His behavior and his story interests were more mature than they had been. By the end of the six months he increased his reading vocabulary to 101 words. But again it was not clear that he read with full insight. His progress in simple num-ber operations was meager. He showed only occasional spon-taneous interest in reading by himself at home. The signifi-cance of these limited responses to more intensive training will be discussed later.

During the four remaining years prior to his death he made no considerable academic gains. He matured, however, in his emotional life and his social interests. He learned to play a simple game of checkers, attending closely for twenty min-utes. He named his moves by vocalizing the number of a checker and indicating right or left by *yes* or *no*. He showed a preference for boy companions of his own age and also gave signs of pre-adolescent bashfulness. He could read the clock and was permitted to play the part of monitor in a rural schoolroom which he attended daily for an hour.

His neurological symptoms were only slightly ameliorated in spite of the fact that physiotherapy treatments were faith-fully continued for years. His coöperation in the muscle train-ing was excellent both at home and at the hospital, and he showed morale in enduring the pain involved. The spasticity of arms and hands somewhat diminished. He learned to open his hand voluntarily on many occasions. He was able to sit for a half-hour supported by pillows without pitching. Salivation decreased and articulation was slightly improved. In the intellectual sphere his rate of later development was distinctly slower than it had been during the first five years of his life. There is evidence that in the emotional and social spheres his development was slowly advancing and that he would have continued to mature during the period of adolescence.

The motor basis of mental growth:

The approximation to a normal as opposed to a feeble-minded mental organization was most convincingly shown in the field of social and emotional behavior. Here A.C. gave evidence of undergoing a steady progress toward mature levels of functioning. He advanced in his play interests; he changed, as just noted, in his attitudes toward children and adults; he showed characteristic pre-adolescent attitudes toward his mother. In spite of the inevitable dependency inflicted by his handicap, he showed considerable morale in trying situations. To be sure he also showed traits which would have been regarded as childish in an unhandicapped child, but it seems important to stress here those behavior characteristics which proved that his central nervous system was not uniformly arrested by the ischemia which so extensively damaged the functions of his tactile-motor system. The vitality and fullness of the mental growth of A.C. were truly remarkable when we consider the paucity and disfigurement of his kinesthetic experience.

How can we explain this significant approximation to a normal although impoverished realization of mental growth? A thoroughgoing motor theory of psycho-genesis would seem to be inadequate to account for the degree of mental growth which was attained. In many respects the handicap of A.C. was more devastating than that of Helen Keller. And he was denied those experiences in the field of kinesthesia and active touch whereby Helen Keller overcame her sensory defects. He was almost postureless and lacking in the simple postural sets which normally lie at the basis of attention and mental adjustment.

It may be argued that the fullness of A.C.'s development depended upon the intactness of his auditory and particularly his visual functions. Visual experience was probably least affected by his brain injury. His eye grounds were normal and the early internal strabismus was self-corrected. He even attained the ability to make eye movements of a reading type. It is possible that the kinesthetic data furnished by his twelve oculomotor muscles supplied the main scaffolding for his mental equipment.

These muscles, it may be contended, were able to muster and maintain within themselves a degree of postural set. By such reasoning the motor theories of mental growth retain their strength. The argument simply states: (a) There is a tendency toward optimal realization and integration of potentialities; (b) This tendency caused the total mental growth complex of A.C. to organize itself about a nucleus of oculomotor experience. It seems to us, however, that this interpretation somewhat strains both the theory and the facts.

How shall we explain the numerous propensities and strivings toward attainments for which this handicapped boy had no equivalent motor realization, or even possibility of motor execution? Even at the age of 6 months he showed an unmistakable propensity to reach for objects, an amazing fact for he never in his whole life time attained a neuromotor equipment sufficient to execute prehension or to exercise in a controlled way the function of active touch.

In reviewing his life history, one definitely gets the impression that his neurological growth did not altogether depend upon the stimulation of motor experience. It is because the unimpaired regions of the brain realized such a full measure of their potential growth that he gave no impression of suffering from a form of secondary amentia.

This does not, of course, mean that his intellectual life was not impoverished. As he grew older, his motor disabilities took a cumulative toll, although his verbal comprehension at a concrete level remained relatively normal. He understood conversation about ordinary domestic affairs, but he showed limited curiosity about affairs remote. He detected verbal incongruities and reacted to them with a sense of humor, but he did not show abstract interest in words, nor did he demand silent reading or reading aloud to increase the scope of his information. Verbal auditory imagery apparently was present, but it lacked the context and vitality of articulatory kinesthesia. He was crippled with respect to "carriers" of notions and ideas. He suffered from a kind of intellectual reduction due to faulty proprioceptive implementation. But even this reduction never brought him into the category of feeble-mindedness strictly defined. In spite of his intellectual poverty, he retained normal modes of thought and a certain perspicacity which clinically was inconsistent with either amentia or dementia.

We infer, therefore, that the insurance factors of maturation bring about a considerable degree of neurological growth in unimpaired regions of the brain, even though these regions are cut off from normal subcortical (tactile-motor) impulses. Such insurance factors enable the organism to some extent to build bricks without straw. It is difficult to think of mental organization apart from tangible (tactile-motor) components. But the new concepts of growth chemistry permit us to believe that the protein molecules of the central nervous system may undergo considerable elaboration and electrodynamic organization without the stimulus of patterned motor reactions.

With such concepts, the evidences of normality in certain cases of cerebral palsy becomes less enigmatic. There is, after all, no inner necessity why profound motor disability should create or produce an equivalent measure of mental defect.

E. PHYSICAL ASYMMETRY

§ 18. B.D.
Hemihypertrophy Associated with Mental Defect
(2 years—15 years)

Hemihypertrophy is a developmental anomaly possibly even more rare than *pubertas praecox*. It represents a partial failure of the regulatory mechanisms which normally bring about symmetry in the two halves of the growing organism. The result is an enlargement of one half of the body and its members, an incipient unilateral gigantism which in B.D., at the age of 2 years, made her left leg 1.6 cm. longer than the right; her left foot, 1 cm. longer; her left arm, 2.5 cm. longer. This physical disparity of the left and right sides resulted in a perceptible limp.

When the mechanisms which regulate symmetry operate with perfection, such disparities do not, of course, occur. Mild asymmetries distributed throughout the body are the rule. Hemihypertrophy is exceptional in extent and comprehensiveness of the asymmetry. It may indeed be interpreted as a minimum phase of double monstrosity which is an abnormal form of twinning.

Twinning is a fundamental manifestation of life. Bateson has defined it as "the production of equivalent structures by division." Newman likewise regards the phenomenon of twinning as a very fundamental process almost universal in the field of biology. For "wherever we have bilateral doubling we have twinning in some form."

The human organism is derived from a single fertilized cell. He is monozygotic in origin. As a singleton he is the end product of bilateral doubling. In the case of true monozygotic twins this process of doubling is carried to such a degree that two offspring result from a single ovum. A perfectly symmetrical bilateral individual, on the one hand, and a perfect pair of duplicate individuals on the other hand, represent the ideal extremes of the process of twinning. Between these extremes there are many gradations and deviations. Some of them are benign; others are monstrous in character. Paradoxically enough, monozygotic twinning not only produces the most perfect resemblances between individuals, but it also produces the most extreme deviations from the normal.

Although rare, hemihypertrophy is an instructive developmental deviation which illustrates the importance of embryonic growth regulation. The embryonic imbalance of twinning may disturb the tissue development sufficiently to produce not only physical symmetry but also mental subnormality.

Case B.D. and the following case, C.E., illustrate this developmental consequence in their curves of mental growth. B.D. was examined three times when she was of pre-school age, namely at 2.25 years, at 3, and at 4 years. Her mental development showed consistent retardation which justified a diagnosis of mental defect of high grade. Now at the age of 15.5 years she is still in a special class for subnormal children. Her developmental level is slightly over 8 years, with an intelligence quotient of 60. Her physical condition is not ameliorated.

Although mental growth tends toward optimum realization, this tendency cannot overcome profound deviations which were initiated in an early embryonic period of development when basic tissue differentiations and symmetries are established.

§ 19. C.E.
*Slow Developmental Rate Combined with Remarkable
Constancy of Performance in Maturity
(12.5 years—36 years)*

Mental growth is not confined to infancy and childhood. Normally it continues into the years of maturity. In certain types of amentia the growth in these later years may be almost imperceptible. The individual, having slowly crept upon a plateau, remains upon it.

The present case illustrates the completeness of arrest which may occur at the close of adolescence in an ament. It also testifies to the stability factors which as a rule insure the durability and integrity of the organism whether normal or subnormal. We first saw this adult when he was a boy of 12.5 years. He then achieved a mental age rating of only 4.5 years. He was unable to count to four. He could not compare the two short Binet lines. On the second examination, at the age of 13 years, he registered a slight gain. He now counted four pennies and he could spell the word *spelling*, for he had had daily spelling lessons during his years in the elementary school. But two and one were seven.

At the age of 20 years his intelligence rating had risen to a little over 5.5 years. He was now able to count thirteen pennies. He could copy a diamond and identify coins. Occasionally he was able to define a word in terms of use. At the age of 25 years his reactions to the intelligence test were identical in almost every detail and his intelligence quotient remained as it had been, 35. At the age of 30 years it again was 35 and the successes and failures on the test questions were amazingly unchanged. His chief intellectual gain was the newly acquired ability to tell how many fingers he had on left and right and both hands. At the age of 36 years his intelligence rating is virtually unchanged. He can now make a distinction between two weights and between right and left hands.

The net result of the foregoing summary shows a psychometric gain of a little over 1 year between the ages of 13 and 36 years; a rise from a mental age of 4.5 years to a mental age of a little over 5.5 years. Practically all of this gain had been accomplished by the age of 20 years. From the standpoint of genetic psychology, the most impressive phenomenon is the incredible stability of his mental performance during

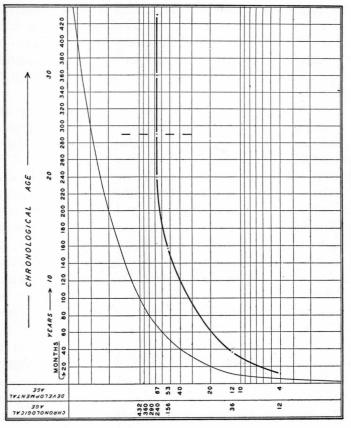

Growth graph of C.E.

the subsequent sixteen years. This stability is reflected in his drawing, in his writing, and in his word definition.

At the age of 20 he spelled and misspelled as follows: *cat, house, it, Mew Haven, Spelling, arithmetic.* At the age of 25 his orthography for these words was exactly the same except that *it* was spelled *ta.* Ten years later we note the erosive effects of time upon the word *house* which becomes *hat.* It is elaborated to *tia,* and the word *Spelling* stands out with granitic integrity in its original perfection, the behavior residuum of countless repetitions of this word at the head of his daily spelling exercises.

The drawings of a bird at the ages of 25 and 36 years remain much the same. In the field of practical judgment there has been an equal degree of stability, and even a slight increment registered in the fact that, whereas at the age of 20 years he could be sent to the store for only one object, he can now be sent on an errand for two or three. There has been no evidence of significant deterioration in his behavior patterns. But this lack of variation in responses and the poverty of his growth, in spite of favorable environmental surroundings, bespeaks again the tenacity of constitutional factors. These factors in all probability operate with comparable distinctiveness in the normal individual, but they cannot be demonstrated with the objective naïvete of the evidence furnished by this defective boy.

The stability of the growth complex was also reflected in the fact that C.E. presented a well-defined case of hemihypertrophy throughout the course of his development. Physical measurements made at intervals showed a marked consistency and persistency of his physical asymmetry. The hemihypertrophy, as suggested also in the case of B.D., probably rose out of a slight imbalance in the twinning process at an early embryonic stage. Yet this imbalance, once established, has projected itself unmistakably throughout the life cycle—an amazing, even if perverse, manifestation of stability. There is a tendency toward a corrective and ameliorative optimum in the developmental process, but this tendency cannot reach the deeper levels of constitutional determination.

F. GLANDULAR AND NUTRITIONAL FACTORS IN
MENTAL GROWTH

§ 20. F.H.
A Mongoloid Growth Trend
(8 years—15 years)

Brief mention is made of this case in our early series (p. 249, "Infancy and Human Growth"). This girl at the age of 8 years rated highest among a group of thirty-eight mongols. Her intelligence was near the 5-year level, with a D.Q. of 60. In temperament she was amenable and good-natured. This degree of mentality, combined with her docility and the exaggerated zealousness of the parents, resulted in early training in school subjects, and at the age of 8 years she was able to write her name and draw a man and copy a square. This is well above the usual level of ability of mongols at this age.

Although F.H. had the standard physical characteristics associated with mongolism, these characteristics were not so well defined as in the typical cases. She presented that milder degree of mongolism which might place her in the mongoloid 'group.

Seven years later, when we made follow-up inquiries in regard to this child, we found that, at the age of 15 years, 'she had a mental age of about 6.5 years and an I.Q. of 45. Such a decline in I.Q. in later childhood is very frequent among mongols. More noteworthy in this instance are the educational ratings in the achievement tests for reading, for writing, for dictation, and for arithmetic. Educationally she rated at the 10-year level with an educational quotient of approximately 70. This disparity of intelligence and educa-tional quotients indicates the disproportionate, though none too well-grounded, educational attainments which are some-times built on a relatively inferior mentality.

§ 21. G.I.
Typical Mongolian Growth Trend
(7 months—13 years)

Mongolism constitutes one of the most distinctive clin-ical types of defective development, whether viewed from the standpoint of physical or of mental characteristics. So characteristic is the behavior complex, that it is highly prob-able that all uncomplicated cases of mongolism have a com-mon origin which dates back to the embryonic period and involves the endocrine regulation of growth.

However, the individual differences in general capacity and specific abilities are considerable. These differences may be due to the differences in the hereditary constitution of the child, and the severity of the developmental disturbance. Where the condition is of mild severity, the child may learn to read and make satisfactory adjustments to the household at a simple level. Other mongols, especially those of definitely neuropathic stock, may be arrested at a low idiot plane.

The developmental quotients of over one hundred cases, examined one or more times at our Clinic, have been tabu-lated. The vast majority of these quotients for the periods of infancy and childhood range between 30 and 60. But there is a very general tendency for the D.Q. to diminish with increasing age. A scatter diagram for the entire group of cases shows an interesting difference in the younger and older cases. Under 4 years of age 76 per cent of the mongols have a D.Q. of 50 or more. Over 4 years of age, the proportions are reversed: 24 per cent have a D.Q. of 50 or more.

The mental growth curve of G.I. showed a fairly uniform and symmetric trend between the ages of 7 months and 2 years. At that age we ventured a prediction in regard to G.I. based upon our previous experience with many mongols of

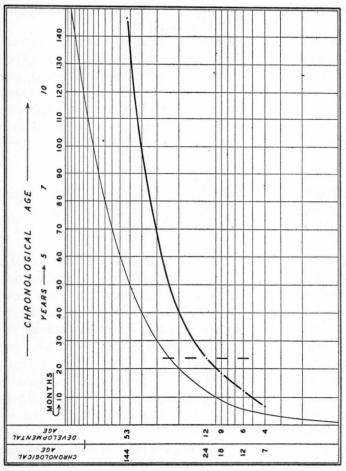

Growth graph of G.I.

different grades of ability: "Her developmental quotient cannot rise above 50 and it is more likely to decline slightly as she grows older." When she reached school age she entered a special class which she left at the age of 13 years. Her developmental level at the age of 12 years was approximately 4.5 years; her developmental quotient 40.

The forecast, in the present instance, was relatively safe. In many other forms of amentia and retarded development, a similar forecast would not have been justified. Indeed, when dealing with retarded children who fall within the range of normality, the probabilities are weighted in a favorable direction; the developmental quotient is, if anything, likely to rise over a period of years. Not so with mongols.

§ 22. H.J.
A Normal Course of Mental Growth Associated with Extreme Physical Precocity in Pubertas Praecox (3.5 years—18.5 years)

In spite of its rarity, the present case deserves inclusion in a clinical volume because of the side lights it throws upon the mechanisms of normal mental growth. The early developmental history of this case was summarized under the name of H.J. in a previous volume. This early history covered the period from 3.5 to 8.5 years of age. It was concerned with a young child who was then attending school regularly, was superficially quite normal in appearance, and gave no obvious evidences of being in any way exceptional. In her general deportment, play life, and school progress she was regarded as an ordinary pupil.

The average age of physiological maturation as evidenced by the onset of menstruation in 487 high-school girls studied by M. Abernethy[1] is approximately 13 years and 6 months. The lowest age of maturation in this group was 10 years and

[1]Abernethy, Ethel M. Correlations in Physical and Mental Growth. Part II. *J. Educ. Psychol.*, 16:539-546, 1925.

only 5 instances occurred at that age. *Pubertas praecox* may be defined as an acceleration of physical development in which physiological maturation occurs well in advance of the age of 10 years.

H.J. began to walk at the age of 11 months. Adolescent changes in body proportion, including enlargement of the breasts, had been noticed even before that age. Menstruation with normal flow of four days began at the age of 3.5 years. In terms of the above-mentioned average, this represents a precocious developmental displacement of ten years. Between the ages of 5 and 14 years the menses were regular. After the age of 14 years they became varyingly irregular.

Height and weight, but not dentition and carpal ossification, were accelerated. At the age of 7 years the height of H.J. was approximately three years above norm. Her dynamometer grip was four years above norm. Beginning at the age of 8.5 years physical measurements were made annually (by H.T.). These measurements showed an early acceleration in growth followed by an early cessation of growth in height and general skeletal dimensions. There was no appreciable change in height and skeletal size after the age of 11 years. The growth in height from 8.5 years to 11 years was due principally to the growth in trunk or body length. This type of growth is normal for girls in their teens and was in a relative sense normal for H.J., for, with respect to maturity of skeletal growth, she was at that time comparable with a girl at the brink of the teens. The patient died from an infection after the removal of a cerebellar tumor at the age of 18.5 years.

In the light of this extraordinary displacement of physiological pubescence, it becomes interesting to inquire into the course of psychological development.

The interactions of the possible growth factors in the present case are so complicated that the psychological development of the patient assumes special significance. Lacking a safe index to the etiological priority of these various growth factors, we may look to the psychological manifestations for some indications of the underlying developmental mechanisms.

Fortunately the psychological data are abundant, a total of sixteen mental examinations and follow-up contacts having been made between the ages of 3 years and 11 months and 17 years.[1] The findings for these examinations, expressed in terms of maturity level, are partially summarized in the accompanying table and growth graph. Psychometric determinations, and clinical impressions as well, point to a rather surprising approximation to a normal course of mental growth. Both in the rate of intellectual progress and in the patterning of her home and school life, there were no striking departures from what is usual or normal. In spite of the extreme physiological deviation, she made average progress through the elementary school, took high-school courses in stenography and typewriting, and developed normal vocational interests. She never became a conduct-problem child, and during her long terminal illness at the hospital she showed a creditable degree of character and stability.

The main characteristics of her mental life may be most briefly and objectively summarized under the following headings: a. Intelligence, b. Motor characteristics, c. Emotional personality traits.

a. Intelligence:

Estimates of H.J.'s intelligence were made from time to time throughout the fourteen years during which she was under observation. At all times she showed relatively normal memory, insight, comprehension, and command of words. When measured by the Yale norms and the Stanford-Binet,

[1] I saw the patient on most of these occasions. The psychological examinations were made by Miss Elizabeth Evans Lord, Mr. Burton M. Castner and by Miss Helen Thompson, who also made supplementary observations in connection with the physical measurements and home visits.

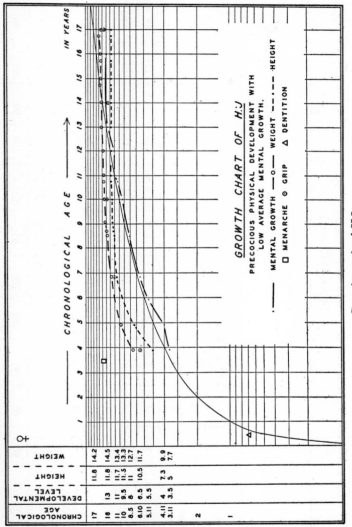

Growth graph of H.J.

TABLE III

DEVELOPMENTAL RATINGS OF H.J.—AGE-LEVEL RATINGS OF DEVELOPMENTAL ITEMS (IN YEARS)

(4 years—17 years)

| | CHRONOLOGICAL AGE AT EXAMINATIONS | | | | | | | | | | | |
	4 yrs.	5 yrs.	6 yrs.	7 yrs.	8.5 yrs.	10 yrs.	10.5 yrs.	11 yrs.	12 yrs.	13 yrs.	16 yrs.	17 yrs.
IMITATIVE DRAWING	4	4.5	5.5	7								
SPONTANEOUS DRAWING	3.5	4	6	6?								
VOCABULARY	3.5	4	5.5	6	7.5	8.5	8.5	10	9.5	12	14	15
DIGIT RECALL	4	4	7	10	10	10	11	12	12	18	14	
READING			6	7.5	8	10	10.5	11	11		12	
COMPREHENSION	3.5?	4	6	6	7	9	10	11	11	14		16
DEVELOPMENTAL LEVEL	3.5	4	5.5+	7	8.5	9.5	10.5	11	11	12.5	13	15
D.Q. & I.Q.	90	80	95	100	100	95	100	100	90	95	80	85

she consistently rated at or near an average level, with the intelligence quotients ranging generally from 90 to 100.

No marked precocities or recessions of ability were noted in the various tests. She excelled herself somewhat in digit recall between the ages of 6 and 9 years, but otherwise per-formed near expected levels. She learned to write, spell, and read at an ordinary rate of improvement. She read orally with moderate fluency; her story interests matured in a natural manner. Her vocabulary increased at a normal rate and fell only slightly below the norms for her age. At the age of 17 years she had a 15-year vocabulary. She graduated from a commercial course at that age, having attained a stenographic speed of 100 to 120 dictated words, and a typing speed of 40 words per minute.

Her progress, in elementary grades and high school, was steady and the quality of her school work was average. Both her intelligence examinations and her educational career certify to an average trend and tempo of development.

b. Motor characteristics:

In motor demeanor H.J. was rather slow and deliberate. This deliberation gave an aspect of poise to her movements in early childhood. Under the stress of play, however, she ran and romped with other children. Her posture and carriage were excellent through the entire period of observation.

There is no evidence of marked acceleration in locomo-tion, body control, or in manual-motor coördinations. It is possible that a careful study of the period of infancy might have brought such evidence to light, because the dyna-mometer records at the age of 4 years, as already noted showed a hand-grip pressure equivalent to that of a girl of 7 years. Strength of grip, however, does not depend only on muscle size and coördination, but upon a capacity to quickly muster and release energy. This dynamogenic capacity is normally increased at the time of adolescence, and its strong manifestation as early as the age of 4 years may indeed be correlated with precocious pubescence.

But in the acquisition of motor skills and in the general character of her movements, there were no departures from the average or normal. One might suppose that precocity in skeletal development would carry with it a corresponding precocity in the development of the skeletal and other voluntary musculature. Nevertheless, the neural organization of the muscles was apparently not hastened. The neurone patterning of motor control proceeded in a conventional way, keeping the usual pace with chronological age.

This is clearly shown in the three specimens of handwriting, made at the ages of 7, 8.5, and 10 years (Fig. 2). These specimens show the usual gradations in amplitude, pencil pressure, size and precision, appropriate to these years. Similar trends show themselves in imitative drawings of geometric figures, and in the spontaneous drawings of a man.

The drawings of a man are reproduced in Figure 3 because they give definite evidence of the same gradual psychomotor maturation which we find in normal girls. The manner in which these drawings were executed also certifies to a typical rather than to an unusual personality makeup at the successive ages.

The 4- and 5-year drawings of the man were slightly below the average, but were made with the uncritical alacrity characteristic of these preschool ages. A central mass with two appendages is normative for the 4-year level of maturity. The drawings show only a slight degree of progress between the ages of 4 and 5 years. This was consistent with other ratings made on the mental examinations at these two ages. The drawings for 6 and 7 years approximate the average.

At the age of 8.5 years, a childlike self-criticism crept into her responses. She made two efforts at drawing a suitable profile, then reversed the paper and needed encouragement from the examiner before she completed the drawing. At the age of 10 years, likewise, there was a good deal of self-

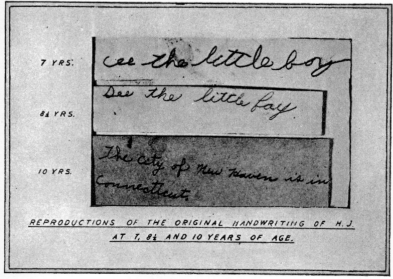

Fig. 2. Handwriting of H.J.

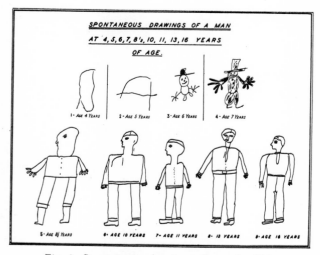

Fig. 3. Spontaneous drawings of man by H.J.

criticism and many erasures. It took her 11 minutes to complete the picture. At the age of 11 years there was not a single erasure and the drawing was completed in 2 or 3 minutes. At the age of 13 years the drawing was again made with dispatch. The series of drawings pictured give a fair objective indication of the general rate of her intellectual maturation.

c. Personality traits:

Personality characteristics as recorded on successive examinations are summarized in the present tense as follows.

On her first examination (4 years) H.J. speaks with a voice rich in timbre, deep in tone, and has a restrained manner. This subdued gravity has a thick, lethargic quality which is unchildlike; but she gives no evidence of advanced maturity in her interests. She plays with dolls, and has a childlike fear of dogs.

At the age of 5 years her gravity is even more conspicuous. She seemed to be mature in her poise, sat quietly in her chair without showing the volatile attention we expect at this age. Some of this "poise" may have been due to the discipline of close association with a dominating grandfather and grandmother. However, H.J. played in a natural way with children of her age. Her mother's estimate is to the point: "She is like other kids, but slow and lazy."

At 7 years, H.J. shows ordinary interest in dolls and dishes and is in no way demonstrative toward parents, siblings, or playmates. Nor is she withdrawn; she shows normal friendliness in her social behavior.

At 10 years she displays an ordinary juvenile interest in reading and in piano-playing. Someday she would like to become a bookkeeper. Occasionally she wakes up with a bad dream of a monster with big teeth and wide-open eyes; but she also has pleasant dreams about lavish gifts.

At 13 years a summarizing note states that the general

character of her personality reactions to the psychological tests remains very consistent. As on previous examinations, she gives quiet coöperation with free responses to all questions, but with very little spontaneous conversation. Occasionally she shows some tenseness by fidgeting and grimacing. However, she is less childlike than a year ago. Her vocational interest and attitude are definitely more serious and mature. In cultural aspects she is now showing adolescent signs which did not accompany her precocious pubescence.

After graduating from a business course in a commercial high school (age 17 years) she showed normal interest in securing a position and held a minor clerical post with success. She joined in social activities of her friends and attended dances. She showed neither reduced nor exaggerated interest in the opposite sex.

The culturally determined aspects of adolescence awaited their appointed time and came into fairly "natural" expression with the teens. It is not without significance that she exhibited typical symptoms of psychological adolescence at the usual age in spite of the precocity of her physiological maturity.

General comment:

The foregoing psychological survey of the career of this girl therefore leads to a striking contrast. Physically she presented an astounding precocity amounting to a whole decade. At the age of 3.5 years she had the configuration and gonadal physiology of an almost mature woman, but her subsequent mental development was scarcely altered in its outward patterns. Apart from her physical anomaly, her career was distinguished only by its mediocre normality.

But in the light of that anomaly, this mediocrity itself becomes distinguished. How can we account for such a remarkable stability and integrity of psychological growth in the presence of the drastic developmental displacement of pubescence?

The morphogenesis of the individual must be conceived in terms both of general and of specific regulators. The pervasive and coördinating controls of hormonal factors do not operate with complete autocracy. There are insurance factors and specific determiners which limit the influence of endocrinological disturbances of development. This limitation comes to beautifully clear expression in the case before us.

The developmental disturbance was so drastic that it must have altered even prenatal phases of the life cycle. Somatic and biochemical transformations which ordinarily occur near the teens occurred in infancy. The feeling tones, the affectivity of childhood were probably altered and took on a mature cast. But aside from this, the central nervous system showed an amazing degree of invulnerability.

This relative invulnerability is a developmental safeguard. Experiment has shown that the nervous system is especially resistant to prolonged starvation and other forms of adversity. In the competition between organ systems, it is favored by certain immunities which serve to protect it from acceleration and distortion in the presence of precocious pubescence. Secondary sexual characters were chiefly affected by the precocity. Skeletal growth was affected, but significantly enough, the outer skeleton of the brain, namely the skull, grew in accordance with normal expectations. This implies independent controls for the development of the cranium or controls which remain subordinate to the growth of the cerebrum.

The present case of *pubertas praecox* affords no warrant for the view that the whole phenomenon of growth is a function of an all-pervading sex factor or libido. On the contrary, it supplies new evidence for the specificity of individual growth components. There are deeply intrenched mechanisms of maturation which tend to preserve the integrity of the nervous system and to promote an optimal realization of the

life cycle. The course of the development of this organ system will, therefore, not be unduly deflected by the precocious
onset of pubescence. Even if we should grant that the
gonadal precocity was initiated by a neoplasm within the
brain, the upshot of the foregoing argument remains. Whatever the rationale, one fact stands in bold relief: the course
of mental maturation was but slightly perturbed.

§ 23. I.K.

Retardation from Hypothyroidism in Infancy Followed by
Normal Mental Growth Trend under Thyroid Therapy
(6 months—13 years)

The case of I.K. is of unusual interest because of the prolonged period during which this girl has been under observation. She was referred[1] to us for developmental examination
when 6 months of age. The diagnosis at that time, justified
since by extensive therapeutic test, was hypothyroidism. The
first developmental examination was made when the patient
was 6.5 months of age, ten days after the initiation of thyroid
treatment. Her body length was 60 cm.; her weight, 5960
grams. She presented a pronounced picture of reduced behavior. She was less reactive than a healthy 1-month-old
infant. She failed to follow either a moving object or a flash-
light with her eyes, but she fixated her head responsively to
the sound of her father's voice. The behavior was superficially comparable to that of a 1-month maturity level. She
did not score a single positive rating on the 3 months normative items.

The early improvement under thyroid treatment was dra-

[1] By Dr. Ethel Dunham, Lecturer on Clinical Pediatrics. We are indebted
to Dr. Dunham, who made her early records of the case available to us. Miss
Elizabeth Evans Lord and Mr. Burton M. Castner of the Yale Clinic of Child
Development secured and analyzed the behavior data. For further clinical report of this case, see Chapter XIII in *Infancy and Human Growth* (ibid.), and
also, Gesell, Amatruda and Culotta: The Effect of Thyroid Therapy on the
Mental and Physical Growth of Cretinous Infants. *Am. J. Dis. Child.*, 52:
1117-1138 (Nov.) 1936.

matic and far in excess of the ordinary rate of development. On the second examination, which followed only three weeks after the first, the behavior picture had advanced to the 3-month level. There was a marked increase of activity. I.K. now held and regarded a rattle. She engaged in mutual fingering hand play. She smiled and even vocalized responsively to social stimulation. She laughed. She closed in with crude coördination upon a dangling ring, but her head and body posture remained limp. The acceleration of mental growth was maintained, and by the age of 18 months she had established a rating near the borderline of normality in general maturity. She earned a D.Q. rating of 75 at that age. She has maintained a similar rating which occasionally has gone as low as 70 and as high as 85 throughout the whole subsequent course of her development. The developmental quotient has gravitated to the 75-80 zone and this is fairly descriptive of the level of general mentality. As the growth graph indicates, there has been a greater acceleration in physical growth and, at the age of 18 months, both height and weight were rated above the average norms for her age.

Personality characteristics have for the most part remained constant and consistent. She has maintained a mild coöperative amenability during the successive examinations. The general course of development, with respect to both physical and mental characteristics, is summarized in the accompanying table. As already stated, the mental status after the age of 18 months has continued at a consistent low average or dull normal level. This consistent mental growth can be confidently attributed to the thyroid therapy.[1]

[1] In a period of twelve years she has consumed well over 1½ Troy pounds of thyroxin with varying daily dosages which are plotted on the growth graph. Irregularities of thyroid intake declared themselves in irritability, constipation, diarrhea, and even convulsions at various times as indicated in the chart. At the age of 9 years, temporary myxedema developed, owing to a pharmaceutical error. The druggist unwittingly performed the experiment. For one month the child was fed thymus instead of thyroid. Cretinous signs at once emerged, but retreated as promptly when thyroid was restored. This child's normality surely hangs on a slender thyroid thread.

TABLE IV

DEVELOPMENT OF I.K.

Sex: Female
Mother: Adenoma of the thyroid
Sibs: Normal
Birth order: First
Birth weight: Normal
Age 1st examination: 6 months
Age when thyroid therapy begun: 27 weeks

Exam.	Age in months	Maturity level	D.Q.	Educational rating	Daily thyroid	Height	Weight	Illustrative behavior increment
1	6½	1 mo.	15		1 gr.	61 cm.	6,400 gm.	Less reactive than av. 1-month baby
2	7	3 mos.	40		1 gr.	61 cm.	5,740 gm.	Adaptive behavior much improved
3	9	4 mos.	45		2 gr.	61.5 cm.	6,460 gm.	Holds head erect. Holds 2 cubes
4	11	5 mos.	45		2½ gr.	73 cm.	7,240 gm.	Picks up spoon but does not regard pellet
5	12	7 mos.	55		4 gr.		8,325 gm.	Picks up pellet. Sits momentarily
6	15	9 mos.	65		4 gr.	78 cm.	9,440 gm.	Sits for long periods
7	17	13 mos.	75		4½ gr.	83 cm.	10,140 gm.	Says 4 words. Tries to release cube on tower
8	17½	13½ mos.	75		4½ gr.	83 cm.	10,480 gm.	Pulls to standing. Combining play
9	18½	15 mos.	80		5 gr.	85 cm.	10,600 gm.	Releases two blocks, nearly making a tower of three
10	19½	16 mos.	80			85 cm.	11,020 gm.	Says more than four words
11	21	16 mos.	75		3 gr.	86 cm.	11,660 gm.	No scorable gain
12	22	18 mos.	80		4 gr.	88 cm.	11,620 gm.	Stands alone. Scribbling improved
13	24½	19½ mos.	80		4½ gr.		25¾ lbs.	Walks alone, unsteadily
14	26½	21 mos.	80		6½ gr.		27¾ lbs.	Asks for things. Tells experiences

#	No.	Age		%	Test / Grade scores	gr.	Height	Weight	Description
15	28	22	mos.	80		6½		29½ lbs.	Piles 3 blocks successfully
16	33	23	mos.	70		2			Builds tower of five
17	34	26	mos.	75		3			Walks steadily
18	35	27	mos.	75			99.5 cm.		Names 5 pictures
19	37	28	mos.	75		4	102 cm.		Makes a horizontal line
20	60	45	mos.	75		4	43.2 in.	44¼ lbs.	Imitates gate. Stands on 1 foot
21	74	53	mos.	70		4	45.6 in.	49 lbs.	Copies square
22	88	66	mos.	75		3	49 in.	54½ lbs.	Describes pictures
					Grade				
23	97	80	mos.	80	Gray reading 2.1 / Iota word lists 2.8 / Written spelling 2.1 / Oral spelling 1.8	2	49.9 in.	52 lbs.	Marked advance in reading and spelling
24	109	90	mos.	80	Gray reading 4.4 / Iota word lists 4.7 / Written spelling 3.2 / Oral spelling 3.4	2			Marked gain in reading and spelling
25	121	102	mos.	85	Gray reading 3.7 / Written spelling 4.4	3	53.5 in.	64¾ lbs.	Improvement in spelling of more than one grade
26	123					2			No examination at this age
27	133	102	mos.	75	Gray reading 4.5 / Iota word list 4.9 / Written spelling 5.9	2–3	55.2 in.	70½ lbs.	Vocabulary score: 19 words / No psychometric gain
28	144	110	mos.	75	Gray reading 5.9 / Written spelling 7.1	3–4	57.4 in.	80½ lbs.	Vocabulary score: 23 words (8 yrs.)
29	156	119	mos.	75	Gray reading 6.4 / Written spelling 8.5 / Oral spelling 8.5 / Vocabulary 10 yr.	2	60.5 in.	100½ lbs.	Vocabulary score: 30 words (10 yrs.)

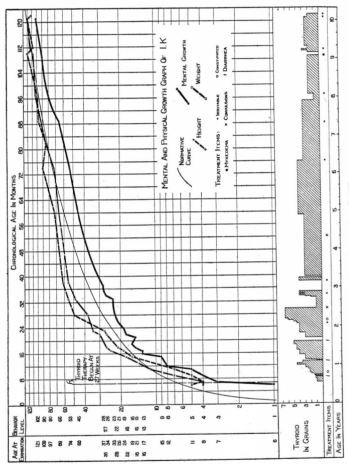

Growth graph of I.K.

To what extent the mental growth trend, so far con-sistently maintained over a period of almost twelve years, is predictive of the future cannot be asserted with confidence. It is highly probable that with thyroid therapy the general level already achieved will be maintained. On the last exami-nation, however, there were premonitory evidences of pu-bescence and we noted a personality change in greater freedom of manner and in increased alertness and social re-sponsiveness. Despite the somewhat improved personality picture, intelligence remained the same as it had been on the two previous examinations (I.Q. 75). A glance at the de-velopment curves shows that the course of mental growth for the last two years has been practically an extension of what it was up to the age of 7 years. The improvement in personality reaction, however, may denote an endocrinolog-ical transformation which may have a favorable accelerating effect upon the total development, including the fields of adaptive behavior. The thyroid gland does not function in complete isolation and independence, and if there is an access of gonadal hormones in store during the immediately forth-coming years, this may exert a palpable influence upon the rest of the life cycle.

G. PREMATURITY AND POSTMATURITY

§ 24. J.L.
Premature Birth Associated with Retarded Development
(3 weeks—12.5 years)

The uterus is the normal environment of the fetus until the end of a gestation period of 40 weeks. But birth with survival may in very exceptional instances occur as early as 24 weeks and as late as 48 weeks—an enormous range of variation in natal age amounting to six lunar months. Varia-tion within a range of two or three months is comparatively common. Prematurity of birth constitutes an abnormal alteration of environment which might conceivably affect the developmental career of the infant.

The life of the child, for a season, may be more precarious than if he had been born at full term. But has he, perhaps, through premature birth, been granted some compensating stimulus in the struggle for existence? One or two months before the appointed time he lives in a world of sight, sound, and social ministrations. Will this confer upon him a precocious adjustment and carry him more hurriedly through his early infancy? Or is this precocious entrance into the world but an incident, and will the nervous system proceed unperturbed in its growth, punctual to the usual program? Such were the questions we asked when we made our first acquaintance with J.L., over twelve years ago.

. He was then "three weeks" old. He had just been transferred from the obstetrical to the pediatric ward. Paradoxically enough, he wore an ancient look on his thin, wizened face, even though by biologic right he was fully five weeks younger than a normal newborn. He had been born with a birth weight of 1,303 grams, and a prematurity estimated at two months. His soft pinkish skin was still covered with lanugo, but his general physical condition was satisfactory. His fontanelle was neither sunken nor bulging; his lungs were clear; his heart sounds of good quality, regular and from 130 to 160 in rate, no murmurs.

Early behavior status:

Our first developmental examination was made when J.L. was 5 months of age. He had attained a weight of 3,440 grams and was ready for discharge from the hospital. His statutory age was 5 months, but his behavior maturity was much less than that.

To characterize his developmental status succinctly we may report selected behavior items, phrasing them in the present tense. J.L. looks at examiner regardfully. Fixates intently on dangling ring; does not definitely close in on the ring, but activity is increased while watching it. Visual fixa-tion on the hand, but no typical 4-month hand play. Head wabbles markedly when he is lifted to shoulder. Does not manipulate or seize paper even when it is placed in hand. Turns head to bell, both right and left.

The general clinical impression of the behavior picture justifies a rating of less than 3 months, or approximately 2.5 months. There is only one item which is rather inconsistent with this generalized rating, namely the response to the ringing of the bell. Further comment on this exception may be offered later.

If the foregoing developmental rating were accepted on its unqualified merit, it would yield a developmental quotient of 50 and necessitate a diagnosis of mental defect. In view of the prematurity, no such diagnosis was considered war-rantable.

Age 7 months. J.L. has made definite behavior gains since the previous examination. He now closes in definitely on the dangling ring. He tolerates the supported sitting posi-tion, although his head plunges forward from time to time. He kneads the table surface when held in the lap. There is "exploratory" inspection of the room. He definitely re-gards a cube when it is placed on the table. On ten successive trials, the span of visual fixation on the cube is uniformly about three seconds. He is socially alert, smiles responsively, coos mildly. A certain quality of normality in the whole be-havior picture restrains a diagnosis of mental defect, though the developmental level is only 4 months and the develop-mental quotient less than 60.

Age 8 months. Although it is only one month since the previous examination, he has made a perceptible gain which permits us to place his developmental level at approximately 5 months. He now definitely clasps the dangling ring. He grasps and manipulates a piece of paper when it is favorably presented. He regards a pellet placed on the table. His head is more erect, but still tends to plunge forward. His head-turning response to the ringing of the bell is very definite.

Age 9 months. The fourth developmental examination was made at the age of 9 months. By that time the problem of developmental diagnosis had become piquantly complex. The infant had taken on a more normal, even pert, appearance. The developmental trend as above summarized had shown a steady advance. But we had learned in the interval that both parents were definitely low in mentality and lived in squalor. On the face of it, the retardation was sufficiently marked to warrant a diagnosis of mental defect, particularly when weighted with these background factors. Our perplexity is revealed in the following clinical memorandum made at the time (1926).

J.L. at the age of 9 months approximates nearly the 5-month behavior picture, from the standpoint of general capacity. He does not present a clear-cut 6-month picture, and there are qualitative imperfections and reductions even on the 5-month items. However, descriptively his status may be generalized as being at the 5.5-month level. He has made perceptible gain in the interval of a month which has elapsed since his previous examination. The items on which this gain can be most concretely formulated are as follows:

Direct grasping by one hand, which during the examination was mainly the right hand, has replaced the cruder closing in observed on the 8-month examination. This reaching has not risen to the 6-month level, but there is definite visual coöperation and there is some facility in reaching situations, if the objects are favorably and closely presented, and if the child is on his back. He probably has not had much opportunity to exercise his capacity through play with toys. His head no longer tends to plunge forward as it did a month ago. His progression reactions in the prone position showed some advance. His hand-to-mouth reaction is not as dominating as it was on the previous examination. Vocalization of eagerness and pleasurable vocalization accompanying frolicsome play were in evidence. On the previous examination the child was almost altogether silent. The visual regard for the pellet also is more clearly defined. Interest in vanishing objects like a disappearing paper is more evident.

While there has been no dramatic gain, these items in the aggregate show a palpable increment, though not necessarily amounting to a full month's gain. The general clinical impression of the quality of the behavior does not decisively indicate mental defect, but suggests borderline inferiority as an alternative diagnosis. However, we recognize the danger of not weighting sufficiently both the qualitative and quantitative subnormalities which have been noted.

Our tentativeness is increased by the fact that we are not certain in regard to the degree of prematurity of birth, and also because there is definite possibility of hereditary defect. In order to make a precise developmental rating at this stage of development, it would be necessary to have finer normative determinations than we can make, and we should indeed have to know the degree of prematurity to the week.

At the age of 5 months, when we made our first examination, a difference of onehalf month in the normative rating has considerable diagnostic and prognostic significance. It is our general impression that the course of development has been relatively consistent, although on a subnormal plane.

The spurious almanac age of this child at the four examinations was as follows: 5, 7, 8, and 9 months, reckoning from the date of birth. The corrected chronological age for these successive examinations would be 3 months, 5, 6, and 7 months—if he was born two months prematurely as we assume. Reviewing all the ratings before us, we may say that the generalized developmental ratings at the four successive examinations are: 2.5 months, 4, 4.5, and 5.5 months. The developmental quotients on the basis of these ratings are all of them approximately 80. To maintain the constancy of this quotient, it was necessary for the child to make a gain of six weeks between the first two examinations, which is a somewhat more rapid rate of development than he has displayed subsequently, but which is not inconsistent if we remember that at the time he was still biologically, if not chronologically, located in the faster-growing period of the life cycle.

The case is a very instructive one from the psychometric point of view, because it clearly indicates the great importance of small durational units and of small increments of development. If we should altogether disregard the fact that this child was born two months prematurely, we should set him down unhesitatingly as being definitely feebleminded. Although this may ultimately be the diagnosis, the present diagnosis is much ameliorated by the fact that his chronological age of 9 months is really a spurious almanac age.

All things considered, we should say that a developmental quotient of 80, although descriptive, is too flattering; and that he may descend somewhat later to a quotient of 70 or 75 and still be clinically classifiable as a borderline inferior with relatively good personality makeup.

Later behavior development:

The last paragraph was a fortunate forecast. As a clinical classification, it is as true today as it was twelve years ago. J.L. was re-examined on nine more occasions between the ages of 9 months and 12.5 years. The developmental quotients have gravitated in the 75-80 zone. On the last examination, age 12.5 years, he earned a quotient of 70. The general course of his development is epitomized in the accompanying graph (Graph 12).

The descriptive characterization of *borderline inferior* made in infancy holds today. We are confronted with a boy who is definitely retarded in his mental development, who barely earns a rating of 8.5 years on the intelligence scale, but who gives sufficient tokens of "normality" to restrain an

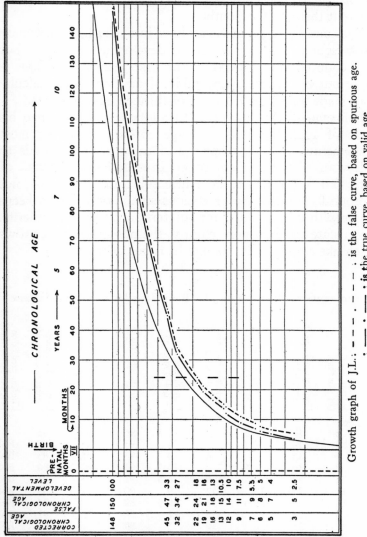

Growth graph of J.L.: − − . − . − . is the false curve, based on spurious age. − . − : is the true curve, based on valid age.

unqualified diagnosis of high-grade mental defect. On a more mature plane, the clinical picture remains essentially what it was at the age of 9 months.

Two months of prematurity have lost their early arithmetical weight in the calculation of developmental status; but they counted very heavily in the first year of life. This is borne out by the following table of developmental calculations made for the entire series of thirteen examinations.

It is evident that the premature infant has more than his share of ages. His biological age appears to be the most fundamental. The development of early behavior tends to follow an inherent genetic order, irrespective of the time of birth. There appears to be a firm substrate of growth, not profoundly affected by precocious stimulation, which keeps the growth curve similar for full-term and pre-term infants. Or to state the fact more bluntly, the pre-term infant grows much like a fetus, even though he is out of the womb.

TABLE V

DEVELOPMENTAL RATINGS OF J.L., BORN TWO MONTHS PREMATURELY

Order of examination	Postnatal chronological age (a) (in months)	Conceptional age (b) (in months)	Developmental age (c)	Corrected chronological age (d)	Genetic age level $= c + 9$ mo. (e)	Genetic quotient $= e/b$	Spurious developmental quotient c/a	Corrected developmental quotient c/d	Clinical prediction BN, borderline normal
	mo.	mo.	mo.	mo.					
1	5	12	2.5	3	11.5	96	50	83	?
2	7	14	4	5	13	93	57	80	BN
3	8	15	5	6	14	93	62	83	BN
4	9	16	5.5	7	14.5	91	61	80	BN
5	11	18	7.5	9	16.5	92	68	83	BN
6	14	21	10	12	19	90	71	83	BN
7	15	22	10.5	13	19.5	89	70	80	BN
8	18	25	13	16	22	88	72	81	BN
9	21	28	16	19	25	89	76	84	BN
10	24	31	18	22	27	87	75	82	BN
11	34	41	27	32	36	87	79	84	BN
12	47	54	33	45	42	77	70	73	B
13	150	157	100	148	109	69	66	68	B

Nevertheless, the premature infant is doubtless a habit-forming creature even during the period of prematurity. He is not altogether impervious to the impact of light and sound, and to the physical ministrations of the nurse. On the basis of this susceptibility to recurrent impressions, very elementary patterns of behavior must take shape; so that he acquires certain "expectations" or "trends of reaction" which could scarcely have been formed within the isolation of the uterus. Whether audition, as such, whether even oculomotor control is hastened by precocious release from uterine protection is not clear. But, as already suggested, conditioned modes of listening or of eye-following, and selective attention to the human face and to the human voice may well be somewhat advanced on the developmental schedule of the premature infant, as already suggested in J.L.

In the habit-forming field of personal-social behavior, expressed in personality, there may be skewing or discrepancy in his apparent favor. Such a personality discrepancy may assert itself with temporary vividness when a newborn full-term infant is compared with a pre-term infant who has had two months of "experience" in a socialized environment. All things considered, however, the extrinsic conditioning factors seem to be of secondary importance in determining the mental growth of the premature child. The substrate of maturation in cases without pathological complications is relatively secure and serves as a developmental safeguard for the prematurely born.

The behavior of the premature infant is not alone a subject of scientific interest from a genetic standpoint; it is a subject of medical significance with direct and indirect bearing upon problems of child protection. Too frequently prematurity is not recognized by physician or nurse, and the child's welfare suffers in consequence. When more is known about the behavior characteristics of the premature, there will be greater accuracy in diagnosing both the presence and the degree of prematurity. Refinements in the hygiene of the premature infant will also come through a better understanding of his behavior limitations and requirements.

§ 25. L.N.
Postmature Birth Associated with Advanced Development
(3 months—10 years)

Postmaturity as well as prematurity exerts a spurious effect upon the calculated rate of behavior development, if correction is not made for chronological age. The mother of L.N. had a gestation history which strongly suggested that her daughter, L.N., was born at least one month past normal term. L.N.'s statutory chronological age, reckoned, of course, from her birthday, was 3 months at the time of the first examination. The level of her behavior, however, was definitely in advance of 3 months maturity. Her eye-hand coördinations were sufficiently advanced to result in spontaneous reaching for near objects in the dressing period. Her adjustment to early training situations and a trace of discriminativeness in her responses to persons indicated a maturity level to which we assigned a value of 4.5 months. The second examination, made at the (statutory chronological) age of 4 months showed a similar advance in the level of behavior. Eight examinations were made prior to her third birthday, and all of these pointed to acceleration in developmental rate. With the results of this series of examinations before us, we were confronted with the question of the probable degree of acceleration. A developmental quotient derived on the basis of the first examination resulted in a rather prodigious value, namely $\frac{4.5}{3}$, yielding a D.Q. of 150. Quotients of this high value, on our present developmental schedules, are extremely rare in the first quarter of the first year. The value of 150 is spuriously high because it ignores the factor of postmaturity. If a correction is made for one month of postmaturity, and a chronological age of 4 months instead of 3 is used for reckoning, we derive a more respectable developmental quotient, namely, a value of 115. Without insisting too much on the numerical precision of these two quotients, the difference does indicate the great importance of accurate determinations of chronological age. The accuracy of our present methods of developmental appraisal would be increased if we had more exact criteria for the determination of true chronological or postconception age. Lacking these exact criteria, due clinical allowance must be made for evidences which point to prematurity and postmaturity. Even after having made due allowance in this case for the fictitious inflation of a month of postmaturity, we adjudged this child to be slightly superior or advanced in her development.

Six subsequent examinations, made between the ages of 3 years and 10 years, have confirmed this judgment. On these examinations the child rated at least one year above her chronological age. A quotient of 115 is typical of her developmental status at 3, 4, 5, 6, and 10 years. By the time she had reached the age of 10 years the distorting effect of one month of postmaturity became negligible in making the appraisal of developmental status. But when she was 3 and 4 months old, this effect was far from negligible.

CHAPTER IV

THE APPRAISAL OF GROWTH CHARACTERISTICS

THE behavior biographies which we have just reviewed give clear evidence of a high degree of latent predictability in the early sector of the life cycle. In the whole series of thirty diversified specimens, there is no instance in which the course or trend of mental growth has proved whimsical or erratic. The case of B.C. showed the most marked reversal of trend. Among the cases which are summarized in Part Two of this volume there will appear other instances of irregularity and apparent accession of new growth potentialities, not recognized in earlier diagnoses. But in comparison with the great mass of cases which remain true to early trends and characteristics, these atypical cases are highly exceptional.

"Exceptional" is a word which needs apology, if it implies something miraculous or outside the realm of natural causes. We use the word here simply to express the fact that under clinical conditions, with the exercise of due caution, and with restraint in over-specific divinations, the growth trends of infancy and childhood can be appraised approximately.

Having strongly urged the need of constant vigilance and prudence, let us for a moment stress the affirmative side of the story. Reliability in the clinical prognosis of behavior development must rest on a judicious weighting of probabilities based upon normative determinations. Prediction can then be carefully graduated to the inherent genetic probability behind the symptomatic behavior patterns.

The term *genetic probability* invites a little philosophizing. This kind of probability is not a mere actuarial probability; nor does it depend upon an indifferent principle of uncertainty, or a neutral condition of utter randomness. The very word genetic suggests a living organism which grows, and which is so charged with certainty that under given, specific conditions it is bound to assume characteristic forms and functions. Webster's definition of certainty serves very well: CERTAIN—"in such a condition or position that failure (to happen or to do a specified thing) is impossible; incapable of failing; destined; sure;—followed by an infinitive; it is as certain to grow as to live."

In this basic sense, an endless number of growth characteristics are *certain*. They are incapable of failing. In this sense also innumerable characteristic sequences of growth products are certain. Such sequences are genetic sequences, and they constitute the essence of genetic probability.

If we seem to be elucidating an axiom, it is because we wish to emphasize the truly enormous scope of developmental prediction. If we add up all the certainties, it may even prove that growth phenomena are among the most predictable in nature. To be sure, we have to assume energy constants which maintain the life of the organism on a more or less even keel. But this is not an extravagant assumption. Even when one risks the astronomical prediction that the sun will rise tomorrow, one assumes certain normal constants!

Assuming normal constants, the zygote is certain to become an embryo, which is certain to become a fetus, which becomes in turn an infant, child, and man. Each punctual and complete fulfillment increases the probability of an impending morphogenesis. For this reason the mode, the rate, and the completeness of attained growth are prognostics of as-yet-unrealized growth. The sequences are governed by inherent genetic probabilities which make prediction possible.

The foregoing generalizations and abstractions are not endangered when we consider the concrete manifestations of growth, whether a limb bud, the optic cup, an ossification center, or a specific pattern of behavior. Each concrete embodiment or manifestation of growth in an organic context presages another more advanced manifestation.

An infant 4 weeks old stares vacantly; at 6 weeks he fixates his eyes definitely upon a window; at 12 weeks his eyes follow the transit of a dangling ring across the field of vision; at 16 weeks he definitely looks at a one-inch cube placed before him. At 20 weeks he closes in on the cube, grasps it on contact; at 24 weeks he seizes it on sight. Here is a genetic series of patterns of eye-hand behavior. The patterns occur as events in an order which is determined by the very mechanics of development.

Once they have occurred we are certain, by inference, that an extremely long and complicated series of antecedent events has already taken place in the prenatal and neonatal periods. By similar inference, there is an almost equally strong certainty that subsequent patternings of basic behavior will occur in a sequence which is genetically characteristic of the species, the type, or the individual (in a specified environment). Prognosis is a forward projection of inference.

Mental growth is a process of progressive differentiation and organization which leads to specific ends. To a considerable extent these ends are inherent in the organism. Mental growth is both labile and stabile. But nature sets metes and bounds to the lability. Variability is constantly channelized. Just as homeostasis safeguards the integrity of the individual on the so-called physiological level, so do closely related mechanisms of maturation give integrity to the growth career. This is the stable aspect of growth.

For such reasons, no genuine miracles can occur in the methods and the issues of behavior growth. It is possible to make errors of diagnosis, to overlook obscure factors which come to light in later weeks or months, or even overnight. When we think of the exquisite plasticities and adaptabilities of the growth complex, our present criteria for estimating growth may well be considered crude; but the very nature of growth confers upon them a great deal of indicativeness. Accordingly, many growth trends can be recognized early and are found to run significantly true to form.

Take, for example, the six siblings discussed in the previous chapter (§ 4: D.E., E.F., F.G., G.H., H.I., I.J.). Three have clung unmistakably to a normal course of behavior development; the other three, as decisively to a subnormal course. It took no diagnostic subtlety to distinguish between these two kinds of growth potentiality on the basis of one behavior examination in infancy. The point is that these infant behavior pictures were unambiguously prophetic of the later careers. The predictions, therefore, were accurate. And they were safe because nature is never so whimsical as to mix up sectors of the growth curves of two sets of individuals as differently endowed as D.E. and I.J.

To a similar degree the predictive estimates of the distinctively superior children like J.K., N.O., O.P. have not missed the mark. The estimates were made before the children could read or write; which means that there was a high degree of indicativeness in the early behavior symptoms.

In less-well-defined behavior pictures, equally confident predictions are not forthcoming because we do not have the techniques or acumen to identify and assess the indicators; but a comparable latent predictiveness resides in these pictures as well.

The illustrative cases already reviewed, and others which are summarized in Part Two, disclose a high degree of characteristicness in the emotional traits and motor peculiarities of children. This characteristicness is so durable that it manifests itself throughout childhood and into adolescence in such well-defined individualities as C.D., V.W., C.E. and H.J. The latent predictability of temperamental traits and psychic constitution in all types of children is probably very great. Science will some day supply techniques and methods for more precise assays of such constitutional factors. But even

now clinical perception can detect numerous traits of individuality, and forecast their persistence in the growth career.
These possibilities will be more fully considered in Chapter VI.

In appraising growth characteristics, we cannot ignore so-
called environmental influences—cultural milieu, siblings,
parents, food, sunshine, illness, trauma, education. But these
must always be considered in relation to primary or constitutional factors, because the latter ultimately determine the
degree, and even the mode, of the reaction to so-called environment. The organism always participates in the creation
of its environment, and the growth characteristics of the child
are really the end-product expressions of an interaction between intrinsic and extrinsic determiners. Because the interaction is the crux, the distinction between these two sets of
determiners should not be drawn too heavily.

When there is a fairly even balance between the endoge-
nous and the sustaining or exogenous factors, the trends of
mental growth, whether subnormal, superior, or mediocre,
are likely to be most consistent. Developmental diagnosis and
prognosis then come nearest to their mark. When, however,
the organism is under stress of distortion, because of unfavorable conditions, then its ultimate adjustments as expressed
in growth characteristics become least predictable. There are
too many variables to appraise. External environment can be
estimated with some shrewdness; but not so readily, the internal developmental reserves.

These hidden reserves are the intrinsic insurance factors
which we have had to mention repeatedly in cases of atypical
and irregular behavior development. The concept of insurance factors is not mystical. It is derived from experimental
embryology and from clinical observation. The surgical ex-
cisions, transplantations, and other interferences with the
growing tissues of laboratory embryos, have demonstrated
that the organism is protected with a remarkable fund of
reserve mechanisms which promptly or gradually move into

every breach and fill it in some way, either through regenera-
tion, or compensatory and substitutive growth. If the lesion
is too great, the organism dies. If the lesion is not too severe,
and the organism not too old, growth may continue in a
normal manner.

In the development of the nervous system and in the onto-
genesis of behavior, the human organism displays comparable
insurance mechanisms. Locked in inner recesses beyond diagnostic scrutiny are reserve factors which may come to the
rescue when development is retarded or impaired. As a poison
stimulates the formation of antibodies, so certain errors or
depressions of development stimulate a regulatory self-cor-
rection. These reserve factors, however, are not a single generalized capacity. They are specific biochemical and somatic
structures, probably almost infinite in number and variety;
and of many degrees of availability. They are present in
defective as well as normal individuals. They are probably
most abundant in the most vital and best endowed. Vitality
is an index of the plenitude and vigor of these very insurance
factors. In spheres of behavior they operate not only during
the period of growth, but also in old age; at least in the most
"vital" individuals.

If there is a principle of uncertainty in the physiology of
development, it is a biological principle which rests upon important individual differences with respect to these insurance
factors. Since they vary in amount, it is difficult to ascertain
their strength in those inscrutable infants who present an
inadequate and yet not decisively defective behavior picture.
Here diagnosis must be wary, sometimes for a whole year or
more. Because sometimes the insurance factors come tardily
and slowly into full force. But if they are present, and if the
attendant conditions permit, they will ultimately assert themselves. When there is no counteracting deteriorating process,
the tendency of growth will be toward something better and
toward an optimal organization of the achieved equipment.

The moral of all this: diagnosis must be cautious whenever

there are strong insurance factors to be reckoned with. In cases of doubt, temper the developmental prognosis favorably or withhold it altogether.

The varied factors which complicate the appraisal of growth characteristics will be further indicated in the series of growth studies which make up Part Two of the present volume. By way of introductory summary the concepts and principles which underly the developmental diagnosis of infant behavior may be outlined in a dozen statements as follows:

(1) The growth characteristics of the infant are primarily determined by hereditary and constitutional factors which undergo their basic organization in the uterine period.

(2) These factors do not operate independently of postnatal environmental influences, social and physical, but they determine the direction and scope of such influences.

(3) Maturational factors impart characteristic trend, tempo, and general configuration to the early behavior patterning of the individual. The resultant characteristicness is amenable to cumulative diagnosis.

(4) Every individual has a distinctive complex of growth; but the infant growth cycle displays fundamental sequences and progressions which are general in nature.

(5) Mental growth is an orderly process of morphogenesis. The reaction system of the infant is a unitary structure which manifests itself in specific and correlated patterns of behavior.

(6) Comprehensively conceived, these patterns embrace the entire organism and include the vegetative, sensorimotor, and symbolic spheres of behavior.

(7) The patterns undergo progressive, ontogenetic changes of form and of correlation with age. These changes can be defined by objective and normative methods, particularly in the fields of posture, locomotion, prehension, manipulation, and adaptive, language, and social behavior.

(8) A developmental norm is a specification of a behavior

pattern or of a behavior characteristic made to serve as a criterion or as a standard of comparison in the scrutiny of a behavior status.

(9) The primary use of the norm is to identify and to characterize observed behavior forms. Because of the rapidity of behavior growth, norms are essential at frequent age intervals.

(10) A norm is a standardized tool for discriminative characterization. Strictly speaking, a norm is not a unit of measurement. It represents a positional value rather than an absolute value in a calibrated scale of equal units.

(11) Growth is a morphogenetic process which produces changes of pattern and progressive degrees of maturity. Growth cannot be measured in the dynamic abstract. It can, however, be characterized. Growth can be examined analytically and synthetically in terms of its patterned products. Norms in a systematic series are aids to such examination.

(12) A norm is accordingly used as a critical device for discovering resemblances and differences. This is comparison rather than true mensuration. But accurate comparison by means of a systematic frame of reference approximates the precision of measurement.

Developmental diagnosis should use methods of analysis and its findings should be formulated in interpretive characterizations to avoid the dangers of biometric over-simplification.

[For readers and students who are not familiar with the ethods of diagnosis used in the developmental examination infants and children, an addendum on page 310 suggests sic manuals and source books which may be consulted.]

PART TWO

H. Superior Mental Endowment   *Helen Thompson*

CHAPTER V

INDIVIDUAL STUDIES OF BEHAVIOR GROWTH

H. SUPERIOR MENTAL ENDOWMENT

§ 26. *Introductory Statement*

THE relationships between accelerated development and superiority of mental equipment were discussed at some length in Chapter III. Four more cases are briefly presented here to further illustrate the diversities in developmental pattern which may occur. It has been demonstrated in Chapter III, § 5-9, that certain signs of superiority appear at a very early age. But in general, the detection of potential superiority in infancy is less certain by ordinary procedures than is the recognition of deficient or average ability. There are several reasons why this should be true. An infant may possess latent language ability which, being latent, has little chance for overt expression in infancy; he may have the capacity for developing powers of abstract thinking not revealed in reactions to infant tests; he may be so keenly and so generally perceptive that his attention, as tested, is distracted from its usual channels and does not measure up even to the average. Furthermore, certain infants of superior endowment may well have a distinct type of behavior growth in which the developmental momentum increases with age.

Greater success in forecasting unusual ability can be attained by further study of the infant behavior of those children who, when older, prove unusually capable. At present, however, it is important clinically to recognize our limitations with respect to prediction. We shall present here two children (Ida and Isabel) whose behavior in infancy was not even up to average standards, but who later gave evidence of superior mental endowment. Irene, on the contrary, was markedly accelerated in infancy, but only slightly so at 4 years of age. Edith, however, represents a more common type in which the early clinical impression of superiority was sus' tained at later examinations.

This diversity of cases will serve to remind us that our present diagnostic measures (and habits of perception) are more suitable for certain forms of superior ability than for others. When we recall how easily genuine superiority is overlooked even in schools and colleges, it is not surprising that we do not invariably detect it in the nursery! More' over, the protean concept of "superiority" is a very loose one which will be abandoned as knowledge becomes more precise. From the standpoint of developmental psychology, both theoretical and applied, our basic problem is to discover distinctive styles of behavior growth and modes of function' ing which are symptomatic of different kinds of adult ability. When we are able to identify such patterns of performance and of personality development, the term "superiority" will lose some of its present vagueness.

§ 27. Ida B.
At One Year Retarded; at 5 Years Superior
(52 weeks—7 years)

According to the laws of heredity we might well expect Ida B. to be a gifted child. Both parents had received college and professional training. Both on the paternal and maternal sides, Ida had distinguished ancestry. Her three siblings like' wise were highly superior. One brother, slow in reaction time, developed at a barely average rate in infancy but clearly dem' onstrated above'average capacities in his second year.

Our first contact with Ida was in connection with an ex' perimental study of adaptive behavior in infancy. Of twelve infants, all 28 weeks old, she was the only one who did not secure a lure placed beyond her reach by pulling at the readily accessible string. We were not greatly concerned by her lack of adaptation in this instance because, with her background, we had no reason to suspect retardation. Again, when she was 40 weeks old she was the only one who failed to solve the "problem." But still we were not disturbed by her failure. However, when she was a year old her mother came to us with serious concern. She reported that Ida was developing very slowly. Would we examine the child and tell her frankly what we found? We were inclined to discount Mrs. B.'s report, but because of her anxiety we were willing to examine the child and, as we thought, allay her fears.

To our surprise, Ida really did not measure up to her age and, furthermore, the reported home behavior gave indication that the test situations were eliciting characteristic behavior. The prenatal, birth, and health histories were negative. Table VI summarizes the course of her behavior development.

On each of the five examinations made between 1 and 2 years, Ida appeared definitely less mature than would be expected of a child of her age. Although at 56 weeks she was inhibited, on subsequent visits excellent rapport was established. We were unable to explain the slowness of her development; she was not premature; she had the same intelligent care under which her brothers had flourished; she had the stimulation of three older siblings; and she had experienced no illness. We wondered if some mild glandular deficiency might be the cause of her immaturity and her lack of spontaneity, but no physical condition which warranted medication was found.

Although her behavior was only at the 18-month performance level when she was 2 years old, we were still unwilling to accept the possibility that she might be potentially slightly below normal, and we suggested that she come to the guidance nursery, where her play would be under close observation. When Ida entered the nursery-school group at the age of 28 months, her behavior corroborated the home report and examination findings. She had not yet progressed beyond the

TABLE VI

IDA B.

Chronological age	Behavior level					Comments
	Postural	Prehen-sory	Language	Adaptive	Personal-social	
52 weeks	38 wks.	40 wks.	44 wks.	40 wks.	44 wks.	Very inhibited; rocks back and forth; sucks thumb. Suggest re-examination
15 months	12 mos.	12 mos.	12 mos.	12 mos.	12 mos.	Friendly, coöperative, and apparently displayed full ability. Does not walk alone. No behavior in advance of 12 mos.
18 months	15 mos.	14 mos.	14 mos.	14 mos.	14 mos.	Good adjustment. No reason to believe that child has greater ability than she displays
21 months	18 mos.	?	15 mos.	15 mos.	18 mos.	Good adjustment but meager self-activity. Happy and docile. Language expression and

Age					Remarks
					comprehension at only 15 mos. level. Development during last 3 mos. in language and adaptation slight
24 months	18 mos.	18 mos.	18 mos.	18 mos.	Slightly more spontaneous, though self-activity still meager. Does not yet put two words together
28 months					Entered guidance nursery for observation. At first, unusually inactive. Watched but did not join the group. Showed more initiative when alone than when with another child. More active out-of-doors than indoors. After 34 contacts with nursery group, learned to enter group play
36 months	M.A. score: 40 months. Developmental ratio about 110				Definite advance in rate of development. Behavior above norm for age in both adaptive and personal-social categories
5 years	M.A. score: 7 years. Stanford Binet I.Q. 140				Replies mature. Especially interested in coöperative play
7 years, 3 months	M.A. score: 9 years, 7 months. Stanford Binet I.Q. 130				Definitions particularly superior in quality. Unusual imagination expressed in drawings. Vocabulary level 10 yrs.

single-word stage and, while she had adequate motor skills for more mature play, she stood watching the children or engaged in some repetitive activity. Even after several periods with the group, she spent by actual count more than 90 per cent of the time simply observing the play of others. Did she not realize that she could do what they were doing? Had she not experienced joy in her own activity, or was the play of others more engrossing?

When brought into the Clinic for special play experience with an adult, Ida utilized all of the materials and occupied herself more normally. "Private tutoring" was continued, usually with one other child present. After four months she was returned to the regular nursery group with astonishing results. She now entered into group activities and spent less than a quarter of her time just looking. A re-examination at the age of 3 years revealed behavior fully normal for her age and even advanced behavior with respect to adaptation and personal-social behavior. On subsequent examinations she gave unqualified evidence of superiority. At 7 years 3 months she has a keen imagination, an unusually out-going personality, and the verbal comprehension and expression of a ten-year-old. She is an incessant talker and a little inclined to be moody.

It is impossible to account for the early lag in development with any degree of assurance. Any clinician will immediately point to the many factors which may have been operating, but the obscurity of these factors must be admitted. It is comparatively easy to interpret when we know the final outcome, but prediction is another matter.

§ 28. *Isabel O.*
*A Foundling. Superiority not Suspected in Infancy but Well
Defined in Fourth Year*
(10 weeks—7 years 3 months)

In contrast to Ida B., whose parents and family were well known to us, we present a foundling whose history was a blank page. A policeman found Isabel O. abandoned in a car, and took her to a hospital. Seven weeks later she was discharged to the child-caring institution, which referred her to us for examination.

We found Isabel to be a dark-skinned infant, with dark-brown hair and eyes. She was placid and presented an appearance of maturity in advance of her general performance. We knew that she must be more than 8 weeks old, yet her behavior, except for postural control, was more comparable with that of the normal 6-weeks-old infant. The second examination, two weeks later, gave a relatively better picture and the outlook was considered "probably average and normal" (see Table VII). But considering the fact that we knew only within certain limits the child's age, we continued to reserve judgment.

On the third examination, fourteen weeks later, or about twenty-four weeks after the child had been found, her behavior was rather consistently at the 20-week level. Physical measurements indicated a chronological age of about 22 weeks. We began to suspect that Isabel was a premature baby. The hospital records were made available and they confirmed our suspicions. When brought to the hospital she was judged to be from 7 to 10 days old; she weighed only 2,130 grams and her length, her head, chest, and abdomen circumferences indicated a gestation age of between 32 and 34 weeks. According to physical signs, then, she was from four to six weeks premature. This finding gave new meaning to Isabel's behavior which was quite up to average when she was regarded in terms of the duration of her life from conception. However, we did not suspect that she had the potential superiority later demonstrated.

On her fourth examination Isabel's performance was entirely consistent with her previous behavior, except in her personal-social relationships, which were better developed than her general behavior.

The fifth and sixth examinations showed a little spurt in

TABLE VII

ISABEL O.

Chrono-logical age	Behavior level					Comment
	Postural	Prehensory	Language	Adaptive	Personal-social	
1. 10 wks.?	8 wks.	6 wks.	6 wks.	6 wks.	6 wks.	Very placid infant. Excellent head control gives impression of maturity in advance of general performance
2. 12 wks.?	11+ wks.	10 wks.	10 wks.	10 wks.	10 wks.	Superior motor control. Developmental outlook is probably average and normal
3. 26 wks.?	20 wks.	20 wks.	20 wks.	20 wks.	20 wks.	Tendency to rock from side to side. Quality of regard immature. Physical measurements indicate CA of 22 wks. Weighed 4 lbs. when found. Premature? Foster home placement
4. 30 wks.	24 wks.	24 wks.	?	24 wks.	26 wks.	Fatigues easily in spite of good physical development. Sensitive to strangers. Normal.
5. 53 wks.	52 wks.	48 wks.	52 wks.	48 wks.	46 wks.	Sturdy-appearing infant who fatigues easily. Outlook at least average
6. 18 mos.	18 mos.	16 mos.	18 mos.	16 mos.	18 mos.	Mildly inhibited during examination. Most mature performance in language field. Placed in home for adoption
7. 3 yrs. 4.5 mos.	Stanford-Binet mental age: about 4 yrs. 8 mos. I.Q. about 135	60 mos.	+54 mos.	+54 mos.	+54 mos.	Behavior well defined and easily elicited. Friendly, responsive, and self-possessed
8. 4 yrs. 6 mos.	Stanford-Binet mental age: about 5 yrs. 7 mos. I.Q. about 125					Most attractive, responsive child. Considerable imagination
9. 7 yrs. 3 mos.	Stanford-Binet mental age: about 8 yrs. I.Q. about 125					Talkative and a little restless during examination. Has many interests

development. On the fifth examination, when her birth age was about 53 weeks, her language and postural development were found to be up to the one-year norm. She walked when

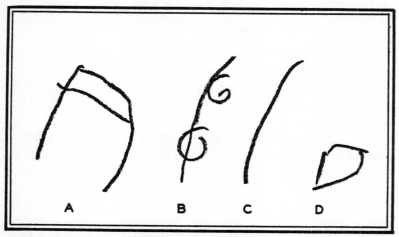

Fig. 4. Drawing of A, B, C, D, by Isabel O., aged 3 years 3½ months.

only one hand was held, and she said "pretty," "kitty," and "by-by," in addition to calling four individuals by a distinctive sound similar to their names. This performance could be considered very good indeed for a premature, but it was not superior. On the sixth examination she rated a quotient of not quite 110 when her age was discounted for prematurity.

We were both surprised and delighted when, two years later, at the age of 3 years 3.5 months, Isabel rated an Intelligence Quotient of 135. Although she failed three of the IV-year tests (matching forms, copying a square, and digit repetition), she passed all of the V-year tests and two tests at year VI (comprehension and identifying right and left). It was of interest that, although she failed to copy the square, she drew A,B,C, and D from memory. She was unable to make corners, but she could reproduce the essential distinguishing elements of these letters (see Figure 4). She had developed a delightfully social personality. After her third failure to copy a square, she gave evidence by her facial expression that she appreciated her inadequacy, then looked up, beaming, and said, "I draw you a prune," which she did with obvious pleasure, matching her task to her ability, the uneven oblong circle suggesting the dried fruit which she had seen at home.

On subsequent examinations there was a drop in quotient, but she still rated as definitely superior. Her imaginative drawings continued to show the same quality we have just described. She is a sensitive, eager, active, sociable child of whom any parents might be proud.

It is important to review Isabel's record to see what factors suggest her present superiority. On the very first examination her head control was described as excellent. This is an item which may have positive diagnostic significance for mental growth as well as for motor growth. (The absence of this item at expected age is, however, by no means always indicative of retardation.) Also Isabel's performance on her first two examinations was superior, if, as we have assumed, she was premature. The third examination elicited the poorest behavior relative to age. Subsequent ratings improved gradually. Were the rocking from side to side and the subsequent tendency to fatigue easily indicative of some health factor which had a counterpart in the behavior picture? The question of race is another unknown factor. Isabel resembled the southern European people in complexion and general features, but the question of her race was even more of a mystery than her age.

It is of interest to note that after placement in a foster home the foster mother reported that the child had an exceptional memory. She was very discriminative with respect to people and situations. We have noticed that infants who have later proven superior are frequently so perceptive in infancy that the behavior examination in strange surroundings and conducted by an unfamiliar examiner inhibits rather than elicits behavior, and that such infants make a relatively poor absolute rating on tests rigidly administered. It may be that perception of surroundings and persons should be highly weighted in certain cases.

But unfortunately we cannot solve the problem of early recognition of superiority by the study of one or two cases. Undoubtedly there are different evidences of superiority in different "types" of infants just as there are different characteristics of superiority in adults. We may have the philosophic type, the deep thinker who becomes absorbed in abstract problems, or we may have the quick, more socially inclined genius, to cite only two examples.

§ 29. Edith T.
Consistent Superior Development
(28 weeks—4 years)

Edith is a child whose superiority was clearly recognizable early in infancy. She is an excellent example of the well-balanced, well-rounded, stable, superior personality type.

Edith first came to our attention at the age of 28 weeks. She had caused a mild furore in the neighborhood by her precocity in the motor field. We found her a very composed, but somewhat inhibited, infant who needed a fairly long "warming-up" period before adjusting to the examination. This type of adjustment is unusual at this early age, and suggested a maturity beyond her weeks. Gross motor development was displaced to approximately the 44-week level. She crept with agility, and on being given her first experience with a staircase, climbed one step unassisted. She sat alone with good control and also pulled to her feet and lowered herself. In other fields of behavior, interestingly enough, the acceleration was much less striking, and her general development was considered near the 30-week level. There was no acceleration in the field of language.

At 40 weeks Edith exhibited the same type of self-controlled and cautious adjustment. The acceleration in development was much more marked, pervading all fields uniformly, and her general level was estimated at 52-56 weeks. An occasional performance was close to the 15-month level. It was interesting to note that motor performance had fallen into line, and in spite of her early precocity, Edith did not yet walk alone, though she could stand momentarily without support.

At one year, the performance was fully 15 months, and the comment was made that many of her responses had a teasing, playful character, unusual for her age. "Her charming personality enhances performance."

Repeated re-examinations, continued through her fourth year, have shown her to be consistently accelerated in development, though the actual amount of acceleration has shown considerable variation. The developmental quotient has fluctuated between 125 and 150, and will probably stabilize within that range.

There have been no difficulties in management, and Edith is describable as an imaginative, resourceful child of superior intelligence. She showed discrimination combined with self-control as early as 28 weeks of age, a sense of her own power to command the examination situation at 15 months, an attitude of coöperation, and insight combined with autocriticism of performance at 2 years. At 3 years she had imaginary playmates, whom she insisted the family must treat with due consideration. At 4 years she had an imaginary other self; this was a serious game but still only a game, and it had no alarming implications.

The early development of this delightful child is interesting in many ways. Although it is unusual to find a measurable acceleration as early as 28 weeks, we were genuinely astonished to find so little (two weeks) in the face of the tremendous advancement in the motor field. Again, early motor acceleration does not necessarily imply early walking. This has been repeatedly seen in institution children who have few toys and little opportunity for play. They are often precocious creepers, but quite as often, delayed walkers. Edith pulled to her feet as early as 20 weeks, but did not walk until she was a year old. This is early but not nearly as early as might well have been expected. Then, too, there was no early (28 weeks) language acceleration, a fairly reliable indicator, when present, of superiority in infancy. Many gifted children show almost no deviation in development during the first year; many others show only varying degrees of acceleration in the field of language. Not so with Edith, whose language development was relatively retarded at 28 weeks and was not accelerated beyond her general level at 40 weeks.

In addition to the intellectual superiority, her emotional maturity, her insight, her command of situations, and her favorable personality were well developed in infancy and have consistently contributed to her performance. They were, perhaps, the very factors which enabled her superiority to manifest itself at so early an age.

§ 30. Irene R.
Accelerated in Infancy; Average at 4 Years
(8 weeks—4 years)

Irene was unquestionably accelerated in infancy. When she was first seen at the age of 8 weeks and also subsequently at 16 and 22 weeks of age she was definitely more mature than is usual. At 8 weeks she was very alert and socially responsive. When approached by the examiner, she increased her activity, vocalized, and smiled. This response was prolonged and vivid. At 16 weeks of age her vocalizations were well developed, with numerous inflections and varieties of attempts to change intensity. She promptly closed on the dangling ring and, when her hands were held, she pulled herself not only to sitting, but also to standing without any appearance of being pulled. Yet she weighed 14 pounds! At 22 weeks she persistently reached for remote objects and sat leaning slightly forward. At 30 weeks she crept very rapidly, pulled herself to standing and stood for as long as fifteen minutes. This behavior was reported to have been initiated four weeks earlier. At 32 weeks she pulled herself to standing and lowered herself carefully, behavior normal for an infant sixteen weeks older.

Thus Irene's advanced motor development was very similar to the motor precocity of Edith T., the case just previously reported. The infants were both generally advanced, but their greatest maturity was with respect to posture.

Unfortunately, there were no observations of Irene's behavior between 32 weeks and 18 months but, unlike Edith T., who did not walk until she was a year old, Irene was reported to have walked at the age of 8 months.

When 18 months of age Irene was still a very dynamic child who combined two words and who on the second trial adapted all three blocks to the formboard without errors, a two-year performance. Her language and adaptive behavior had caught up with her motor skills.

But when Irene was reexamined at 4 years of age her performance, measured by either the Stanford-Binet or the Yale Developmental tests, was high average rather than superior. The vivid dynamic qualities noted in infancy were no longer observable.

Why did not Irene, like Edith, continue to grow behaviorally in accordance with her early tempo? There were, of course, many differences between Edith and Irene. But which factors were the crucial ones in determining the continued accelerated development of one infant and the reduced development of the other infant? Only through more systematic research and detailed histories of individual growth careers can we arrive at answers to such questions.

I. Language Problems   *Burton M. Castner*

I. DELAYED LANGUAGE DEVELOPMENT IN EARLY CHILDHOOD

§ 31. *Introductory Statement*

Early language development, as a general rule, takes place in orderly fashion and at a rate consistent with that of growth in other fields of behavior. Satisfactory norms have been established, and appear in testing schedules covering the first year of life. During the earliest years, however, language is far from being the satisfactory index of general mental development that it comes to be in later life. The close interrelationship with other behavior, which comes with the ability to verbalize activity of all kinds, is a matter of later development and learning; and language at first functions in a relatively independent manner. As a result, it is more subject to independent variability at this time, and more likely to be specifically affected by differences in constitution, environment, and training, than is the case later on.

This variability is reflected in the studies which have been made of the development of vocabulary in young children. In the case of the appearance of the first word, any age between 9 and 15 months may be regarded as normal, although it is not uncommon to find an earlier or later date. Reported vocabularies of normal two-year-olds range from a few words to more than two thousand. The language norms for the second year of life in the Yale Developmental Schedules call for two words at 12 months, four at 15 months, and five or more at 18 months. Joining of two words is expected by 21 months, and combining words in short sentences at two years.

From the standpoint of prognosis in the language field alone, a certain amount of delay in achieving these stages is not too disturbing, when development otherwise appears satisfactory, and when the child shows some comprehension of spoken language. Practically all children of normal intelli-gence learn to talk satisfactorily in the long run, and more harm may be done by trying to "teach" talking to a child who is slow than by ignoring the problem completely. In cases of persistent delay, however, the situation warrants careful clinical study to determine whether or not it is the result of unrecognized handicaps which need correction.

Some of the more important possible explanations for slow language development may be summarized as follows:

1. *General mental retardation.* When this can be deter-mined with confidence, and language is found not to be sig-nificantly retarded below other types of behavior, the lan-guage problem is not a specific one and calls for no special attention in itself. There are cases in which developmental diagnosis is difficult because of the absence of language, and because the disturbing factors responsible for delayed speech may also cloud the general picture. Because of its relative conspicuousness in the child's behavior, however, backward-ness in talking may be the only aspect of a general retardation which has concerned the parents. Many seriously retarded children are referred with only the complaint that they have been slow in learning to talk.

2. *Physical factors.* The most obvious physical handicap which would be expected to affect the development of lan-guage, is total or partial deafness. This is a condition which it is extremely difficult to determine with any assurance in the case of very young children. Auditory tests of various sorts may be used, and it is necessary to depend to a large extent upon improvisation. Failure to obtain a response to sound is often a matter of attention rather than lack of hearing. Even when the child gives a response to certain loud or sharp sounds, this is no indication that hearing is sufficiently acute to distinguish sounds within the range of the normal speak-ing voice. The response to softly played music, or the ability

to carry a simple tune, as well as the tone quality of the child's vocalization, may be very enlightening.

Specific motor defects in the speech mechanism may be responsible for failure to talk. In some cases, careful physical and neurological examination, taken in connection with a thorough developmental examination, may reveal the presence of an obscure cerebral injury. "Tongue-tie" is rather frequently suspected, and suggested by parents or physicians, but it is actually a very rare condition, and tongue-clipping is seldom necessary or helpful.

3. *Laterality.* A factor of interest in its implications with respect to language development is manual ambidexterity, or, more correctly, delayed development of preference for one hand. The fact that such delay is often accompanied by lateness in starting to talk has been long familiar. In most cases the outlook, as far as language is concerned, is definitely favorable.

4. *Emotional factors.* Inhibition based upon fear or anxiety seems to account for certain cases of delayed speech. In some cases the repression may be traced with some certainty to a specific emotional episode; in others it may be the characteristic response of an emotionally sensitive child to chronic disturbing factors in his environment.

5. *Social factors.* A child who does not hear words will not learn to say words. Some children are talked to very little in the home, and get little opportunity to acquire a vocabulary. This situation is encountered frequently among children in institutions, even when "excellent physical care" is given.

The point has sometimes been made that the child whose needs are always anticipated will not learn to talk because he has no need of language. This is not altogether true, since most early language behavior has little relation to needs, but is for the most part a form of play activity. There can be no question but that the practice of constantly anticipating a child's needs may slow down the later stages of language development and the acquisition of vocabulary, but it will not account satisfactorily for a complete failure to talk.

The cases of Rose L. and Sarah O., discussed in the following pages, give an account of two children, each of whom was first seen at the age of 27 months with an almost total absence of speech. The two cases are highly similar in many ways, the chief differences being in the home situation and the type of coöperation received from the family in attempting guidance. Both children have proved to be of average intelligence or better, and both, when last seen (at nine and ten years, respectively), gave evidence of satisfactory personal-social adjustment and school progress. Both eventually came to talk normally, but progress was much more rapid in the case in which full coöperation was received from the family.

§ 32. Rose L.
*Retarded Language Development. Corrective Program
Attempted but Family Uncoöperative and
Little Improvement
27 months—10 years*

Rose was referred to us by her parents at the age of 27 months because of her failure to learn to talk, although in other respects her development had seemed to be satisfactory. In the Clinic she appeared as an attractive little girl of normal appearance with curly dark hair, small of stature but of stocky build. She was the youngest of three children, the others being a girl of six years and a boy of four. The father was a clothing merchant with a small business of his own.

At the age of 10 months Rose had started to use "mama" as a word. Later she had added "bye-bye." By the time we saw her these were the only words that had been heard, and they were seldom used except imitatively. Wants were usually indicated by pointing, and when she was not given what she asked for she regularly had loud crying spells. Her most frequent type of vocalization consisted of a little grunting sound, but occasionally there was something approaching a conversational jargon, from which no meaning could be derived. Humming was another favorite vocal activity, and she could carry a simple tune quite recognizably.

Walking had begun a little late, at 18 months, but had developed satisfactorily. She had apparently few play interests; a favorite occupation reported was to sit for an hour at a time carefully turning over and "reading" the pages of a blank composition book.

Developmental examination at this time was unsatisfactory from the standpoint of effort and attention, as well as the lack of speech. Language excluded, her performance scattered from fifteen months through thirty months. She scribbled spontaneously—though not very vigorously—with a crayon, but would not attempt imitation of the examiner's stroke, nor did she differentiate between the stroke and a circular scribble. She placed cubes in a row imitatively to make a "train," but did not add the block for a "chimney." She piled a tower of eight cubes, but had to support it with her free hand to keep it standing. She adapted to the reversal of the formboard but not on the first presentation. Although in general she showed comprehension of spoken words, she did not point to any of the test pictures when they were asked for by name.

Despite this relatively poor showing, the general impression of basic normality remained, and in view of this and the complications in the examination, it was determined to proceed tentatively on the assumption that we were dealing with a child of potentially average development. Events justified this assumption; at 31 months, still without language, but with excellent coöperation, she gave a performance at the 30-month level, and her intelligence quotient between the ages of 6 and 11 years has ranged between 95 and 105.

In attempting to get at the basis for Rose's failure to talk, the following factors were among those considered:

1. *General mental retardation.* Although the first developmental examination did not absolutely rule this out, we did
not accept it as an explanation, for the reasons stated above.
In any case, she gave definite evidence of a level at least up
to 21 months, and this would not account for so serious a
backwardness in the language field. As has been pointed out,
Rose proved to be of average intelligence.

2. *Physical factors.* Although response to words was irregular, responses to a low voice were frequent enough to
rule out any question of her being very deaf. The tonal quality of her vocalizations was excellent, and she carried a tune
quite well for her age.

Physical examination revealed no evidence of any condition which might explain the backwardness. There was no
history of any illness which might have given her a setback
in language. During the first few weeks of contact with her,
she was heard at various times to make most necessary speech
sounds sufficiently well to have made use of them in talking.

3. *Ambilaterality.* In general, Rose preferred the right
hand, but was observed to use the left hand rather more than
is usual in children of her age. The mother reported at this
time that there had never been any noted tendency toward
sinistrality in Rose or in others of the family. Several years
later, however, she reported that all the children had seemed
lefthanded at first, and that she had trained them to use the
right hand. In view of the fact that she seldom seemed to
have much time to give to the care of the children, it seems
doubtful that the sinistral tendency was very strong, and
quite probable that Rose's was more a case of delayed unilateral dominance. As late as 7 years she was still quite ambi-
dextrous, and showed consistent left-eye dominance.

4. *Emotional factors.* These were prominent in the home
and family relationships. Rose had been an unwanted child,
and there was little evidence of affection for her on the part
of parents or siblings. The mother was fond of afternoon so-

cial activities, and found little time to spend with her children. She could not, however, afford a high type of help in
the home, and the children had been left much of the time
to the care of a series of young and untrained girls, who had
the responsibility for most of the housework as well.

Several home visits revealed a chronic state of emotional
tension and unhappiness in the home, between the parents
themselves and between parents and children. The children
were always quarreling; the older child dominated the second, and both dominated Rose, pushing her aside when she
attempted to join their play. Mealtimes were always unpleas-
ant, the older children objecting to many foods, while Rose
was learning to imitate them.

During some of our home contacts with the family, relatives dropped in for visits. These visits were always accompanied by overaccentuated displays of affection toward the
children, including effusive demands for kisses and embraces.
Rose rather withdrew from this type of advance, and much
was made of this, with a great deal of shaming of the child.

5. *Social factors.* Some of these have been indicated under
the preceding heading, considered from the standpoint of
their emotional effects. Rose was little talked to. Her wants
were, as a rule, ignored; her absolute needs were attended to
without her having to take responsibility for indicating them,
mainly as a matter of saving time. When a question was addressed to her, the older children would rush to answer it,
asserting, "Rose can't talk." She had little opportunity to
play with children outside the family, and little encouragement to play with those inside. It was almost true that she
was never played with in a normal, pleasant manner by
anyone.

Another factor of doubtful significance, that should be
mentioned, is that of heredity. The other children are reported to have talked at "the usual ages" (no specific times
could be furnished), but the father stated that he had not
begun to talk until the age of three years. No details were

obtainable of the actual history of speech development in his case.

It will appear from the above discussion that Rose's speech backwardness might be considered only as a single symptom of a complex family emotional problem. This problem, how-ever, was never admitted by the mother, and she had no de-sire to enter into any program for improving the general situation. She wanted Rose to talk primarily because her failure to do so reflected upon herself, but she was quite un-willing to make any changes in her established routine of everyday life that would have helped in the process. She showed a great deal of superficial interest, but this extended only as far as bringing Rose to the Clinic and talking about the problem with members of the staff. She was quite un-reliable in her reports as to how far she was carrying out suggestions made to her, and occasional unscheduled home visits revealed that she was actually doing practically noth-ing along this line. Ordinarily, so complete a lack of coöpera-tion would have led to the case's being dropped, but because of special interest in the speech problem, a long series of guidance nursery contacts was kept up.

Rose adjusted very well to the nursery situation, and showed real enjoyment in coming. At first she was seen alone, but was soon introduced into small groups of two or three children, and later into a group of four to six of about her own age. She entered into the group situation pleasantly, and developed a stronger attitude of affection toward mem-bers of the Clinic staff than she was ever observed to show at home.

Effort was made to release tensions through establishing freedom of play and general activity. Considerable response was obtained as far as behavior at the Clinic was concerned, but there was very little carry-over to the home, where the general situation, despite guidance, remained essentially un-changed.

At first there was no attempt to attack the speech problem

directly. As Rose became adjusted to the situation, she was asked, with increasing frequency, to repeat words appro- priate to situations encountered in the nursery. Failure to do so was never followed up, but such failures were common only at first, and increasing willingness to respond was en- countered within a very few weeks. No progress was ob- served within this time, however, in the matter of sponta- neous talking.

At the end of three months, Rose was taken for a week's visit to the home of the guidance worker. During this visit she showed more happiness and satisfaction than she had ever been observed to show before, and, for the first time, several words were heard spontaneously. Upon her return home, however, she lapsed into her former attitude.

From September to June of the first year there were sixty- seven visits to the Clinic. Although she would regularly say words when asked to do so, there were, by the beginning of the summer, only two or three words that came spontaneously in response to appropriate situations. There had been striking improvement in freedom of play and in general behavior at the Clinic, but this had carried over to only a limited degree at home, where there had been no significant change in attitudes.

At the end of the summer Rose was seen again. Continued gain in animation and spontaneity of play was observed, and she now would frequently respond appropriately with single words to such questions as, "What is this?" Some improve- ment in the mother-child relationship was traceable to the fact that during the summer an artist had become attracted by Rose's appearance, and had asked to paint her portrait, which was hung at a summer-colony exhibit and attracted favorable comment. From this time her mother gave more attention to Rose, took more interest in her dress and appear- ance, and took her about with her regularly for the first time in the child's life. During the winter season, however, she returned to her round of social afternoons and found time for no more personal attention to her children than before.

Less intensive work with Rose was carried on during the second Clinic year. There were, in all, twenty-five visits, a number of them in the company of a neighborhood playmate of about the same age but talking well, with whom Rose had established a good relationship. During the year speech advanced, but very slowly, and by the end of the year, at the age of 4 years, she was speaking in short simple sentences, of the type characteristic of 24 to 27 months. These tended to fall into stereotypisms—the same sentence being repeated over and over during the course of a morning, with slight variation. During the morning of her last visit of the year, for example, she spent a good part of her time making sand pies, and her conversation consisted almost altogether of such phrases as "I make pie, see?" "I want pie," "I make one, two pies," over and over during the visit.

From this time on there were no more than one or two contacts a year. At 5 years sentences were longer, but the same tendency toward stereotypy was observed. Playing with large blocks throughout her morning at the Clinic, she repeated, with minor variations, "Now I make sidewalk, see?" "See, I make sidewalk," "Now I make sidewalk." A full year later, the record of a morning's activity and conversation was practically identical with this. She answered questions and talked freely in the routine situations of everyday life, but vocabulary seemed limited. Articulation was quite readily understandable, despite some residual infantilism. A trace of this remained at 9 years, in a tendency to pronounce the "r" sound as "w."

Later growth has been accompanied by a series of minor problems, some of which seem to be associated with the early speech difficulty. At the ages of 5 and 6 years the mother reported that Rose stuttered. This seemed to occur only at home, and was never heard at the Clinic or at school. There was a recurrence of this home stuttering at 8 years, but it did not last long, and no further recurrence has been reported. She made slow progress in reading during the first two grades, but improved spontaneously, and her achievement in reading and spelling was almost up to the average by the time she reached the fifth grade.

At the age of 10 years Rose is a slightly shy, quiet child, whose conversation suggests no special complications in the matter of speech. In school she is regarded as a little slow, but not seriously backward. She appears moderately well adjusted, but there is always the suggestion of a basic unhappiness. There seems to have been little change in family attitudes and understanding over the years, but Rose has shown fewer serious results from these than might have been expected after such a poor start, and there is an excellent possibility that she may work out a satisfactory adult adjustment.

§ 33. Sarah O.
Retarded Speech Development with Rapid Gain following Improvement in Social and Environmental Conditions
(27 months—11 years)

Sarah was the third child in her family, born six years after her next older sister. The family on both sides came from old American stock, with a distinguished social history, and her father was a successful professional man.

Our first contact with Sarah was at the age of 27 months, when she was referred because of her failure to talk. At this time she was reported to have said only one word, "bye-bye," and this only responsively. Most of her communication needs were fulfilled through gestures, which were vivid and readily understandable by those about her. Development in other respects had seemed normal. She sat up alone between the ages of 7 and 8 months, and was walking well by 14 months. She had two teeth at 4 months, eight at 8 months, and sixteen at 16 months.

The home situation was one involving pleasant family relationships, but Sarah's own place in it was extremely limited. She was under the care of a nurse who had been with the family for years, having cared for all of the children. The older children, however, had now outgrown her care; so that her entire time, and apparently her entire emotional interest, was spent in Sarah, whom she mothered practically twenty-four hours a day. She had never had the child try to dress or undress herself, always sat by the bed holding her hand until she was asleep, and had never thought of having her feed herself. Sarah had been bottle-fed until the age of 15 months. At the age of 27 months almost every mouthful had to be put into her to the accompaniment of coaxing and story-telling.

There had been almost no opportunity provided for Sarah to play with little children. Her sisters were fond of her, and enjoyed playing with her as frequently as could be expected, in view of the difference in age and the fact that they were at school most of the day; but they, of course, were as ready to interpret her gestures and vocalizations as were adults.

In the Clinic, Sarah appeared as a sedate little girl of attractive normal appearance. There was never any doubt of her complete normality of development in other fields than spoken language. She showed a fully normal comprehension of spoken words, pointing correctly to eight of the ten test pictures without hesitation when their names were given. She had a vivid gesture-language at times, and "named" the picture of a watch by leaning forward in a listening attitude and cupping her hand over her ear. Her response to the three-figure formboard was excellent for her age; the adaptation to reversal was made thoughtfully, without the usual "trial-and-error" technique.

Play interests seemed of a normal type for her age. Her activity appeared a little slowed down in comparison with that of other two-year-olds, but would be more adequately characterized as deliberate rather than lethargic.

No physical handicaps were observed which might account for the failure to talk. She was clearly not deaf. She was

predominantly dextral. The question of hereditary predis-
position might be raised, since the older children had been
a little later than the average in talking, but neither had
shown the amount of delay encountered here.

There was no observation, and no reported history, of any
marked fears or emotional episodes. It was noted that she
held her lips lightly but firmly compressed together during
most of her play and other activity. This might well have
been the result of persistent attempts to feed her against her
will. She showed great emotional sensitiveness, and was
greatly distressed at the sight of another child crying, although she seldom cried over anything directly concerned
with herself.

Since there was no opportunity at this time to arrange for
intensive follow-up in the Guidance Nursery, the following
program was suggested to be carried out at home:

1. Decrease dependency upon adults. Encourage self-feeding and
   coöperation in dressing. Gradually withdraw her dependency upon
   the presence of an adult in going to sleep.

2. Encourage talking by not being too ready to understand her gestures and undifferentiated vocalization. Try to get some effort at
   saying a word before responding. (Caution: Be careful not to
   force to the extent of increasing her negativism with respect to
   speech.)

3. Provide frequent opportunities for contact with children of about
   her own age. Encourage play, but stand aside as far as possible and
   let her work out her own adjustments.

4. Encourage play calling for free activity of body and limbs. Stimulate
   her to shout in connection with rapid activity. Have her try to
   hum little tunes with her mouth open and using various syllables—
   "la-la-la" etc., instead of only vowel sounds or droning. Develop
   interest in nursery rhymes; when she has become familiar with one,
   break off toward the end of a line or phrase and have her try to
   finish it.

5. Avoid a worried attitude or other show of over-concern with respect to speech. Sarah can talk, and will talk in time, since she is

a perfectly normal child. If those about her expect that she will talk, she is likely to do so a great deal sooner.

The mother showed full understanding of these principles, and did her best to see that they were followed out, devoting more of her own time to the child than she had done in the past. The nurse, however, proved unwilling or unable to adjust to them, and at the end of two months there was no more tendency to talk than before.

When we next saw the child, at the age of 33 months, there had been a complete readjustment of her social situation. Although we had not specifically advised it, the mother had of her own accord dismissed the first nurse four months previously. During the summer months a second nurse had improved Sarah's feeding habits somewhat, but had accomplished little more. The third, and present, nurse had shown much more understanding and willingness to deal with the problems. At first, when Mrs. O. had told her to appear stupid and not understand gestures, the nurse reported that this was next to impossible, since they were so vivid and expressive; but she continued to make the attempt. Little progress had resulted; Sarah called by name one child in a play-group into which she had been introduced, but used no other words spontaneously.

At 35 months it became possible to arrange regular Guidance Nursery contacts, and the following general program was outlined:

1. Have Sarah come as often as possible. At first have her play alone, then introduce her into small groups of children near her own age.
2. Try to develop first an interest in free, active, social play; secondarily, try to encourage free vocal expression, including talking. Work along the lines suggested in the home guidance program, with the same caution against developing increased negativism.
3. Have regular contacts with mother and nurse. Let them observe the child from behind the one-way vision screen. See that they understand what we are trying to do and our methods of going

about it. Advise them as to fitting the home methods in with those used in the Nursery. Encourage them to expect improvement, even though it comes slowly.

The new nurse proved entirely coöperative in bringing the child, accepting guidance, and carrying out suggested ideas at home. Improvement in language began to be noticed, slowly at first, but with rapid acceleration. Table VIII indicates progress noted in the development of speech.

At 35 months, Sarah's vocabulary was scarcely above that of an 18-month-old child; at 40 months her language development was well within normal limits for her age; and at 5 years it was definitely superior. It will be noted that her speech did not suddenly jump to an advanced stage, but went through the normal phases of development—from single words and rote phrases through short spontaneous combinations, simple sentence constructions, to relatively complex sentences with proper use of parts of speech. The gain coincided very clearly with marked improvement in personal-social behavior. Her play became more free and spontaneous; she lost the mild but constant tension that had marked her manner at first, and she entered more and more into group play. At the same time she became more independent of adults in her home habits, dressing and feeding herself, and no longer requiring company in going to sleep.

The similarities between this case and that of Rose L., (§ 32) at the age of 27 months, were many. The outstanding differences were in the emotional attitudes within the respective families and the type of coöperation encountered in connection with the guidance program. There is every reason to suppose that, under favorable conditions similar to those we were able to bring about in the case of Sarah, Rose also would have begun to talk normally at a much earlier age than she did.

It should be emphasized again that in neither case was the guidance program based upon the concept of a problem simply calling for "speech training." The language retarda-

TABLE VIII

SARAH O

Age	Status of Language Problem
27 months	Only reported word is "bye-bye," given responsively. Says "choo-choo-choo" with adult when playing train. Obtains wants by vocalizing "a-a-a-m!" in a shrill voice, or by means of gestures. Vocalizations during play, "ah-ooh! oh!"
29 months	No significant change noted or reported.
33 months	Says "bye-bye," "all gone," "ta-ta," "Mary." Has said "daddy" and "key," but dropped these. Says "yes" in answer to question.
34 months	Tries to repeat words at times. Calls cup " 'up."
35 months	No spontaneous speech beyond above.
35–36 months (7 Nursery contacts)	When a point is made of it, will sometimes say what she wants. Progress is rapid during this month. At first she uses only single words and syllabified jargon. Later some two- and three-syllable words and phrases are heard — "ki'(ddy)-kar," "sank you," "shee-shaw" (for see-saw). On the fifth visit of the month, between eighty and ninety attempts at words, many being repetitions of the same words, were heard. At the end of the month she would say into the toy telephone, "Do (hello); g'bye; te'phone."
37–38 months (6 Nursery contacts)	On the first visit of the month, forty-three words and short phrases, including many repetitions, were heard: "a ball;" "Sa'ah p'ease," "do this." On the last visit, such phrases were heard as "that's mine," "p'ease go," "push Sa'ah."
38–39 months (10 Nursery contacts)	Will finish lines of nursery rhymes—"get a pail of water," etc. Will start some rhymes spontaneously, and says nearly all of first four lines of "Sing a song of sixpence." Aside from this, she still confines herself to single words, short phrases, and interjections. These are heard more frequently, as many as 150 in an hour being recorded.
39–40 months (3 Nursery contacts)	On the first visit, talks to herself almost constantly under her breath; the words cannot be distinguished. Three weeks later (with no visits in the meantime) she is talking in short sentences, using pronouns, adjectives, etc.: " 'Ey a box dere"; "Dat turtle all green, I want it"; "No, you bring it"; "De're more kitties in dere." There are occasional regressions to

TABLE VIII (*Concluded*)

Age	Status of Language Problem
	earlier speech habits, but in general she is talking quite freely, both at home and at the Clinic. On the last visit of the Clinic year, "Dere's one [kitten] dere; he's running after a f'y."
44–46 months	Four contacts, more for observation than for guidance, since use of language is now normal. Articulation is slightly defective in a manner suggestive of immaturity rather than serious defect. During one hour, with a familiar group of children, she is heard to use 552 words (including repetitions).
5 years 1 month	Psychometric re-examination. Mental age score 6 years, intelligence quotient approximately 120. She talks freely and often at considerable length; definitions are superior to use, and in describing pictures she makes use of such phrasings as, "These two old men are sharing the newspaper"; " . . . and a plate for a little child who is too small for a big plate." She says "free" for "three," "bastik" for "basket," and has some difficulty with *n* and *m* in "animal." She is making excellent kindergarten adjustment.
6 years	Mental age score 7 years, intelligence quotient approximately 115. Responses are rather more wordy than the average. In Group VIII she passes the "superior to use" definitions, and all three comprehension questions; at IX she passes the rhymes test very quickly. Articulation is perfectly normal.
11 years 3 months	Mental age 13 years, intelligence quotient approximately 115. Reading is above 8th-grade norms on the Gray Oral Paragraphs, and written spelling is at a good 6th-grade level. She is being promoted to the 7th grade, with a good scholastic record. She now appears well adjusted, mature, and coöperative, and is an unusually talkative child. Her mother remarks that she long ago restored the average for the years she did not talk.

tion was considered as simply one aspect of a problem in personal-social adjustment, and attempts at encouraging speech were deliberately made secondary to the attack upon the major problem. Our experience with Rose, moreover, furnishes a good demonstration of the principle that such problems cannot be adequately handled by means of a pro-gram which deals with the child as simply an isolated in-dividual as encountered under clinical conditions at a given time. He must be constantly thought of as a member of a family and of the larger social group, and his problem must be considered in dynamic relationship to the total develop-mental history, if the results obtained are to be more than superficial.

J. Reading Disabilities   *Burton M. Castner*

§ 34. *General Statement*

Among the children referred to the psychological clinic for guidance during the pre-school years, there are many who will prove, after they have entered school, to be handi-capped by a specific weakness in reading. This problem, so commonly met with among school children who receive clinical study, has received a great deal of attention in its more advanced stages. Methods of remedial instruction have been extensively developed and are being constantly im-proved. Nevertheless, in the majority of school systems it is unlikely to come to attention for several years after a child has entered school, by which time the emotional complica-tions resulting from failure, humiliation, and misunderstand-ing have often so overshadowed the basic handicap that the child is as apt to be referred because of behavior difficulties and social maladjustment as because of failure in school. In addition to this, the reading problem itself has become more difficult to treat: the necessary gain to bring the child up to age and grade is greater, faulty reading habits and atti-tudes must be overcome, and aid beyond reading alone must frequently be given because of the effect of this specific weak-ness on other school subjects.

Early diagnosis and guidance are therefore of the greatest importance from the standpoint of satisfactory social and emotional adjustment as well as educational progress. If these children show any indication during the pre-school years that they are likely to suffer later from a reading handicap, we may, in many cases, insure against serious complications by arranging to have such children followed up during their first years in school, and giving guidance on the basis of their progress at that time.

In 1935[1] the writer described a clinical method to detect such cases prior to entrance into the first grade. This method made use, not of special tests to be added to the regular examination, but of various characteristics of performance and personality to be noted in the course of the normal clinical study of the child. In all, more than thirty cases indicating potential reading disability have been followed up through an age at which the correctness of the prediction could be checked with some confidence. Not all of these children have proved to be handicapped in reading to a serious degree; not all have required remedial teaching, since a number—especially those with psychometric ratings above the average—have shown spontaneous improvement after two or three years in school; but, with only two or three exceptions, all have been seriously retarded in reading during the first year or two in school, and in a large proportion of cases the clinical picture has been consistent with a definite diagnosis of specific reading disability. In a number of instances it seems probable that more serious permanent problems have been averted as a result of guidance given on the basis of the early recognition and analysis of the problem.

The nine items which appear to be of the greatest predictive significance are listed below. While some of these are of greater value than others, no one of them seems to be of paramount importance in itself; they are found in various groupings, none appearing in every case studied, and all of them being found together only in rare instances. Interpretation of the various combinations that are found must still depend somewhat upon clinical familiarity with the problem; but in cases between the ages of 4 and 6 which show several of the factors it is good insurance to arrange for follow-up study during the first year in school to check the child's reading progress.

1. *Scattering and inconsistency of the individual developmental examination.* This factor, when present, stands out conspicuously because of the way in which it often complicates the interpretation of the test results. It seems to be most marked during the younger pre-school stages, between the ages of 2 and 4 years, decreasing with advancing age, and is most significant when encountered at 4 years or above. In some cases, of course, it appears simply to be the result of incomplete coöperation or some identifiable organic or environmental complication; but in many instances no such explanation seems satisfactory.

2. *Inconsistency of results on successive examinations.* This is usually observed in the form of an increase in developmental quotient on later examinations as compared with earlier ones; though a decrease in relative score, or fluctuation in both directions, may be of even greater significance. The rise in developmental rating is explainable, in some cases, in terms of the decrease in scattering with advancing age, mentioned in connection with Item 1, but is sometimes found also in cases which have shown no marked scattering at any time.

3. *Specific weakness in drawing tests.* Many of these children, whose general intelligence appears to be fully average, show a definite weakness on drawing tests as compared with tests of other types of ability. This weakness is particularly evident in connection with the copying of the cross, square, triangle, and diagonal, as included in the Yale Developmental Schedules (see Fig. 5). It may appear to arise from weakness in form perception, in manual coördination, or in both. Free drawing (*e.g.*, of a man) is likely to be inferior as well, although in some interesting cases this does not hold true. In the free drawing, conception may be superior to execution—for example, the drawing may be quite unrecognizable, and yet have more parts designated by the

child as features, limbs, etc., than are usually included by children of the age in question.

This item seems to be one of the most significant of all those listed, being encountered in nearly all of the cases

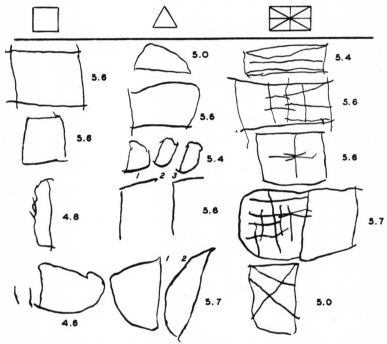

Fig. 5. Responses to drawing tests made prior to first grade entrance, in cases in which reading difficulty was correctly predicted. All are by children within average range of intelligence (I.Q. 90-110), and above the age at which satisfactory copying of the model is expected. The reproduction is made from ink tracings of the original pencil drawings; while some effort has been made to differentiate between extremely light and extremely heavy lines, some gradations in the strength of stroke have been lost.

studied. It is not found in all of them, however, and there is no evidence that it is of special diagnostic value for the reading problem in the absence of others of the items listed.

4. *Specific weakness in number concept.* In addition to the counting of four, ten, and thirteen pennies, this ability

is informally tested in pre-school children by presenting a pile of blocks and saying, "Give me *just two* blocks," "Now put *just one* over here," "Now *three* over here," etc. Many of the children who later have trouble in reading are considerably later than the average in developing these concepts, and the counting test in Group IV of the Stanford Scale is, after the drawing of a square, the test most frequently failed below age at 5 years.

5. *Sinistrad or other atypical directional tendency in drawing, or a tendency to reversal in making letters and numbers.* The atypical drawing tendency will be found in the drawing of horizontal lines from right to left, vertical lines from the bottom up, etc. Because of the emphasis which was formerly laid upon the factor of reversal in reading disability, there is likely to be a tendency to overweight this single item in making prediction. It is, however, quite frequently encountered among children who never have the slightest difficulty in learning to read. Until its relation to the reading problem is more fully understood, it should probably be included as a possible predictive factor when it appears with unusual persistence, or in conjunction with other traits described here.

6. *Presence or history of sinistrality, total or partial, in the child or his immediate family.* The same general caution as to overemphasis given with respect to Item 5 is necessary in interpreting this item, since the relationship of sinistrality to reading difficulty is now generally agreed to be much less clear than it was formerly considered. There is some evidence, however, that sinistrals, and particularly mixed lateral types, are a little more likely to develop reading difficulties than are the pronounced dextrals.

A number of observations as to manual preference may be made, using either a standard procedure or informal observations. Drawing, throwing, kicking, batting, pointing to pictures or to parts of the body, counting a row of pennies, represent simple sources of data. Eyedness may be tested by means of the Miles V-scope. Information as to early lateral tendencies and the presence of left-handedness or ambidexterity in other members of the family should be obtained from the parents.

7. *History of reading disability in older siblings or in parents.* So many instances are encountered in which a reading problem is found in more than one member of a family, that this item should be given considerable weight.

8. *Atypical factors in speech development.* Since reading and speech are both major aspects of the language function, it is not surprising that deviations in both fields sometimes occur in the same individual. In the cases studied, the language complications have taken the form of late talking, defective articulation (including unusual persistence of infantilism), and occasionally stuttering.

9. *Immature or excitable personality.* Many of these children are of the active, energetic type, frequently referred to the clinic by harassed mothers with the general complaint of being "hard to manage." They are apt to be hard to examine, not because they are actually uncoöperative, but because of immature control of attention and diffusely directed physical activity. Occasionally these traits are suggestive of more or less serious instability; more often they indicate only a certain immaturity of personality which becomes less disturbing as the child grows older. In many cases there seems to be some immaturity of physical development as well.

It is to be emphasized again that, in the cases which later show difficulty in reading, these traits occur in varying degrees and combinations. No one of them is, in the absence of other signs, especially significant from the predictive point of view. To a considerable degree the use of these items as a simple check list will be of value in selecting the cases to be followed up, but personal judgment based upon clinical experience undoubtedly facilitates their use.

The usual procedure in arranging the follow-up study is

to call back the child for re-examination after two or three months in the first grade, with later examination at intervals determined by the findings at that time. Little achievement, as measured by standard reading tests, is expected at the time of this first visit, but some idea can usually be obtained of how well the child is responding to his first instruction in reading, and particularly of his general response and adjustment to the whole school situation. It is usually undesirable to raise the question of a reading handicap in talking to the parents until it is felt with some certainty that such a problem is present. Guidance during the early stages should take the form of guarding against the development of emotional problems arising from failure, counseling patience with respect to school work, the maintenance of an attitude of encouragement, and avoidance of overemphasis upon the importance of rapid early progress in reading and spelling. Remedial tutoring may be necessary later, but, so long as the case is receiving attention, it may safely be postponed in most cases for a year or even more from the time of first-grade entrance. If "reading readiness" classes, or some similar facilities, are available, their use will of course be considered.

A word of warning here against judging reading progress by the school report alone, may not be amiss. We not infrequently encounter cases of first-grade children who bring a report of excellent reading achievement from their teachers, but who prove on standardized tests to be definitely retarded, or even completely lacking in reading ability. In many such cases, the children have been making such excellent use of memory and alertness in picking up the thread of a story as to deceive both teachers and parents. This seems to account for many of the cases of older children of whom we are told that they did well in reading at first, but later lost their ability.

The cases to be described in the following pages are chosen from among those in which a difficulty in reading was correctly predicted before the age of first-grade entrance. Selection has been primarily on the basis of illustration of differing combinations in which the predictive items are encountered.

§ 35. Phebe S.
Reading Disability Predicted at 5 Years 4 Months in a Girl of High Average Intelligence
(5 years 4 months—7 years 6 months)

Phebe was referred by her mother at the age of 5 years 4 months to determine whether she should be allowed to enter first grade or whether she should wait another year. No kindergarten was available in her school district, and children of appropriate mental age level were sometimes permitted exemption from the minimum age requirements for school entrance. Phebe was seen in September, about three weeks after the opening of school.

Two earlier examinations, at 20 weeks and 104 weeks, had been made in connection with a research study of normal children. On both she had been rated as "high average." On this examination she earned a mental age score of 6 years, with an intelligence quotient of approximately 110. This score would satisfy the requirements for admission to school. The following observations were made on the predictive items for reading difficulty, starred items having possible predictive importance:

1. *Scattering of performance:* Negative. All V-year tests were passed, with five out of six at VI, and one success, giving the number of fingers, at VII.
2. *Variation in I.Q.:* Negative. The present examination gives a slightly higher rating than the infancy examinations, but all have agreed in placing her above average.
*3. *Weakness in drawing:* Very marked. Her copy of the square barely passed, her lines being weak and poorly controlled. The triangle and diagonal were badly failed.

4. *Poor number concept:* Negative. The VI-year test of counting thirteen pennies was passed, above her age.

*5. *Directional tendencies:* Doubtful. Her mother reports that she has shown a tendency to make letters backward. In the Clinic she can make only the number 1 and the letters in her name, all but one of which are not reversible when made as capitals. (This of course applies to her actual and not to her fictitious name.) In writing her initials she reverses the order of the two letters. Data considered too meager to draw definite conclusions.

*6. *Sinistrality:* Right-handed in drawing, throwing, counting, and right-footed in kicking a ball. Left eye preferred on eight of ten trials with V-scope. (On subsequent examinations she was consistently right-eyed.) Considered possibly significant, since right-handed left-eyed children seem a little more likely to develop reading trouble than the complete dextral.

7. *Reading disability in family:* Negative. There are no older siblings, and parents are not known to have had trouble.

*8. *Speech complications:* Slightly defective articulation. Speech is a little infantile, and the "l" sound is consistently pronounced as "w."

*9. *Personality:* In general, her personality was pleasing, but a bit babyish. She was less spontaneous than most children of her age during the examination, and there was definite blocking and lack of confidence on language tests.

The prediction of reading disability was made with less confidence in this case than in many others, because of the relatively slight strength of value of the positive items, with the exception of drawing. For this reason, no specific recommendation against having her attend the first grade was made, but a note was entered in the Clinic files to insure that her school progress would be checked regularly.

Reading progress:

The following table represents her reading progress over a period of two years from the time she entered first grade.

Scores are in terms of grade norms, tenths of a grade being equivalent to months:

Age	Gray Oral Paragraphs	Written Spelling	Oral Spelling
64 months (age of entrance)..	1.0	1.0	1.0
69 months...................	1.0	1.0	1.0
6 years, 6 months...........	1.0	1.0	1.5
6 years, 9 months...........	1.4	1.0	1.7
7 years, 6 months...........	1.9	1.8	1.7

At the time of the examination at 7½ years, Phebe had been in school two years and two months, and had made just nine months achievement in reading—about 40 per cent of normal progress. She was in the second grade, having repeated the first, so that her backwardness relative to her grade was less than when considered in relation to her age and intelligence.

Phebe had received no remedial tutoring, since the parents could not afford the expense. As the problem became apparent, its nature was explained to both mother and teacher. The mother was advised to maintain an attitude of encouragement, to minimize failure, and not to urge promotion until it was earned. Toward the end of the first year she was told how to help understanding of the fundamentals of reading by simple word games, and, a little later, by encouraging the reading and re-reading of primers at home. The problem of attitude was emphasized, however, since it was felt that this was a case in which spontaneous improvement might take place if emotional complications could be kept at a minimum.

The results, in general, have been favorable. Some discouragement has shown itself at times, but slight gains, being noted and praised by the mother and teacher, have helped to offset this, and she is now quite interested in school. The rate of reading gain has shown acceleration during the past few months and she is now, in terms of grade, only slightly below the average for her group. The general outlook appears good.

§ 36. *Robert V.*
Reading Problem Predicted at 5 Years 6 Months; Serious Personal-Social Complications
(5 years 6 months—7 years 4 months)

Robert was referred by his parents at the age of 5 years 6 months because of concern over a number of aspects of his general behavior. He was reported as destructive in play, unable to amuse himself, wanting his own way when playing with other children, and "hard to reason with." The destructiveness complained of proved to be not of a willful type, but mainly a kind of immature awkwardness and forgetfulness. His playmates were practically all older than himself. He had attended kindergarten for six months when seen. Deportment was reported as generally good, but with a tendency to tease and annoy the children at times.

The clinical study showed a pleasant-mannered boy, cooperative enough in his attitude, but active and restless in his behavior. There was an automatic defense response to any test situation to which he could not immediately see the appropriate answer—"I don't know," "I can't make it very good," etc. Drawings were carefully shielded by his free hand while he was working, and he showed them at the end with some reluctance. Despite these complications, he earned a mental age score equivalent to his age, with an I.Q. of 100.

Future difficulty in reading was suggested by the following factors: *Drawing:* The pre-school drawing tests were passed at a level consistent with age. His procedure, however, was extremely slow and laborious, and control of lines was weak in comparison with the performance as a whole. *Sinistrality:* At this time he appeared predominantly right-handed and right-eyed. The father, however, was left-handed, and reported that up to between the ages of 2 and

3 years he thought that the boy would be left-handed also. He stated that the dextral preference had developed spontaneously, and that no attempt had been made to force it. *Language:* There was a history of delayed development in this field; Robert did not begin to use words until the age of 20 months. *Personality:* As described above, this appeared characteristic of the type found in many children who prove later to be handicapped in reading.

The factor of variation in examination results was inapplicable because there was no record of an earlier examination. The present examination showed no scatter. Number concept was satisfactory for his age. He was reported to make letters and numbers backward, but in the Clinic the only letters he could make were his two initials, neither of which was reversible as a capital; he did, however, make the second initial first, although he printed them from left to right. Two older siblings were reported to have made normal progress in school.

Because Robert lived in another town, at some distance from the Clinic, frequent follow-up contacts were impracticable. A second visit, at 6 years 1 month, just after first-grade entrance, revealed that the adjustment problems were still giving difficulty. Detailed guidance was given both teacher and parents, in an attempt to stabilize the personality picture and increase the satisfaction and interest in school work and in his daily life.

Further attempts to secure a check-up examination fell through until the age of 7 years 4 months, in midyear of Robert's second grade. Improvement in general behavior was reported at this time, but school work was reported as unsatisfactory, except in arithmetic. After a year and a half of school, he showed an achievement of four months on the Gray Paragraphs, and of seven months on the Iota lists of single words. Oral spelling was at a lower level than his reading, but written spelling was at a beginning second-grade level. His spelling was done very slowly, however, and he sounded out and spelled a word over and over under his breath while writing. In this he gave evidence that he had obtained some grasp of phonetic principles. Drawing, from being a specific weakness, was developing into an outstanding ability, and was the activity in which he showed the greatest interest.

This is a case which will require understanding and exceptionally careful management if serious personality and adjustment problems are to be avoided. The interrelationship of the educational handicap and the personal-social difficulties is such that each tends constantly to intensify the other, in the manner of a vicious circle. Such progress as has already been made is encouraging as far as it goes. Within six weeks of his entrance into first grade, Robert had been labeled by his teacher as the "bad boy" of the room, and was being sent to the principal's office almost daily, kept after school three or four times a week, and isolated from the other children at work and play. This sort of handling was modified somewhat after the Clinic visit at this time, but it is far from certain that his problems are really understood at school. Progress is actually being made in reading, although the rate is very slow. If the more drastic disciplinary measures can be held off, and the necessary aid given in reading, there is a chance that future school achievement may eventually approach the normal.

§ 37. *Victor P.*
Reading Disability Predicted at 5 Years 1 Month
Confirmed Later
(5 years 1 month—7 years 9 months)

Victor, the son of immigrant Italian parents, was examined at 5 years 1 month, prior to commitment to state care. His mother died soon after his birth, and he has been boarded with a neighbor ever since. His father, finding it difficult to meet the expense, has now asked state aid.

On psychometric examination, Victor earned a mental age score of about 4 years, with an intelligence quotient of approximately 80. Because of the type of scattering and the quality of his best responses, it was felt that he was essentially close to average, and this was confirmed by an I.Q. of approximately 95 on later examination. The following items suggested the likelihood of trouble with reading.

1. *Scattering of performance.* This did not cover a wide range but within the range from III through V there was considerable variation in the quality of his performance on tests of equivalent difficulty in terms of age.

3. *Weakness in drawing.* The square was badly failed. Asked to draw a man, he produced an unrecognizable group of disconnected lines and a crude small circle. Coöperation was good, and he seemed satisfied with the result.

4. *Poor number concept.* Failed the counting of four pennies, counting them "1—2—5." Differentiated "just one" and, doubtfully, "just two," but not three or more.

6. *Laterality.* Mixed. Prefers the right hand as a rule, but transfers pencil to left for the left side of the paper. Uses left a good deal in manipulating cubes. Throws a ball with the right hand, but kicks with the left foot. Is right-eyed on ten trials with the V-scope.

8. *Speech complications.* Significance doubtful. Speech is not very clear, but there is the suggestion of foreign-language influence. He talks and understands English, however, and his performance on the verbal items of the examination is not below his general level.

From the standpoint of personality, Victor appeared as a pleasant boy, small for his age, with an attractive smile and manner. He was a little explosive in his speech and behavior but not outstandingly so.

Reading progress:

At 6 years 8 months, toward the end of his first year in the grades, Victor had made no measurable progress in reading. He was promoted to the second grade, and in November was reported by his teacher as doing excellent reading. On the easiest of the Gray Oral Paragraphs, however, he made ten errors, requiring nearly two minutes to get through the paragraph. When he could get through a few consecutive words, he read with fairly good expression.

At the age of 7 years 9 months, at the end of the second school year, his reading score was equivalent to the fourth month of grade I. The same paragraph mentioned above was now read in thirty-five seconds, with only four errors. The second paragraph in the series required fifty-one seconds, with six errors. Beyond this the performance deteriorated rapidly.

Remedial teaching has not been possible because of the social situation. Victor has been a great favorite with his teachers, and he is eager and interested in his attitude toward all school work. He is to be promoted to grade III, a step concerning which we may feel somewhat dubious. The outlook, as far as school achievement is concerned, appears questionable, but there is no suggestion as yet of emotional complications, probably largely because the teachers have not recognized any problem, and have taken a friendly and encouraging attitude toward him throughout.

§ 38. *Raymond D.; Thomas D.*
Prediction of Reading Difficulty in the Case of
Two Brothers: Prediction Fulfilled
Raymond: 4 years 3 months—8 years 2 months
Thomas: 5 years 5 months—9 years 8 months

These two boys were referred for study before commitment to state care. They had been for two years in a foster home, the parents being separated and unable to provide for them. In the case of Raymond, no personal problems were reported; Thomas was reported as "nervous," with a tendency to stutter at times. Neither had attended school. Both scored at a low average level (about I.Q. 90) at the time of the first examination, and both have since scored between 95 and 100. Both were placed in a boarding-home under the care of a foster mother who has seemed pleasant, cheerful, and fond of children, but rather ineffectual from the standpoint of training and insight into problems.

In the case of Thomas, reading disability was suspected on the basis of marked weakness in drawing, left-eyedness (he was right-handed), slight backwardness in number concept (he counted four pennies correctly, but was lost at five or more), and the slight stuttering tendency. Personality type was also consistent with the prediction; he appeared as a rather tense highly-strung child, showing some emotional blocking in the examination. The performance was not scattered. In drawing, he copied the cross satisfactorily, but with rather wavering lines; his square barely passed in one out of three trials, and his attempts at the triangle were quite hopeless.

Raymond gave a slightly irregular performance, scattering from 36 through 54 months on the developmental examination. Drawing was definitely below the general level of his performance. Although no speech problem was reported, he was observed to stutter slightly at times during the examination. The suggestion of a probable future handicap in reading in the case of the brother strengthened the impression that Raymond also might face such a problem. The personality type was rather similar to that of Thomas, allowance being made for the difference in their ages.

On the basis of these observations, both cases were set down for follow-up study in connection with school progress. It proved impossible, however, to get them in for three years from the time of the first contact. At the end of this time, they were again referred by the original agency, with complaints of behavior difficulty in school and failure to make normal progress. Such follow-up contacts as it has been possible to secure have showed the following test results.

TABLE X

THOMAS

Age:	8 yr. 4 mo.	9 yr. 0 mo.	9 yr. 8 mo.
Years since first-grade entrance..	1.8	2.5	3.1
*Reading achievement (Gray Paragraphs)................	1.3	1.1	.8
Reading quotient..............	.72	.43	.29
*Spelling achievement (written).	.7	.8	1.4
*Spelling achievement (oral)....	.7	.8	.9

RAYMOND

Age:	7 yr. 3 mo.	8 yr. 2 mo.
Years since first-grade entrance..	1.8	2.7
*Reading achievement (Gray)...	.0	.0
Reading quotient..............	.0	.0
*Spelling achievement (written).	.0	.0
*Spelling achievement (oral)....	.0	.0

* Reading and spelling achievement is given in terms of school years and tenths of school years, and is obtained by subtracting 1.0 from the scores in terms of grade equivalents. The reading quotient is obtained by dividing the achievement by the number of years in the grades.

The decrease in reading score shown by Thomas over a period of a little more than a year is atypical; but the scores are not entirely representative of his actual progress. At 8 years 4 months he read very slowly, a word at a time, following with his finger, and totally without expression. At 9 years he showed no increase in reading score, but read more quickly and smoothly, though with about the same number of errors as before. The latest examination was made shortly after the opening of school in the fall, and perhaps shows the effect of lack of practice during the summer. A difference of two or three errors at this early level of reading will, of course, make more difference in score than it will later on. It is of interest that, during this period of lack of gain in reading, the behavior difficulties complained of at school have undergone distinct improvement. The school system involved happened to be one in which some consideration is given the problem of reading disabilities, and, although remedial teaching was not at the time available in the school attended by these boys, it was possible to explain the situation to the school authorities and aid them to handle it with more complete understanding than is usually the case. He was given encouragement and some opportunity for leader' ship, and, as far as possible, such help as would keep him from being held back too much in other subjects by his diffi' culty in reading. It is hoped that remedial tutoring will be made possible for children in his school within the near future.

The behavior difficulties in the case of Raymond have been much less serious than in his brother. His effort and interest in school work are irregular, and he becomes discouraged easily, but he responds fairly well to encouragement. The foster mother characterizes him as a very active, energetic, mischievous boy, but not presenting any disturbing problem.

Neither boy has developed the slight stuttering tendency noted at the time of the first contact. If it proves possible for them to have the necessary special aid during the next year or two, the outlook for future school and social adjustment may be considered fairly good, although both will require some watching. If they do not receive the remedial work, the outlook is unpredictable; there may be spontaneous improve' ment sufficient to take them through the grades, although at a rate slower than average; but this, of course, cannot be expected with confidence.

§ 39. Owen T.
*Reading Difficulty Predicted at 4 Years, 9 Months:
Reading Progress Slow, with Improvement under
Remedial Teaching
(4 years 9 months—8 years 6 months)*

The prediction of reading difficulty in this case was made with some hesitation, largely because of the fact that drawing at the time of the predictive examination, so far from being a specific weakness, was exceptionally good for the age rep' resented. Both in copying tests and free drawing, Owen's performance was characterized by a precision above his age.

The boy was referred primarily because of defective speech.

He had not begun to say words until the age of 3½ years, and was still difficult to understand, although definite improvement had been noted since he had entered kindergarten, five months before our contact with him. An older brother, previously seen, had been handicapped in reading. Both parents were college graduates.

On developmental examination there was a slight scattering, from 48 through 66 months. At 54 months he failed in counting four pennies, the number concept not running above three. On the Detroit B vocabulary test (Action-Agent) he scored at the level of five years, and at 5½ years his drawing of the diagonal figure was a definite success. Comprehension questions at the five-year level were failed. The intelligence quotient was between 105 and 110.

Owen was right-handed and right-eyed. The mother was a converted sinistral, and the older brother had developed dextral preference relatively late. This brother was reported also as having shown very slow speech development in infancy.

In personality, Owen gave no indications of instability, and there was no problem in attention control. Otherwise, he seemed rather babyish in behavior as well as in speech and general appearance, giving the impression of being younger than he actually was.

From the standpoint of predicting reading disability, the picture was not strongly suggestive. In most cases hitherto encountered, the factors of drawing weakness and unstable attention had been outstanding, one or the other, if not both, being observed in practically all cases. Here was one in which drawing was exceptionally good, and personality, though immature in some respects, definitely not so in the matter of attention control.

Nevertheless, the factors of number weakness, familial sinistrality, defective speech (with the history of delayed early development), and the presence of a reading handicap in the older brother, led to Owen's being entered in the follow-up index as a child to be watched in the matter of reading progress as well as speech.

The speech problem showed rapid improvement during the next year or two, with a few traces remaining at 6 years; by the age of 7 years articulation was practically normal. In large part, this improvement was spontaneous, direct attempts at correction being kept at a minimum—a procedure which seems indicated in the case of many children at this early age.

In reading, early progress proved to be very slow, the picture being consistent with the familiar type of reading disability. In this case, no blame could be laid upon the factor of attention; his teachers reported that in school he maintained the same kind of interest, willingness, and application to the work that he has shown regularly in the clinical contacts. During his first year in the grades, as has been the case with many of these children, his alertness and excellent memory for stories misled his teacher into thinking that he was making excellent progress in reading, although his performance at the Clinic showed that this was far from being the case. By the end of the year this was apparent to the teacher as well, but his progress in other fields had been so good that he was promoted to the second grade in the hope that the retardation was only temporary.

Owen was 6 years 3 months of age when he entered first grade—a little over the average age. There were several clinical contacts during this year, showing a very slow gain in reading vocabulary. By the end of the year he had learned a handful of words, but had still no idea at all of how to recognize a word which had not been specifically learned, and his performance on the Gray Oral Paragraphs was below the lowest first grade norms. This was still the case toward the middle of the second grade, when he was 7 years 8 months of age. His performance at this time on the Iota reading tests—lists of single words—was similarly retarded. On the Ayers-Monroe spelling tests, he was also at a low first-grade level, although on the oral spelling test he did a little better than on the written.

At this time no especially trained person was available for tutoring. At our suggestion, however, the mother engaged a woman with teaching experience to work with him, and arrangements were made that she should work under our direction, following methods that had been found helpful in similar cases, and bringing him in so that we could check on his progress at intervals. This work was not done as inten-sively as might have been desired; the tutoring could not be done during school hours, and it was felt undesirable to add another hour to the school day four or five times a week in the case of a child as young as this. The number of hours a week varied from two to four, and during four or five weeks of the summer tutoring was omitted altogether because of a vacation trip.

Under this arrangement improvement was slow but defi-nite. In November of his third year in the grades—he was now in the third grade, and 8 years 6 months of age—he was slightly above a beginning second-grade level in both reading and spelling. Interest and effort continued to be good; he liked school and seemed to enjoy reading. Achievement in other subjects was excellent. Tutoring is to be continued as long as it seems necessary, and the general outlook is con-sidered good. The original speech problem, as indicated earlier in this summary, has disappeared.

K. Irregularities in Early Mental Development
Burton M. Castner

§ 40. *General Statement*

One of the basic assumptions made in using tests of mental development is that such development takes place at a relatively uniform rate in relation to chronological age. This assumption, as a general principle, has been repeatedly borne out by experiment, and most standard tests have been shown to have a satisfactorily high degree of reliability. The psychologist who deals regularly with problems of deviation and maladjustment, however, must never lose sight of the fact that among his examination subjects there is likely to be a high proportion of those individuals who prevent such statistical measures from approaching absolute reliability. Regularity of development is the rule, even among cases presenting clinical problems, but the psychologist's responsibility requires that he be constantly aware of the factors that lead to variation, and that, as far as possible, he learn to recognize their presence and take them into account in interpreting test results.

These factors are particularly important in their effects during the pre-school years. Although the behavior growth processes have tremendous power to overcome obstacles, the underlying mechanisms are complex and delicately integrated, and the headlong rapidity of their development in the early years of life makes them particularly susceptible to temporary disturbance during that period. As a result, we encounter among infants and pre-school children more fluctuations in development, more inconsistencies in the clinical picture, and more difficulties in diagnosis, than are found in later years when the organism has become more stabilized, habits of behavior more set, and environmental experience, as a result

173

of school attendance and greater freedom of social activity, more uniform.

The usual effect of these irregularities is to give the impression, at some stage, of a lower level of intelligence than is actually present or potential in the child being tested. As in the case of older children and adults, the familiar principle holds true that the subject may for many reasons make a lower score than the one of which he is fundamentally capable, but cannot make a higher one. There are apparent exceptions to this—children who at some stages of their growth careers make deceptively high scores that are not confirmed by subsequent examinations—but such cases are rare.

Personality differences play a far greater part in determining the character of the psychometric performance during the pre-school years than they do in later life. Even without strong interest and motivation, the mature individual is able to control his attention and concentrate his effort sufficiently to make a representative showing on examination. Young children, however, show extreme variability in this respect, regardless of relative intelligence. Defective attention control is often found associated with retarded mental development; yet many normal and some quite superior children have shown a degree of distractibility in the early years that served effectually to conceal their true intellectual status. First-hand familiarity with many growth careers will usually permit a qualified examiner to detect and give weight to the often subtle aspects of behavior that distinguish such children from those who are actually retarded, but he will also recognize the likelihood of error, and will be correspondingly cautious in interpreting and reporting his conclusions.

Personality complications of the type referred to seem often to be the result of delayed integration of function in the growing organism. Children in whom this is encountered may appear as immature, distractible, and overactive, sometimes to an apparently abnormal degree. In some cases the whole developmental picture is affected; in others one or more of the specific behavior fields will show little or no effect. Again, some such children will present a consistently retarded performance, while others will show a wide scattering, with some inferior-level tests failed and other, relatively difficult, ones passed.

It is interesting to note that this slowness in integration seems frequently to be associated with a delay in the development of unilateral dominance. This factor is discussed elsewhere, in connection with retarded language development and also with the pre-school indications of specific reading disability. Reference to its presence will be found in a number of the cases reported in the present chapter, including the extremely atypical Melissa T.

While there is some tendency among these children to group as a recognizable clinical type, the individual variations of response are great. In some, the outstanding trait is a high degree of emotional sensitivity, with more susceptibility to disturbing influences, such as impermanence of home background, or prevailing emotional tensions in the home, than is found in the average child.

The problem of diagnosis in these cases presents the most difficulty, in general, below the age of 5 years. There are notable exceptions, but in a large proportion of cases there is a rapid acceleration of the integrative processes between 5 and 7 years, the resulting gain in stability being reflected in the psychometric performance.

Some of the more extreme personality deviations of the sort described may raise the question as to whether or not some pathological condition of the organism is present. In the case of Kate P., for example, the marked tremors of the mouth at 27 weeks, and of the hands at 26 months, were sufficiently impressive to lead us to request a thorough neurological examination, which, however, revealed no specific basis for the behavior. The difference between children like Kate and perhaps also Clara B., and the generally tense ex-

citable child like Dorothy S. who is more commonly encountered, is probably one of degree, though it may be that
research in clinical neurology will eventually reveal some
more definite explanation for the extreme cases.

Cases involving gross physical handicaps can, of course,
be expected to present difficulties in developmental diagnosis
and departures from the normal course of mental development, some of which are illustrated in § 60-71 of the present
book. Physical handicaps may operate directly upon the
organism to prevent the development or the demonstration
of certain potential abilities, or indirectly through limiting
the child's experience. The effect upon personality also may
be great.

The effect of environmental differences upon the psychometric history is most sharply indicated in cases in which
a distinct change in the developmental rate follows a change
of environment, as when a child is transferred from an institution to a family home, or from a poor family home to a
better one. The factors in such atypical social histories which
can be expected to affect the psychometric showing operate
in two ways—by failing to provide in the early environment
opportunity for acquisition of the specific abilities to be
tested, and through the development of personality traits
which interfere with the acquisition of these abilities or
inhibit their operation in the test situation. The specific
effects of prolonged institutional life in infancy and early
childhood need detailed study; clinical experience suggests
that they may be considerable. They may occur in any of the
developmental fields. Language is apt to be retarded, while
motor development may even be slightly accelerated. Personal-social items and adaptive behavior seem to be more
irregularly affected.

The insecurity felt by the institution child in dealing with
strangers in an unfamiliar environment may lead to emotional blocking and suppression of responses in the develop-

mental examination. This situation, of course, is by no means encountered only in children from institutions, but it is more commonly to be expected in such cases, and in those of children who have undergone recent or frequent changes of home. It must be pointed out, however, that these factors do not operate in any consistent and readily predictable way, but are modified in their effects by other, less tangible, factors, including basic personality differences.

While clinical responsibility points the need for caution in making interpretations of cases similar to those which are here described, and particularly in reporting conclusions to outside agencies, evidence which may be taken into account is seldom altogether lacking. Flashes of higher abilities than are shown by the general performance are frequently encountered, sometimes even in conversation and play outside the examination proper. Reports of "bright" behavior at home should be critically considered, but by no means ignored. In a scattered performance, careful consideration must be given to the highest successes when these are not plainly fortuitous.

In spite of all caution, cases will be encountered in which no hint of potentially higher abilities, discovered to be present on later examination, can be found in the early growth career, and no satisfactory explanation for the developmental delay can be found. Such a case is that of Ida B. reported in the chapter on superior children, in whom there was only the superior family history to give us pause.

It is clear that, even in the absence of overt indications of higher ability, developmental diagnosis and especially prognosis should be guarded in the case of young children whose histories and personality traits show the type of complications which have been discussed. Fortunately, the better pre-school scales are much more liberal than those intended for older subjects in the matter of allowing the use of clinical judgment, both in giving and interpreting the tests. Strict ritualistic methods of test presentation will fail to elicit representative performance on the part of a large proportion of pre-school children, while assignment of developmental age on the basis of straight plus-and-minus scoring and counting up of tests passed will in many cases lead to grave injustice.

It may be argued, in this connection, that the psychologist's sole task is to evaluate the child's ability at the particular time he is examined, and that prediction of what it will be at any future time is not called for. This is all very well, but the fact remains that, for all practical purposes it is impossible to make such a diagnosis without at least implying a prognosis. A classification made at a particular age and reported to an outside agency, may remain in the child's record as a basis for judging his ability long after he has outgrown the factors which caused him, at the earlier age, to score below his full capacities. Nor can we hope to avoid this risk altogether by means of a note attached to the report, calling attention to any doubts that we may have. It is unfortunately true that, in many cases, the only part of such a report that is attentively read and remembered is that which describes the examination results in terms of mental level or I.Q. Qualifying or cautionary comments are overlooked.

Fortunately, even in the pre-school years, developmental classification can be made with confidence in the great majority of cases. When there is any doubt of the adequacy of such classification, however, it is wise to state it clearly and request a re-examination after a suitable period. The need for immediate and accurate prognosis is seldom so urgent that a general statement will not suffice until further examinations can be made. Frequently, when actual mental deficiency can be ruled out on the basis of the first examination, this will suffice as far as the immediate problem is concerned, and closer estimation of the relative degree of normality can wait until later. The occasional inconvenience that may be caused by the delay is less important than the injustice that may be done by a premature and possibly inaccurate diagnosis.

§ 41. Matilda V.
Highly atypical and irregular behavior in infancy; improvement of prognosis at 4 years
(50 weeks—5 years 11 months)

Variation in development:

From a "borderline—dull" rating at 50 weeks to average (I.Q. 100) at 5 years, 11 months.

Social history:

Admitted to institution at just under 9 months. Previous history unspecified. Mother reported "of low intelligence," fabricates tales of past life, apparently definitely unstable. Child placed in foster home at 1 year, and has remained since in same home, where her mother pays her weekly visits. At 5 years 11 months is reported well adjusted, friendly, without fears of any sort, and not at all shy.

Summary of examinations:

In the following summary the factors which were adjudged to be of probable diagnostic significance are italicized.
I. *50 weeks.* "Probably borderline; possibly dull normal." "Gross motor behavior, 40 weeks; fine motor, 36 weeks —; language, 34 weeks; adaptive, 36-44 weeks; personal social, 38 weeks." "This child presents an *uneven development; imitative ability and persistence are quite in advance of motor and analytic ability.* She is not up to average, and *her pattern of behavior is not characteristic of a normal infant at any age level.* Since *certain aspects suggest dull normal,* although the general picture is suggestive of borderline ability, it seems best to defer classification until later examination. A very interesting type of *withdrawal from the environment* was

noted when she could not get what she wanted—*a persistent rocking back and forth*. She needs suitable toys to play with, and should be placed in a family home."

II. 48 months. "Dull normal; possibly borderline," Stanford score 38 months; Yale Developmental Schedule performance about 42 months. Highest performances: Matches 4 Stanford forms; *copies cross* (with inferior control); enumerates objects in Dutch Home picture. "A *very active and restless child* who *resists quiet activity* but enjoys housekeeping play with dolls and helping foster mother with household tasks. According to foster mother, she is very set in her wants, but this has created no serious problems. Although her behavior is not up to age, I am of the impression that *some of her failures were the result of faulty attention* and that *there is a possibility that later progress will approach the normal.* If these same characteristics persist, however, she may prove to be dull normal and slightly unstable."

III. 5 years and 11 months. Mental age score 6 years, intelligence quotient 100. An even performance with all tests passed in age-group V, five out of six in group VI, and one in group VII. The failure in group VI was naming missing parts of pictures; she named two correctly when three were required. The success in group VII was giving the number of fingers. Drawing tests were passed at age, though control was poor. She was somewhat flighty and very talkative, "Oo, I can't make that," etc., but entirely coöperative, and good effort could always be elicited through encouragement. She was in and out of her chair constantly throughout the examination. She was able to print her name, but had been in school too short a time for us to judge academic progress.

Summary:

Factors which might have been taken as casting doubt upon the raw performance rating at 50 weeks: (1) The apparent relative neglect in her own home up to the time of transfer to the institution. (2) Lack of normal stimulation during the 12 weeks in the institution. (3) Response to frustration by going into her habit of rocking. (4) Irregularity of her performance, "not characteristic of any age." (5) Flashes of imitative ability and persistence in advance of actual achievement.

At 4 years the attention factor was properly given weight in evaluating her performance, and the likelihood of a later rise in the relative score was indicated. This prediction is fully justified by the performance at 6 years.

§ 42. Theodore S.
Rise of Eighteen Points in Intelligence Quotient over Period of Eleven Months
(5 years—5 years 11 months)

Theodore S. referred at 5 years in connection with plans for future placement. Re-examination, prior to court hearing on commitment action, at 5 years 11 months.

Family background:

Theodore is the ninth of ten children in a family of Polish parentage. The father was a general laborer, who had worked in factories, on farms, and as garbage collector; reported as having been a chronic alcoholic. Polish was spoken in the home up to the time of the death of the parents. The mother died in childbirth when Theodore was 37 months of age, and the father died ten months later of pneumonia. Siblings are considered of normal mentality; three, on whom psychometric examinations have been made, have shown intelligence quotients between 85 and 95.

Following the death of the father, the home was kept together a few months by the older sisters. When Theodore was 50 months of age, the five youngest children were committed to state care, and he was placed with two brothers in a foster home, where he has remained. Excellent adjustment is reported both in the home and in kindergarten, which he has been attending for four months. The foster mother reports that he is friendly and gets on well with other children, and that he enjoys wiping dishes and otherwise helping her.

History of clinical contacts:

Examination I—age 5 years. Stanford mental age score, 4 years, intelligence quotient 80. Tests of counting and digit-repetition were failed at the 4-year level, while weight-discrimination and definitions were passed at 5 years. The drawing performance was below age, but better than his general level on tests of other types. Personality appeared a little immature, but potentially favorable. He was mildly talkative and distractible, but less so than many children of his age. Because of these factors and the slight irregularity of the performance, the impression was recorded that a gain of between 5 and 10 points on future examination appeared not unlikely.

Examination II—age 5 years 11 months. Stanford mental age score 5 years 10 months, intelligence quotient 98. All 5-year tests were passed, with four out of six at 6 years, and one—copying a diamond—at 7 years. He appeared weakest on tests of a verbal-ideational nature, and best on direct performance responses.

Theodore has remained in the same foster home, and has continued to improve in his adjustment. He seems very fond of his foster mother. He has been a little over three months in the first grade, and hates to be late for school or to miss a day. He seems to have made no achievement in reading, recognizing only the capital A on the Gray Oral Reading Paragraphs.

Discussion:

This case illustrates particularly well the need for caution in interpreting psychometric results in the case of pre-school children whose home and social background have been in any way atypical. Superficially, there seemed at the time of the first examination to have been fewer and less serious effects from these atypical factors than in most other cases. He had been in the foster home ten months, and in school four months, and was happy and well-adjusted in both. The effect of the foreign-language home during his first 4 years seemed minimized by the fact that one of his highest successes was on a test of language ability.

The prediction of a probable rise of 5 to 10 points was made on the basis of the slight irregularity of the record and the relatively slight immaturity in control of attention, in the light of experience suggesting that some gain is likely in cases with a history like that of Theodore. There appears, however, to have been no overt reason for expecting so dramatic a rise as actually took place—a gain in scoring ability of 22 months in an 11 months period, with a rise of 18 points in the intelligence quotient.

§ 43. *Nicholas C.*
Marked Fluctuations in Psychometric History
(50 weeks—6 years 6 months)

Nicholas C., dependent, examined four times between the ages of 50 weeks and 6½ years. Referred for guidance in connection with placement.

Family history:

Nicholas is the third of three children of Italian parent-age, the other two being, respectively, four and six years older than himself. The father is a laborer, reported as fond of his children and unwilling to relinquish guardianship of them, even when they have become dependent upon the city because of the inability of the mother to care for them. At the time Nicholas was first referred, the mother was handi-capped by a post-encephalitis condition; she died a few months later. No further details as to the family were obtain-able through the referring agency.

Personal history:

At the age of 3 weeks, Nicholas was placed in a boarding home, where he remained up through the time of our first examination at 50 weeks. The foster mother considered him a normal baby. Details of the birth history were not obtain-able. At the age of 17 months he was transferred to another foster home, in which he has remained ever since.

History of psychometric examinations:

Examination I—age 50 weeks. Developmental level 10 to 11 months, slightly below average. General outlook consid-ered average.

Examination II—age 43 months. Developmental level about 42 months. Stanford mental age score 3½ years, range from III through IV, intelligence quotient 97.

Examination III—age 5 years 8 months. Developmental level 4 to 4½ years. Stanford mental age score 4 years, range from III through VI, intelligence quotient 70.

Examination IV—age 6 years 6 months. Stanford mental age score 5 years 4 months, range from IV through VI, intel-ligence quotient 82.

Discussion:

At the time of the first two examinations there was a definite impression of basically average development, even though on both occasions he fell slightly short of a fully average performance. Since he was in a bilingual home, allowance was properly made on the second examination for his failures on specific language tests, but his adaptive behavior was essentially normal for his age. He seemed at this time a good deal lacking in self-confidence, and the variability in effort might well have raised the question at this time as to whether an "average" rating would in fact fully represent his basic capacities. Cases have not infrequently been seen in which a picture of this sort between 3 and 4 years has been followed by a rise in the intelligence quotient to a superior level as the child grew older. In the present case, however, we have, on the contrary, a drop to a borderline score at 68 months, rebounding to an intelligence quotient of only 82 at 6½ years. How is this sort of fluctuation to be interpreted?

An examination of the record of the 68-month examination furnishes some explanation for the sharp falling off in the score. It is recorded that the boy was extremely active and distractible, with attention to the tests hard to obtain and poorly sustained. Successes were scattered; counting and drawing were failed in group IV, and there was one success each in groups V and VI. It was felt that several failures were the result of a too precipitate attack on the problem, and too little attempt to plan. Nicholas had recently entered the first grade, somewhat under age (no kindergarten was available), and the same tendencies observed in the Clinic had disturbed the teacher and made her feel that he was unable to learn.

If the falling off shown in the third examination had been primarily due to attention factors, a sharp rebound in the score might be looked for as better control of attention was developed. The fourth examination, nearly a year later, shows a clear shift in the direction of normality, but does not approach an average performance. Attention was, in fact, much improved at this time. Scattering of performance was markedly reduced, though still a little greater than is found in most normal cases. Drawing was extremely poor. It may be expected that further gains in general stability, with a consequent evening out of the performance, will result in further gains, but there is no clear suggestion, except on the basis of the two earliest examinations, that he is likely to go beyond a low average level.

§ 44. Philip D.
Consistent Psychometric History Despite Shifting Home Background
(39 months—8 years 11 months)

Philip D. was referred for examination at 39 months; reexamined at 8 years 11 months.

Family history:

Philip is the illegitimate child of a woman of Scotch-Irish descent who is employed as a sales clerk. The father is reported to have been employed as a hatter; little is known of him. The mother lives at home with her parents; her own mother is the only member of the family who knows of the existence of the child.

Personal and social history:

Delivery was normal, at full term. Philip is reported to have walked alone at 11 months, and to have talked in sentences by 2 years; other information as to early development is lacking. The child was born in an institution and remained there until he was 23 months of age, when he was placed in a foster home with the prospect of adoption. At the end of three months, however, he was returned to the institution because of the death of the foster father. At 37 months he was again placed for adoption. In this home he was entered in a nursery school but, because of difficulty in management and failure to make adjustment to the nursery group, he was referred for examination and guidance.

Summary of psychometric findings:

Examination I—age 39 months. Developmental level about 36 months. Impression of average development.

Despite a rather unfavorable report of behavior from the nursery school, there was no great difficulty in making the examination. He was restless, but amenable if allowed a little freedom in leaving the table at intervals. Language develop-ment was below average, but in other respects he approached a normal performance. He worked with concentration on the Goddard formboard, reducing his errors in the course of the three trials from 20 to 2. He was friendly throughout the visit, and showed no apparent feeling of insecurity. Although the distribution of scores in itself indicated a low average level, the general quality of the performance was suggestive of fully average ability. The foster mother's impression of the child was somewhat more favorable than was that of the nursery school.

Examination II—age 62 months. Mental age 4 8/12 years; intelligence quotient 90.

Within two weeks after our first contact the foster parents removed to another state and returned the child to the orig-inal institution. Four months later he was placed in another foster home. A few months later he was reported from this home as "troublesome, lacking in affection, stubborn, dis-obedient, restless, falls out of bed, cries and screams at night." This was the complaint when the second examination was made, at another Clinic. The very brief report of that examination which we have, records that at this time he spoke with a slur, was nervous and very distractible, showed considerable instability. The score, however, was not sig-nificantly lower than when we first saw him.

Examination III—age 8 years 11 months. Mental age 8 years; intelligence quotient 89.

Following the second examination, he was returned to the institution and immediately placed in a fourth foster home, at the age of 5 years 2 months. During the succeeding year he had severe attacks of pneumonia and scarlet fever. At 7 years he was reported to be in good physical condition. When referred for his second examination by us, at 8 years 11 months, he was still in his fourth foster home, and was reported as presenting a behavior problem in school—"restless, frequently tardy, no application, listless." He was repeating the second grade, and said to be doing passing work.

The intelligence quotient at this time showed no significant change from what would have been expected on the basis of the two previous examinations. He was under considerable tension throughout, was restless, and bit his nails, but was cooperative as far as willingness went. There was no unusual scattering or inconsistency in his performance. Reading and spelling were at a second grade level, but were both somewhat irregular in quality; many of his errors were on words which, when his attention was specifically directed at them, he could read correctly. The poor reading was considered to be the result of personality complications rather than of a specific disability.

Discussion:

Despite an institutional and foster-home background which had involved three changes up to the time of the first examination, and despite reported instability and specific retardation in language, Philip D. gave as satisfactory a psychometric performance at 39 months as he has been able to give up to the age of 9 years. There was, indeed, an impression at that time that he was probably fully up to the average. It may be pointed out that the adjustment difficulties have become rather worse as he has got older, and that the personality complications may still, at 9 years, be acting to reduce his score. This may well be true. There is, however, no suggestion that he is actually above average, and if I.Q. 100 represents approximately what he would be capable of under favorable conditions, the earlier scores earned cannot be considered to have been so low as to misrepresent significantly his potential ability.

§ 45. Clara B.
Judged Defective Throughout Infancy:
Superior Endowment at Three Years
(28 weeks to 36 months)

This child is presented as a rather unusual example of irregular development. Her background, as far as it is known, is of considerable interest. The mother's I.Q. is reported to be 59. She attended school until she was 16 years old, but was never promoted above the 4th grade. She has had five illegitimate children, Clara being the fifth. A brief report on the first child at 12 years of age states that he had done some third-grade arithmetic and some reading with the second grade, but was finally expelled from school because of troublesome behavior. There is no information available on the second child except that she was placed in adoption. The third child died shortly after birth. The fourth child was examined at this Clinic and his development was normal at 45 months of age. Details about the mother's family are lacking and nothing is known of Clara's father.

Clara was born in Institution A; of her birth we only know that she weighed 7½ pounds and that she had gonorrheal vaginitis, which responded to treatment in 6 weeks. At 3 months of age her general physical condition was good. At 15 weeks of age she was placed in foster home B but was removed shortly after because the family objected to the history of vaginitis. She was then placed in foster home C. The foster mother was a nurse, and the agency caring for

Clara took advantage of the superior physical care and more professional attitude available in this home, placing physically and mentally subnormal children under her care. Clara remained in this home up to the age of 13 months, when she was placed in foster home D.

The course of her development may be summarized as follows:

TABLE XI

Exam.	Age	D.L.	D.Q.	Classification
I	29 wks.	18 wks.	65	Borderline defect
II	36 wks.	20 wks.+	55–60	Defective
III	52 wks.	32 wks.+	65	High-grade moron or borderline
IV	21 mos.	18–20 mos.	85–95	DN to low average
V	36 mos.	42 mos.+	115	Superior

At the time of her first examination, Clara had been in foster home C, with the nurse, for 3 months. Her physical condition was good, she was friendly and smiling, and made a completely undiscriminating adjustment to the examination. Her behavior was very characteristic of the 18-week level of development. In the supine position she assumed symmetrical attitudes, engaged in simple rattle play and hand regard. At the sight of the dangling ring and rattle she brought her hands together in a crude ineffective closure. In the prone position she held the head one to two inches above the platform; when pulled to sitting there was no head lag, but postural control in the supportive chair was poor. The dictated report of her performance with the pellet and bell is given in full:

PELLET: Watches Ex's hand as pellet is presented, follows withdrawing hand. Mouths her hands. Looks at the pellet (?), then at her hands. Vocalizes. Looks at the ceiling. Continues to mouth, scratches table, and then quite definitely regards pellet briefly, then her hands. Pellet is moved to left to check regard; again she regards her hands as they scratch table. Then brings them back to her mouth, gurgles as she looks at Ex. Regard for the pellet was questionable.

BELL: Regards it intently, scratches with right hand. Brings hands together, looks at hands, at bell, brings hands to mouth, scratches table, separates hands and again brings them in, contacting bell momentarily. On none of these contacts (cubes, cup, bell) was the hand adjusted for grasp.

At 36 weeks her development reached the 20 week level, except in the gross motor field, where it was 28, and in the language field where it was questionably 28. At 52 weeks the developmental level was approximately 32-36 weeks. A few peculiarities of behavior were then noted for the first time. She occasionally showed tremulous excitement in manipulating toys, stiffening the arms, clenching the hands, trembling, using her hands in a peculiar rotary manner in transferring and manipulating toys. At other times her exploitive play had no unusual characteristics. Selected parts of the dictated report of her behavior with the cup and spoon are illustrative:

CUP AND SPOON: Picks up spoon with right hand, turns it about, looks at it very intently. Now picks up cup by rim with left hand, looks from cup to spoon. Thrusts end of spoon in mouth; she has released the cup. Now as she accidentally knocks the cup over, she stiffens, becomes excited, lifts cup to mouth, bites rim.—Picks up spoon, mouths it, looks up at light, looks at spoon again. Her arm is shaking tremulously. Transfers spoon and it hits cup, looks at cup, at spoon, and mouths spoon.—She pursues spoon in an awkward manner without picking it up. Becomes excited when spoon rattles on table. Finally picks it up in a backhand manner, carries to mouth, mouths it with occasional excited movements. Glances at cup, approaches, scratches handle with index.

Re-examination at 21 months, 8 months after removal to a new foster home, showed striking improvement, and there was no longer any question of her essential normality. She was somewhat excitable and silly, and development was slightly inferior, but further improvement was considered possible. Her progress during the following year, however, exceeded all expectations.

At 36 months her general maturity level is 42 months+, and she is an attractive, amenable child of superior intelligence, with no evidence of personality deviations. She prefers the left hand for most activities.

Discussion:

The occasional infant one encounters who is retarded in infancy and who later attains a normal development is usually either only mildly retarded and presents fairly obvious environmental factors, or else shows atypical behavior and scattering or other evidences of personality deviation or instability. In the present instance the retardation was serious and apparently simple. The social responsiveness, while attractive, could not mask the inadequacy of the performance. No abnormalities, other than the retardation, were noticed until the examination at 52 weeks; the excitement, tremulousness, and mannerisms at that age have been described. Scattering was never marked. She was placed in a boarding-home at a relatively very early age, and the social agency considered the home above the average; certainly many children develop normally under poorer conditions.

Here we have a potentially normal infant, who shows a definite and serious degree of retardation throughout the first year of life, and who fails to give any indications that this does not represent her real endowment. We can look for causative factors; we can ask, in retrospect, if a home with a professional attitude, caring for subnormal children, is particularly conducive to optimum development; we can ask if it is possible for 3 months of institution life (the first 3 months) to cause such a deviation in the normal curve of development; we can postulate obscure endocrine factors, or neurological factors (physical examination to the contrary); even if we find them, the fact remains that they were not recognizable during that first year. The signs at 52 weeks of age which might have suggested instability are not borne out by her past record, nor by her present status. We can only conclude that it is possible, in our present state of knowledge, though in our experience it is extremely exceptional, for a potentially normal, even superior child to go through a prolonged developmental phase without revealing her normality.

§ 46. *Eugene M.*
Atypical and Retarded Behavior in Infancy:
Superior Development Later
(50 weeks—48 months)

Eugene was the second illegitimate child of an Irish domestic, aged 27, of normal mentality. His birth was normal and at term, and his neonatal period was uneventful. Eugene lived in Institution A from age 10 days to 10 months, in Institution B from 10 to 11 months, in foster home C from 11 to 30 months, when he was placed in foster home D. His health history was normal.

Examination was requested at 50 weeks (while in Institution B) because his behavior was so abnormal and retarded. He was reported to be very unobservant, to laugh and cry without reason, to hold his head up poorly and to use his hands "only for exercise."

Examination I—age 50 weeks. Eugene looked like a 9-10 month infant; he was almost constantly active, kicking, rolling, pivoting, sitting, and rolling again with considerable abandon but with poor balance and control. He sat with the back bowed and the head drooping forward. He was completely absorbed in his own activities, and apparently did not notice his environment or persons near him. The examiner stood beside him for fully twenty minutes before he noticed her, and when he did he was completely uninterested. When sitting he stared at his knees, and a hand passed back and forth before his eyes did not distract him even momentarily. Attention to test materials, however, was surprisingly prompt, but prehension was unsuccessful, often not even attempted. He exploited toys chiefly by poking and scratching. After repeated attempts to place an object in his hand, he finally held it and later once succeeded in grasping this same object without help. Hand postures were bizarre, and grasp was defective. Neurological examination was negative except for an external strabismus of the right eye with poor eye coördination.

His behavior scattered from 3 to 9 months and no classification was attempted. The impression was that this boy had a secondary defect of obscure etiology, but the factor of institutional life could not be entirely ignored.

Examination II—age 15 months. Eugene's behavior scattered from 8 to 12 months, showing essentially the same characteristics as before. "Child has many normal potentialities and is not in the strictest sense feeble-minded." Ophthalmic examination suggested the possibility of myopia. At 3 years he had only a mild refractive error.

The following table summarizes the course of his development:

TABLE XII

Exam.	Age	Develop-mental level	D.Q.	Classification	Comment
I	50 wks.	3– 9 mos.	?	Unclassified	Atypical behavior
II	15 mos.	8–12 mos.	?	Unclassified	Atypical but many normal potentialities
III	18 mos.	12 mos.	65	Borderline defective	More normal quality. No marked hand preference
IV	24 mos.	15–17 mos.	65	Borderline defective	Again a more normal quality Left hand beginning to be preferred
V	36 mos.	42+ mos.	116	Superior	Well adjusted. Definitely left handed
VI	49 mos.		116	Superior	

On his last examination, despite a slightly scattered performance with specific backwardness in drawing and number-concept, he again earned a superior rating on both the Stanford and the pre-school scales. He appeared to be somewhat subject to over-fatigue, and it was reported that he tended to stagger noticeably when over-tired. He still preferred the left hand, and there had been no interference with this preference. In view of certain aspects of the picture which

resemble those found in many children who later give evidence of a specific reading disability, it will be desirable to
check his school progress after he enters the first grade.

Discussion:

Nothing in Eugene's past record had prepared the examiner
for his performance at 3 years. As his peculiarities of behavior
faded, the retardation persisted in spite of a good adjustment
in his home. After his examination at 2 years we were fairly
well convinced that Eugene had shown his maximum improvement. A year later, however, although this boy had
recently suffered a change in placement, he was no longer
dull, but was definitely above the average.

The evidences of normal potentialities glimpsed at 15
months should have received more respect. We can now
postulate that the multiple factors of defective vision, personality deviations, institutional environment, and a mild
motor handicap, as evidenced by poor head and trunk control
and manual incoördination (birth injury?), combined in this
child to exert a malignant effect on his early development.
Time, compensatory reactions, and subsequent good environmental circumstances have permitted his superior intellectual
endowment to assert itself. Obviously there may be unknown
factors operating on one or both sides of this reaction. Eugene
remains an odd little personality, and how he will react to
the trials and tribulations that his social situation alone will
bring is not known.

§ 47. Melissa T.
*Apparent Mental Deficiency at 50 Weeks, with
Average Intelligence at 5 Years and Later
(50 weeks—7 years 9 months)*

At the age of 50 weeks, Melissa was referred to us by
a child-placing agency for examination to aid in estimating

her suitability for adoption. The parents were married, but conception had taken place three months prior to the marriage, and to cover the situation they had decided to give her up. The ancestral stock on both sides was American for several generations. Heredity, so far as known, was negative from the standpoint of its bearing on the problem of developmental diagnosis. The parents themselves were reported as apparently normal, except that the father had a slight tendency to stutter.

Birth was at term, following a normal pregnancy. Instruments were not used. When she was received by the agency, at 5 months, the baby showed signs of rickets, and was "tongue-tied" (we have learned to accept reports of this condition with some skepticism). Before the tongue was clipped (at about 6 months), and for a time afterward, it was characteristically slightly protruded. There had been an attack of whooping cough from which she had reportedly not entirely recovered when we saw her; this had not been exceptionally severe, but she was about five pounds below average weight. She had begun to sit up at 10 months, and, at 50 weeks had two teeth.

Twelve days after birth, Melissa was placed by her parents in a home where four or five other children were boarded. At 5 months, feeling that she had been neglected there, they asked the agency to take charge. She spent six weeks in the agency's nursery, and was then placed in another foster home.

In facial appearance, Melissa at 50 weeks appeared relatively normal, and her wide-open eyes even gave an impression of some alertness. Alertness did not appear, however, in her behavior, which was seriously retarded for her age. The fact that she sat alone with steady head posture caused her gross motor development to be rated ahead of other fields of behavior. Even this, however, had been relatively late in occurring. She failed to secure the pellet, though she approached it with hand pronated. She showed selective attention for the handle of the cup, but there was no combining activity with cup and cubes or cup and spoon. Banging, patting, brushing, and transfer, were conspicuous in her manipulation. Characteristic vocalization was mild fretting or a thin, slightly inflected whine of pleasure.

The most frequent spontaneous activity consisted of a fixed staring at her hands, which were held before her eyes, the fingers flexing and extending constantly, while the index finger was wagged laterally. This activity alternated or was combined with rocking back and forth as she sat. Similar behavior, noted at 5 months, had caused the agency to suspect that she might be mentally retarded, and to hesitate in considering her as a possible adoption candidate.

On the basis of this first examination, we made a diagnosis of mental deficiency, assigning a general developmental level of approximately 7 months. A second visit, made two weeks later for the purpose of obtaining physical measurements, brought out nothing to conflict with this judgment.

At 19 months Melissa's adaptive, personal-social, and language behavior were still below the 12-month level, with motor behavior at 13 to 15 months. Again it was noted that her general appearance was suggestive of normality, and there were snatches of behavior that had a normal adaptive aspect. She walked alone, with an almost normal gait. Three or four words were reported, but all that was heard in the Clinic was a jargon of repeated monosyllables indicative of desire or protest. Emotional adaptation in personal-social situations appeared shallow, and attention was poorly sustained. The general pattern of her behavior, in terms of both total situations and specific features, still appeared consistent with serious retardation.

We did not see Melissa again until 4 years 11 months, and were somewhat taken aback to encounter a normal-appearing little girl who, despite a somewhat scattered performance, earned a Stanford intelligence quotient of approximately 100. The test results of this and subsequent examinations are summarized in the following table:

TABLE XIII

Age	Mental age score	I.Q.	Educational measurements
4 yrs. 11 mos.	4 yrs. 10 mos.	98	
5 yrs. 9 mos.	5 yrs. 4 mos.	92	
6 yrs. 4 mos.	6 yrs. 4 mos.	100	
7 yrs. 3 mos.	7 yrs. 2 mos.	98	Reading: Grade 1.0; Written Spelling 1.0; Oral Spelling 1.8
7 yrs. 9 mos.			Reading: Grade 2.1; Written Spelling 1.3; Oral Spelling 1.9

There is no question but that Melissa is of normal intelligence, and, after a slow start, she seems off toward a normal achievement in school subjects. We are happy to report that her early retardation did not debar her from ultimate adoption. She was adopted when 6 years of age, and is making an excellent adjustment in her home.

In looking back at the detailed records of her examinations in infancy, it is difficult to see how her later normal development could have been predicted. We do have the observations as to her normal facial appearance at 50 weeks, but this is surely no reliable indicator, in the presence of consistently defective behavior. At 19 months, snatches of apparent normality in behavior were noted, but these were not sufficiently marked, in the opinion of experienced examiners, to be considered as other than the type of pseudo-normal flashes not infrequently met with in defective children.

It is unfortunate that so long a period elapsed between the second and third examinations, since a record of the actual rise to normality might have thrown more light on the causes for the inconsistency. In the absence of such a record, certain possibilities may be considered.

Even during the first year of life, personality differences among children may play a significant part in affecting the behavior picture. Certainly, in the case of Melissa, the peculiarities were very marked. Her prolonged and habitual hand-regard and the shallowness of her interest in the test materials indicated tendencies which could be expected to affect her developmental showing, both through limitation of her experience in daily life, and through interference with optimal responses in the examination.

In other cases such factors have been observed to have a generally similar effect, but there is seldom so complete a blocking out of the normal patterns as was encountered here. If they had resulted in her giving practically no response at all to materials, we should have been much more doubtful than we were about the diagnosis, but there was definite manipulation and exploitation characteristic of the lower age level.

The fact that Melissa had recently had whooping cough might be felt to have played some part in confusing the picture, but this fact was minimized, since the peculiarities of behavior had been observed as early as 5 months. The point could hardly have been considered significant when she still appeared retarded at 19 months.

Specific information is lacking as to the actual degree of neglect she suffered in her first foster home, but it was quite possibly sufficient to have caused this particular child to develop the peculiar habits of hand-fixation to a point which had caused them to persist.

The factor of lateral dominance is one which has been prominent in this case, as it has in many others showing deviations from the normal course of development. At 4 years 11 months Melissa was very nearly a true ambidexter. Drawing was about equally good with either hand, and both were used spontaneously. The right hand was used for throwing, and the left foot for kicking, a ball. In counting a row of pennies, different hands were used on different trials; with the right her counting was sinistrad, and with the left dextrad—the reverse of the usual direction in each case. She has been consistently left-eyed.

The ambilaterality was still marked as late as 7 years 4 months, but the left hand has gradually come to be preferred exclusively for drawing and writing. It may be significant that the reading and spelling showed marked acceleration during the period in which the tendency to use both hands was finally dropping out.

§ 48. Dorothy S.
Irregular Development
(40 weeks—41 months)

Dorothy's mother was one of several children of a "plain, respectable" family. She left school at 15 years, having completed the sixth grade, and entered a factory where she was a good worker. Her I.Q. was reported to be 55. Dorothy is her second illegitimate child. The father is unknown. The birth was normal and Dorothy was cared for in an institution from 10 days of age to 16 months. She was then placed to board with an elderly woman; there were no other children in the home.

Developmental history:

Examination I—age 40 weeks. Her general maturity level was approximately 36 weeks, with gross motor development at the 44-week level. She was described as wiry and active; her behavior was undiscriminating, details were not investigated, fine adjustments not made. In the institution she was reported to throw all her toys to the floor and to be interested only in motor activity; she rocked back and forth in the creeping position, a "habit" common among institution infants. She was classified as low average.

Examination II—age 20 months (4 months after placement). Although Dorothy did not show any timidity, she was almost completely uncoöperative, and the examination was very incomplete. She ran around the examining-room, hurling toys about, laughing excitedly, screaming and kicking if any attempt was made to restrain her. There was no constructive play, no response to commands or demonstration, and attention was very scattered. Outside of the motor field, no behavior above the 12-month level was seen. She had no words, did not feed herself, and had not responded to toilet training. Her behavior at the Clinic, it should be added, was described as precisely like her behavior at home. The foster mother admitted herself at a loss to deal with Dorothy. No rating was attempted, but the outlook was not considered to be very bright, particularly from the standpoint of personality. The fact that behavior had deteriorated after placement was regarded as a somewhat ominous sign. The home was considered good, however, and no change was advised. The foster mother was given general advice and guidance.

Examination III—age 27 months. At this time there was some improvement in adjustment, but Dorothy was under terrific pressure to *do,* over-responding to all situations. Although she stood, sat, stood on the chair, the table, sat again, and so on *ad infinitum,* she did not leave the examination table until permitted to do so. In resecuring the rod from the performance box she pounced on it with such wholehearted abandon that she crashed head-on into the box; subsequent resecurals were more restrained, but even so her violence was not curbed enough to prevent her from bumping her head each time. To get any attention to verbal commands, a favorable moment had to be selected and she had to be helped by contact to direct her attention to the examiner. She screamed in protest at leaving, and had to be carried bodily from the room, but a moment later smiled good-by.

At this visit her development showed scattering from the 18-21 month levels, and the comment was made that "it is possible that the over-activity and attention difficulties are masking abilities that will assert themselves if and when Dorothy becomes less volcanic and driven. On the basis of this examination she is considered inferior and unstable."

Examination IV—age 33 months. Dorothy was wilfully perverse and negative for the first fifteen to twenty minutes of her visit, but finally became interested and coöperative. She was still under pressure and had difficulty in doing anything requiring control, patience, or sustained attention. She threw the ball so hard she almost fell down and literally threw herself at the ball to retrieve it.

Her behavior was in the 27-30 month zone. Although the foster mother reported that Dorothy still had an "awful" temper, her training was succeeding, for Dorothy took full responsibility for her own toilet needs, put on her own shoes and shirt, and wiped and put away dishes!

Examination V—age 41 months. Dorothy was more cooperative than at the time of any previous examination, but there was still a good deal of difficulty in control of attention, and again there was the definite impression that her maximum potential ability was not being demonstrated. The examiner (who had not previously seen the child) was of the opinion that she might eventually prove to be at least close to average. Actually, in terms of the test situations, she did not definitely demonstrate ability more than slightly above 36 months. Flight of attention, and heedlessness in response to instructions were the chief factors which were considered to be lowering her score.

Discussion:

Obviously this story is incomplete. As far as the developmental quotient goes, here is a child whose D.Q. was approximately 90 at 40 weeks, 60 (on very incomplete data) at 20 months, 65-75 at 27 months, 80-90 at 33 months, and 85 at 41 months. The apparent variation in D.Q. is probably more a reflection of extraneous factors than a real fluctuation. The description of her behavior which is given in some detail shows temperamental difficulties that can easily be considered sufficient to affect her ability to score on a developmental test. It may be added that while such terms as "volcanic, terrific, etc." may seem extravagant to the reader, to the writer they seem more inadequate than anything else.

There is ample cause for emotional disturbances in this child's history. She spent her first sixteen months in an institution. The last two months of that time she had gonorrheal vaginitis and was isolated, a traumatic experience in itself, particularly for a child who perhaps had no other source of the feeling of security than the other children in the institution. It is not known what treatment she received for her infection, but it may well have been disturbing. Then, too, the change from institution to foster home requires adjustments that are difficult for most children.

It is not easy to predict Dorothy's future. We consider her relatively normal in intellectual endowment. Her emotional adjustment will probably depend largely upon the vicissitudes of her life within the next few years. The foster mother is no longer young, and cannot be counted on to provide a home for Dorothy indefinitely. The outlook for adoption is too risky to be considered at present; it is particularly risky for Dorothy, for an unsuccessful placement at this time might be disastrous. Adoption may be a possibility later, but Dorothy is rapidly passing any semblance c f the "cute" stage, and it is not easy to find adopting parents for an older girl with a difficult and unappealing disposition. Dorothy's independence of spirit is one of her greatest assets and it may be her saving.

§ 49. Madeline D.
Child Emotionally Unstable in Infancy; Behavior Average.
At 4 years 3 months, Intelligence Quotient about 120
(14 weeks—4 years 3 months)

Madeline was born out of wedlock. Her mother, of Italian parentage, was a bookkeeper; her father was unknown except that he was Jewish. The hospital report was "Normal,

full term delivery. Weight at birth 5 pounds 14.5 ounces."
When 4 days old Madeline was placed in a foster home. She
remained there until she was 6.5 weeks old, when she was
placed in a child-caring institution.

The nurses called our attention to Madeline when she was
14 weeks old. They were amazed that when they placed her
standing at the side of the crib, she would stand as long as
they held her hands. She was a mature-looking child, with
long almost black hair and a small face with pointed chin.
We briefly tested her behavior at this age and retested her
more fully when she was 17 weeks old. On each occasion we
found her adaptive behavior to be slightly below her chronological age. Perceptively she was very alert. Her maturity of
posture was unusual and colored the impression made by her
general behavior which was near, but a little below, the average for her age.

Madeline was again referred to us when 35 weeks old because of her habit of masturbating. All of the nurses and
nursing attendants were agreed that the habit was a very
pronounced one. Examination of Madeline's behavior development revealed a marked scattering of performance. Although she crept rapidly on hands and knees, she could not
sit alone. When placed sitting she violently flung herself
backward. She did not use her thumb in grasping, but instead
she raked at objects and grasped them interdigitally. She disregarded the string in her attempts to secure the ring, but she
banged objects on the table with vigor, anticipating the noise
by blinking her eyes. Her behavior was as intense as her posture and this intensity colored all of her adaptive responses,
producing a distorted behavior pattern.

When we attempted a retest a week later, she sucked her
thumb audibly and so vigorously and persistently that we
were unable to divert her attention to the test toys. She was
reported to react strongly to people, favoring some and showing strong dislike of others. We made recommendations con-

cerning her care and suggested that a foster-home environ-ment where she could have more consistent handling and where she would not be subjected to many different person-alities was essential for her improvement.

When she was 21.5 months old she was brought to us with the question of adoption. She had been in a foster home for a year and a half and had shown improvement in all of her habits. At the Clinic when she recovered from her scream-ing, she apparently adjusted very well and a full examination was obtained under somewhat informal conditions. Again the behavior was irregular, but her language expression and comprehension were both up to her age level. However, after she had been standing at the table between 15 and 20 min-utes, her legs and body trembled so that it was impossible for her to manipulate the cubes. Because her general make-up suggested the possibility of an unstable personality, we recom-mended that the question of adoption be deferred.

We visited Madeline in her foster home when she was 2 years old and found that her improvement was all that the foster mother claimed. Madeline had changed from a child who screamed violently when she saw a stranger even on the street, to a child who was not only friendly but affectionately demonstrative to strangers who came to the home. Only occasionally did she show her former outbursts of crying, screaming, and trembling all over. However, she was almost as intense in her affection as she had been in her withdrawal from people.

Four follow-up examinations have been made (see Table XIV), the last when Madeline was 4 years 3 months old. Improvement in general adjustment has continued, and with it improvement in behavior ratings. On our last examination she definitely scored superior, although the scoring scattered over four year levels. She has been legally adopted and to date there are no reported problems in the adoptive home.

TABLE XIV

MADELINE D.

Chrono-logical age	Behavior level					Comment
	Postural	Prehen-sory	Language	Adaptive	Personal-social	
14 weeks	General impression of about 12 weeks maturity					Child very tense. Examination brief
17 weeks	15 wks.	?	15 wks.	14 wks.	15 wks.	Perception better than manipulation. General muscular tension confuses estimate of motor development
35 weeks	28-38 wks.	31 wks.	31 wks.	30-36 wks.	31 wks.	A thin almost rigid child. Very reactive. Quality of responses normal. Scoring of behavior scatters markedly
21.5 months	−21 mos.	20-22 mos.	21 mos.	?18 mos.	21 mos.	Violent screaming at first followed by later adjustment. At times when standing at table, her body and hands shook so that it was not possible for her to build with the cubes. Talked freely
30 months	27 mos.	30 mos.	26 mos.	−29 mos.	?	Performance irregular, articulation poor
37 months	34 mos.	+36 mos.	+34-36 mos.	−39 mos.	+36 mos.	Friendly and chatty. Articulation infantile. Attention difficult to maintain
43 months	+42 mos.	42 mos.	+48 mos.	45 mos.	45 mos.	Overactive. Slight infantile articulation. Tendency to perseverate
4 years, 3 months	Stanford-Binet Mental age score: 5 years, 2 months. I.Q.: about 120.					Failures range to year 3, successes to year 7. She cannot copy a square but she repeats 5 digits. Has had no schooling

§ 50. Kate P.
Irregular Development Associated with Feeding Difficulties and Tremor of Hands
(12 weeks—5 years 3 months)

Only a few of the facts of Kate P.'s history are available. Mrs. P. married when she was 16 years old. She had one child and then she separated from her husband. Kate was illegitimate. Her natural father was a sailor and for a few weeks after her birth she was cared for at his home, where he lived with his father. Mrs. P.'s family did not know of Kate's existence. Mrs. P. finally left town and Kate was placed in a boarding-home. When she was 12 weeks old she was transferred to a children's institution.

When born, reputedly at full term, Kate weighed only 3 pounds. Nothing is known of her health history until she came under the care of the institution. At the age of 12 weeks she weighed 9 pounds 1 ounce and was 22.5 inches long. A behavior examination showed her to be somewhat inactive but to have considerable body tension. Otherwise she was normal and average. When she was re-tested at 16 weeks and again at 18 weeks, her behavior appeared to be up to her age level. When 19 weeks old, however, her behavior began to lag. We could elicit regard for neither the pellet nor the cube. She regarded her own hands rather than the rattle. She was both a very tense and a very social infant. She vocalized and laughed when socially stimulated. The muscular tenseness noted when she was 12 weeks old was still present. We considered her potentially low average or possibly dull-normal.

Kate was again referred to us at the age of 27 weeks because she was a child who might be considered for adoption, and also because she had become a serious feeding problem. Observation revealed that she fed very slowly; in 45 minutes she consumed only 1.5 ounces. She was easily distracted and we noticed a marked tremor of tongue and chin after she had taken about an ounce of her formula. The tremor occurred rather frequently during the hour of observation. A behavior examination showed that her skill in prehension was retarded. She could not grasp a cube placed well within her reach on the table, although she attempted to do so. Even her gross motor behavior was not up to her age. We advised postpone' ment of the question of adoption and suggested immediate foster home placement.

After placement in the foster home, Kate's feeding be' havior improved and her development regained its former tempo. She was still a very tense, active child and occasion' ally refused to eat.

On re'examination at the age of 2 years 2 months we noted a marked tremor of the hands and a tendency to use the left hand rather than the right, which had been preferred at 16 months. She was reported to take "hours to go to sleep." Feeding behavior continued to improve, but she was a "slow eater." Her behavior rating showed a slight lag but it was well within average limits for her age. Because of the history of jaw clonus during feeding and hand tremor while block' building, we sent her to a neurologist. No deviations were found. The tremor was explained in terms of her high'strung personality.

When Kate was 5 years 3 months old she was again brought to the Clinic. She was then mentally superior. She easily passed all of the 6'year'old tests and one at the 7'year level. She showed a slight tendency to repeat phrases, but the habit could not be described as a definite speech defect. Her foster parent reported hand trembling, but only when she was very excited. She had reverted to her original right'hand preference. A serious congenital heart condition had been discovered which ruled out the possibility of adoption, since she would probably need very special care at an early age.

This case interested us greatly because there seemed to be a close relation between the child's physical condition and her behavior development. It is very difficult to know when allowance for failures in adaptive behavior should be made because of physical disability. Instead of being a dull normal child, as the examination at the age of 27 weeks tended to indicate, Kate actually was potentially superior. Other cases which we have studied have not improved. Our problem then is to distinguish between the two types of cases. At present we can specify no rule except this: give the child the benefit of his optimum behavior until it is clearly proved that the behavior is really spurious.

§ 51. General Statement

It would be a great aid to developmental diagnosis if we always knew how old a child is when he is born! Notwithstanding centuries of observations and the aids of modern science, we have no exact method of determining the maturity of a newborn infant. In obstetrics, a *mature* infant is one born at term—that is, with a post-conception age of from 270 to 290 days. An infant with a gestation age between 28 weeks and 38 weeks is regarded as *premature*. An *immature* infant, from a clinical standpoint, is usually one whose birth weight is less than 2,500 grams (5½ pounds), and who is physiologically inadequately prepared for extra-uterine existence. Such an infant may be born prematurely, at term, or even postmaturely. Birth weight alone does not establish a diagnosis of prematurity. The physician has to take into account somatic and functional indications of the degree of maturity. The menstrual history of the mother and the calculated date of confinement[1] throw some light on the probable gestation age of the child, but such calculations likewise are subject to errors and variations.

Does prematurity have any significant effect upon the character and course of mental growth? This question is frequently raised by parents. There can be no simple, general answer. Prematurity of birth takes place under such a diversified array of conditions, that at the one extreme there is the certainty of permanent defect or of early death; and at the other extreme, the full assurance of normal development and

[1] The calculation is made by adding seven days to the date at which the last menstrual period appeared and then counting back three months.

ultimate maturity. The developmental fate of the prematurely born infant is always an individual matter, depending upon the severity of the associated complications, the cause of the prematurity, whether spontaneous or induced, and upon his primary growth potentialities. There is always the logical danger that we shall ascribe to prematurity consequences which arise out of more fundamental or associated factors. These factors, among others, include constitutional disease and chronic infections in the parents; undernourishment, physical shock or acute illness of the mother; asphyxia of the fetus; and multiple pregnancy.

Detailed study of individual cases of uncomplicated prematurity strongly suggests that the general course of development is not markedly accelerated or retarded by mere precocity of birth, when due allowance is made for the prematurity in reckoning the true chronological age. The central nervous system, unless it is actually impaired, tends to mature in accordance with inherent determiners, so that the cycle of behavior growth is not greatly altered by the birth displacement.

These facts have already been considered in our report of child J.L. (§ 24). They are also exemplified in child Jane S. (§ 52). The following thumb-nail sketch illustrates the principles involved when the prematurity of birth is uncomplicated by any serious pathological conditions:

An infant, 24 weeks of age, was brought to the Clinic for a developmental examination. He had an unusual birth history and the parents were somewhat concerned about the possible effects of a prematurity of 8 weeks, a birth weight of 3½ pounds and considerable early retardation in physical development. At the time of the examination the infant had attained a weight of 14 pounds and was vigorously reactive, without, however, showing any desire to sit up.

He was examined in the supine position in the clinical crib and his behavior was observed. Expressed in the present tense the observations were as follows: He lies with head in the midline and maintains this mid-position for prolonged periods. He rotates the head freely and turns it fully from one side to the other. Only traces of the tonic neck reflex are seen. His arms are symmetrically active; they are predominantly flexed and the hands usually fisted. His legs are acutely flexed at the knees and the hips externally rotated. He rolls freely to the side without assistance. He is regardful of his surroundings. He brings his hands to the midline, where they engage. . . . He perceives a dangling ring when it is presented in the midline and gives it immediate and prolonged regard. While he inspects the ring he brings his hands together over his chest, but he does not prehend the ring. He repeatedly follows it with his eyes and over a distance headward and forward and through an arc of 180°. He shifts his regard to the examiner's hand which holds the ring. When the examiner places the dangling ring in his hand, the infant regards it and carries it to his mouth. . . . When pulled from the supine to the sitting position he tenses his shoulders and shows no head lag.

The foregoing patterns were all observed in the course of fifteen minutes. These patterns are unquestionably less mature than we ordinarily expect in an average 24-week-old infant. They are less mature than those of the 20-week level, but they are definitely more mature than those of a normative 12-week-old infant. They are, in fact, highly characteristic of the 16-week level. But this infant was 24 weeks of age.

Ordinarily a retardation of 8 weeks at a chronological age of 24 weeks would constitute a developmental ratio of 2/3 and denote a seriously unfavorable condition which might even be indicative of a high-grade mental deficiency. In the present case, however, the behavior picture was quite normal. The corrected chronological age of the child, allowing for 8 weeks of prematurity, was 16 weeks. The retardation was a fact, but it was an artifact. The parents were assured that the developmental outlook was favorable. They were also advised to restrain their tendency to over-stimulate the

child's development to make up for the prematurity. The subsequent growth history of this child has justified the assurance. At the age of 6½ years he is well above an average
level of intelligence.

This case illustrates the importance of post-conception age
in the developmental diagnosis of immature, premature, and
postmature infants. The problem of diagnosis has an added
piquancy when we deal with foundlings for whom birth history and even birth data are entirely lacking. In these instances we are obliged to make a highly critical use of behavior norms as diagnostic indicators of a most probable
birthday. It is peculiarly difficult to diagnose at one time
both chronological age and biological age.

The three cases which are summarized in the present chapter illustrate the practical issues which may arise in clinical
service. Appraisal of behavior status would have erred in the
case of Jane S. (§ 52) if allowance had not been made for
six weeks of prematurity. . . . In the case of Janet P. (§ 53)
the suggested complication of prematurity was not fully confirmed by the developmental history. . . . In the case of
Horace T. (§ 54) immaturity was at first mistaken for prematurity, with some distortion of the developmental estimate.
These cases show the importance of a reliable medical diagnosis of prematurity whenever this factor is in question.
Neonatal "immaturity" must be differentiated from prematurity and also from developmental retardation. It refers
specifically to a physical or functional unreadiness for the
physiological demands of extra-uterine life.

§ 52. Jane S.
*Consistent Development When Proper Allowance Is Made
for Premature Birth*
(28 weeks—10 years 3 months)

Jane S. was brought to the Clinic at the age of 28 weeks
because her mother, who had two other girls, realized that

Jane was not doing what her sisters had been able to do at that age. Was she normal?

Mrs. S. had had a series of colds while pregnant, but otherwise her health had been good. Six weeks before term, Mrs. S. went on a five-hour trolley ride and that night, after being taken to the hospital, she gave birth to Jane, a physically normal premature weighing 5 pounds 1 ounce. Jane had a slight mouth infection in the hospital. After this healed at the age of 4 weeks, she began to gain. No other illness was reported when she was presented to us for examination at the age of 28 weeks.

When due allowance was made for premature birth, Jane's

TABLE XV

JANE S.

Chronological age	Behavior level				
	Postural	Prehensory	Language	Adaptive	Personal-social
28 weeks	22 wks.	22 wks.	22 wks.	22 wks.	22 wks.
36 weeks	30 wks.	30 wks.	30 wks.	30 wks.	30 wks.
42 weeks	36 wks.	−36 wks.	−36 wks.	35 wks.	36 wks.
46 weeks	40 wks.	40 wks.	40 wks.	40 wks.	40 wks.
58 weeks	51 wks.	51 wks.	51 wks.	−52 wks.	−52 wks.
80 weeks	Behavior consistent with former examinations. Uses 10–20 words freely, accepts 4 cubes, imitates stroke and looks at pictures in book, turning pages				
36 months	36 mos.	36 mos.	?	36 mos.	36 mos.
5 years, 2 months	Stanford-Binet mental age score: 5 yrs., 2 mos.				
10 years, 3 months	Stanford-Binet mental age score: 10 yrs., 4 mos.				

behavior was found to be normal and average. We reassured Mrs. S., but suggested that we follow Jane's development to confirm our findings. The results of our nine examinations (Table XV), the last at the age of 10 years and 3 months, represent very steady and consistent growth. Had the child's prematurity not been taken into account we should have erred seriously in our early diagnosis. It is interesting that the illnesses (measles at 32 weeks and whooping cough at 1 year) which Jane experienced, produced but little if any change in the course of her behavior growth.

§ 53. Janet P.
Development only Slightly Retarded in the First Year; Borderline at 8 Years 5 Months
(5 months—8 years 5 months)

Janet P. came to our attention when she was a little less than 6 months old. She was then residing in a child-caring institution, convalescing from a siege of pneumonia. Her available history was meager. Her mother, a former domestic and factory worker, had had one legitimate child three years before Janet was born. After the birth of her first child, Mrs. P. separated from her husband. Janet was illegitimate and nothing was known of her natural father. She had been born in a doctor's office and had then been placed in a boarding-home in the country. When 1 month old she was brought to a hospital. Hospital records described her as "a tiny marasmic baby, weighing 2,100 grams." The diagnosis was "Premature infant. Indigestion acute, with intoxication. Malnutrition with atrophy." The degree of prematurity was not stated in the diagnosis, but elsewhere it was estimated that she was a month premature. She remained in the hospital nine weeks and weighed 4,020 grams on discharge. When 4 months old she developed pneumonia, was hospitalized, and then as a convalescent was sent to the institution which referred her to us.

The behavior examination at the age of 5 months 24 days revealed a socially responsive infant who momentarily sat alone; grasped a cube placed within her reach; visually pursued dropped objects; and vocalized during her play. This behavior was up to the 5-month level. It represented a very adequate performance for a premature less than 6 months old. We expected her to develop normally and eventually to attain an average level of ability.

Janet was re-examined at the age of 9 months, when she was recovering from a heavy cold. We again found her behavior suggestive of average mental endowment. She used thumb and index finger to grasp the pellet; she inspected the bell, poking at the clapper; she retained two cubes and accepted a third; and she secured the ring by pulling the attached string. Surely, considering her history, this was creditable behavior. It was true that her postural behavior was deficient. She needed a pillow for support when sitting; she did not pivot, creep, or regress when prone; and she could not pull herself up to sitting from supine. However, in view of her recent illness, she was entitled to some lag in postural behavior.

Although Janet's postural behavior did recover from its depression, her mental development did not take the expected course. When she was 16 months old her adaptive behavior was only slightly more mature than it had been at 9 months. She had a serious furuncle and we wondered if her listlessness should be weighted in interpreting her performance. But at 22.5 months her general behavior was rated as of borderline grade. This estimate was justified by subsequent examination at 3 years 6 months and again at 8 years 5 months. On the last examination, particularly, there was no indication that Janet was capable of more than her actual performance. Adjustment to the examination was good and she showed relatively favorable personality traits.

TABLE XVI

JANET P.

Chronological age	Behavior level			
	Postural	Language	Adaptive	Personal-social
5 months, 24 days	+5 mos.	5 mos.	5 mos.	?
9 months, 1 week	7 mos.	−8 mos.	9 mos.	−8 mos.
16 months	15 mos.	−12 mos.	+9 mos.	−10 mos.
22.5 months	18 mos.	+12 mos.	+12 mos.	+15 mos.
42 months	36 mos.	27–30 mos.	27–30 mos.	27–30 mos.
8 years, 5 months	Stanford-Binet mental age score, 6 years, 2 months. I.Q. 75. Classification: Borderline Inferior.			

Discussion:

As we restudy the record, we wonder if the child was really premature. The first medical record available carried a diagnosis of prematurity (age 1 month). It is possible that she was in reality a full-term infant and that her condition simulated prematurity because her physical growth had suffered from the faulty care of her boarding-home. Actually her behavior showed rather marked irregularity even for a full-term infant. Illness and hereditary factors might have accounted in part for her mental-growth failure.

No harm was done by our optimism when Janet was 9 months old. However, if on the basis of our estimation of potential normality, she had been placed in an adoption home then, the consequences might have been more serious. When hereditary factors and birth history are unknown, it is best to delay placement with a view to adoption until behavior is convincingly normal. In the present instance, health factors were in any event a deterrent to adoption. It is possible that these health factors were themselves indicative of a generally defective constitution.

§ 54. Horace T.
Immaturity Confused with Prematurity. Development Consistent
(12 weeks—5 years)

Horace T. was referred to us as a 12-week old infant whose history was at that time unknown. His behavior was in no respect up to his age level. The most mature responses which we could elicit were in the adaptive-behavior field, and they were not up to 8 weeks' maturity. Horace was a small infant for his age, and we wondered if possibly he was a premature.

When re-examined at the age of 17 weeks, again not only his actual behavior, but also the quality of his responses, was very poor for his age. However, experience had taught us to be cautious in our prediction. We reserved judgment until we made another examination at the age of 40 weeks. At that time it appeared to be quite certain that Horace was a defective, immature child rather than a normal premature whose behavior level would eventually coincide with his age. His perceptive behavior was particularly deficient. When he dropped an object, he might glance at it, but he made no attempt to retrieve it. His attention, instead of being alert, was difficult to obtain. Thus, while he actually rated a 20-22 week score, there was a defective quality to his perform-ance which could not be explained in terms of prematurity.

Shortly after this examination, we received his birth his-tory. He had been delivered by Caesarian section at term, when his mother was sterilized. She was definitely feeble-minded and had had one feeble-minded child three years pre-

TABLE XVII
HORACE T.

Chronological age	Behavior level				Comment
	Motor	Language	Adaptive	Personal-social	
12 weeks	−4 wks.	+6 wks.	−8 wks.	4 wks.	Outlook depends on history. Child small for age. Premature?
17 weeks	Better than 8 wks. but not up to 12 wks.				Regard stary, but little exploratory inspection. Closure delayed and appears reflexive rather than adaptive
40 weeks	20 wks.	22 wks.	−22 wks.	20 wks.	Inactive, listless. Laughs out loud on social stimulation, but other responses weak and hard to elicit. Defective
21 months	General pattern of behavior, 8.5 mos.				Record incomplete because child adjusted poorly. Objects barely and rarely combined
46 months	36 mos.	24 mos.	33 mos.	27 mos.	Attention excellent. Good imitation and form identification but general ability definitely defective
5 years	Developmental level about 42 mos.				Somewhat distractible and uncritical of own performance. Defective: moron to borderline

viously. Horace's father was considered to be of low-grade mentality.

Table XVII shows that our prognosis, made when Horace was 40 weeks old, was borne out by subsequent examinations. This was not surprising when his inheritance was revealed. Had we known the facts of his history earlier, a correct diagnosis might have been determined sooner. Birth history is of considerable importance in the clinical appraisal of the behavior of young children. Without it even the experienced clinician is likely to err if diagnosis is not deferred or carefully qualified.

M. Twinship *Arnold Gesell*

§ 55. General Statement

The study of twins has almost attained the dimensions of a subscience. Literally hundreds of books and monographs have been written on the normal and the abnormal aspects of twinning. There remain, however, many superstitions and erroneous ideas in regard to twins.

The developmental significance of twinning has been partly considered in Chapter III in the case of B.D. As was pointed out, twinning is a process of bilateral doubling. In a sense this process is manifested even in the genesis of a single individual derived from a single zygote. Twinning produces the two equivalent halves of the individual. If the process of duplication of a single zygote (monozygote) is carried beyond the usual limitations, two offspring may result from a single ovum. If the process of duplication is very nicely balanced, a perfect pair of duplicated individuals, namely monozygotic twins, results. Approximately 15 per cent of our twin births have a monozygotic origin. The remaining twin pairs are dizygotic, and as is well known, result from two separate zygotes.

Because of this difference in genetic origin, the growth careers of monozygotic twins are very much more alike than are the careers of dizygotic or fraternal twins. It must be remembered, however, that although the tendency is toward duplication in monozygotic twins, the conditions of intra-uterine life sometimes favor one twin at the expense of the co-twin. The favored embryo may appropriate a disproportionate amount of blood in the placental circulation. For this reason, in some instances, monozygotic twins may be extremely unlike rather than extremely similar. The incidence of congenital mental deficiency is somewhat greater among twins than among the ordinary population, because of special hazards during gestation and birth.

In spite of these physiological hazards, it is quite unjust to assume that twins as a rule have an inferior developmental outlook. Superior endowment is frequently found among twins. The highest intellectual level which we have encoun' tered in our long series of cases at Yale was attained by a pair of monozygotic twins whose developmental precocity was manifest soon after birth. These twins were reported under the names Alpha and Beta in an earlier publication.[1] Their development was followed over a period of ten years. At the tender age of 10 months, these twins were combining words into phrases and sentences in a manner characteristic of 18 months. At the age of 9 years, their language ability and vocabulary were at an average adult level. When 7 years old their mental age was 13 years. In the decade between 7 and 18 years these twins not only graduated from elementary school, high school, and college, but simultaneously earned a post-graduate degree with similar distinction. The marked resemblances and precocities of the first year of life were highly predictive of their later growth careers. Twinship surely was no handicap. Indeed, with their exceptional abili' ties, which tended to set them apart from children of their own age, twinship had definite social advantages. Each twin served as a stimulating companion for the other.

Incidental reference may be made here to the fraternal twins Y and Z who were pictured in a previous volume[2] These twins consistently exhibited contrastive emotional be' havior as early as the age of six weeks. They have maintained this contrast throughout the following 10 years, during which they have been under observation. This pair of twins illus'

[1] Gesell, A.: *The Mental Growth of the Preschool Child. A Psychological Outline of Normal Development from Birth to the Sixth Year, including a System of Developmental Diagnosis.* New York, Macmillan, 1925, p. 447.

[2] Gesell, A.: *Infancy and Human Growth.* London, Macmillan, 1928, p. 418.

trates the persistence of individual differences among frater-nal twins even when reared together in apparently identical "environments." Inasmuch, however, as any psychological environment is a function of the individual's capacity to re-act, we should not assume that the environments of fraternal twins can be actually alike. In highly identical monozygotic twins there is indeed more similarity in their environments, because of the primary similarity in ability to react.

The three pairs of twins considered in the following sec-tion suggest a variety of developmental problems and mech-anisms. Twins Olga S. and Orma S. exemplify the remarkable physical and mental correspondences which frequently occur in monozygotic twins. Twins Laura T. and Lewis T. illus-trate the consistency of individual differences in fraternal twins. The individual growth careers of these twins are com-parable to what we might find in two ordinary siblings. Twins Jessie R. and Joan R. are monozygotic and illustrate a type of benign developmental retardation which may be due to monozygotic twinship. This pair of cases at least raises the question whether the physiology of development in mono-zygotic twins may not in some instances so alter the bio-chemical determiners of growth that the rate of maturation is somewhat atypical. The growth potency was apparently reduced in infancy, but ultimately the children reached a plane of full normality. Twins more frequently than single-tons are born prematurely. This fact must also be taken into account in appraising their early development.

§ 56. *Twins Olga S. and Orma S.*
Extraordinary Physical and Mental Resemblance, Including
Bilateral Macular Coloboma
(8 years 7 months—12 years)

The choroid is a dark-brown membrane situated between the outer covering of the eyeball and the retina. It consists mainly of blood vessels united by delicate connective tissue.

A coloboma of the choroid is a congenital defect of this membrane and of the retina which shows itself to the oculist in a large white patch. This defect arises extremely early in the embryonic period when the minute optic cup from which the eye is derived is in process of formation.

Here is a physical complication so deep seated that the physician cannot eradicate or forestall it. Fortunately, colobomas do not occur often, but when four of them appear in a pair of twins, one in each eye, and when these colobomas prove to be strikingly alike they assume great significance for anyone interested in the mechanisms of child development. (See Fig. 6.)

Physical and psychological characteristics:

Except for their eye defects, Olga and Orma were a pair of relatively normal twins. In spite of their eagerness and vivacity they had been handicapped in their school progress because of their defective vision and were referred to the Yale Clinic of Child Development, where physical and mental measurements were made. The measures and comparative data when the twins were 10 years old are summarized in Tables XVIII and XIX.

The resemblances, both physical and functional, were impressive. Olga was slightly superior in height, weight, intelligence, and reading ability. The differences, however, were almost negligible and were much less than those found among ordinary siblings. In numerous items the similarity was thorough. In a vocabulary test the children succeeded and failed, with only one exception, on the same words. Even their errors in spelling were often similar. Their temperamental traits, tastes, sense of rhythm, inflections of the voice and phonetic deviations also were alike. When they sang a duet the harmony was complete. The twins were clearly monozygotic.

Examination of the eye grounds (fundi) by Dr. E. M.

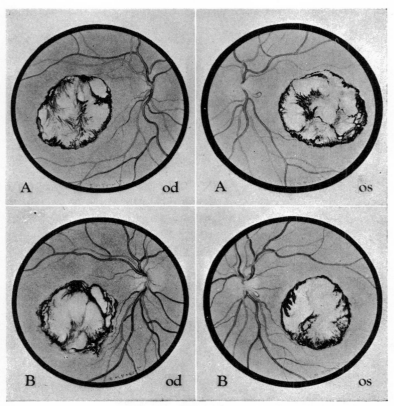

Fig. 6. Eye grounds of twins Olga and Orma.

TABLE XVIII

PHYSICAL CHARACTERISTICS

Item	Olga S.	Orma S.
HEIGHT		
Vertex	144.7 cms.	142.05 cms.
Suprasternal	116.7	115.05
Symphysis	77.0	76.5
DIAMETERS		
Biacromial	31.8	30.5
Mesosternal	22.1	20.8
Iliocristal	22.1	21.6
HEAD GIRTH	49.9	49.8
WEIGHT	72.75 lbs.	66.75 lbs.
TEETH		
Carious	3	4
Form of molar cusps	Similar	Similar
Eruption	Remnant, deciduous upper left first premolar	Remnant, deciduous upper left first premolar
		Lateral incisor erupting
	Upper central lateral incisors sharply angulated	Upper central lateral incisors sharply angulated
Maximum transverse diameter		
Upper palate	6.5 cms.	6.5 cms.
Lower jaw	6.5	6.3
Antero-posterior diameter		
Upper palate	5.2	5.0
Lower jaw	5.0	4.2
Maximum width		
Upper central incisor	9.0 mm.	9.0 mm.
Lower central incisor	6.0	6.0
HAIR		
Color	E to B	E to C
Texture and abundance	Similar	Similar
Whorls	Counterclockwise	Clockwise
EYE COLOR	Equal in both eyes, Norm 6	Equal in both eyes, Norm 6
PALMAR PRINTS	L: 11–9–7–5 R: 11–10–8–5	L: 11–9–7–5 R: 11–9–7–5
DERMAL CHARACTERISTICS	Similar 5 moles; 2 freckles	Similar 5 moles; 2 freckles
VISION (corrected)	R: 4/200 L: 10/200	R: 4/200 L: 10/200

TABLE XIX

PSYCHOLOGICAL CHARACTERISTICS

Item	Olga S.	Orma S.
MENTAL AGE	8 years 7 months	8 years 7 months
INTELLIGENCE TESTS ADMINISTERED	18	18
Identical successes	7	7
Identical failures	8	8
READING		
Speed: Paragraph 1	16 sec.	23 sec.
Paragraph 6	33	65
Errors: Paragraph 1	2	2
Paragraph 6	5	10
ORAL READING SCORE	3.7	2.8
WRITTEN SPELLING SCORE	1.5	1.5
ORAL SPELLING SCORE	2.05	1.8
VOCABULARY SCORE	18	18
PORTEUS MAZE	Similar	Similar
DRAWINGS	Similar	Similar
MOTOR COORDINATION		
Block building, aver. time	12.85	15.71
VOICE	Similar	Similar
MISPRONUNCIATIONS	Similar	Similar
MISSPELLINGS	Similar	Similar
PREFERENCES	Similar	Similar
GAMES PLAYED	Similar	Similar
REACTIONS TO DISCIPLINE	Similar	Similar
APPETITE	++	+
SPONTANEITY	++	+
SMILING	++	+
LATERALITY		
Writing	Right	Right
Throwing	Right	Right
Batting	Right	Right
Kicking	Right	Right
Thumbs up in folded hands	Right	Right
Eye dominance	Right	Left

Blake[1] disclosed a remarkable duplication of bilateral coloboma. In each eye there was a conspicuous roundish whitish
patch, roughly 4 diopters in diameter, occupying the macular
area. In the left eye of each twin there was a fetal remnant of
the hyaloid artery. This artery normally disappears before a

[1] Gesell, Arnold, and Blake, Eugene M.: Twinning and Ocular Pathology,
with a Report of Bilateral Macular Coloboma in Monozygotic Twins. Arch.
Ophthalmol., 15:1050-1071, (June) 1936.

child is born. All four eyes were myopic, although of slightly different degree. There was a divergence of the right eye of one girl and of the left eye of the other, explained by the difference in visual acuity. Neither child had ever worn glasses. Vision was seriously retarded. Olga could count fingers at six feet with the right eye and at three feet with the left. Orma counted fingers at four feet with the right eye and at ten feet with the left eye.

Attendance at a sight-conservation class was recommended. In two years, during which the twins have been subsequently observed, there has been no demonstrable change in the condition, except that the visual acuity is somewhat better as a result of wearing glasses for the correction of myopia. There has been also a diminution of nystagmus, often seen with increasing years or through correction of a refractive error.

Significance of developmental correspondences in twins:

Medical literature includes many case studies of twins which point to the importance of constitutional factors in the production of physical defects and deviations. One study reports a pair of twin boys in whom the identity included nose as well as eyes! In addition to identical refraction errors, the nose of each boy showed a distinct deviation to the right. A group of twelve pairs of monozygotic twins showed complete similarity of the eyes with respect to corneal curvature, astigmatism and refraction. Another study reports a dozen different kinds of tumor occurring simultaneously and symmetrically in a dozen different parts of the body in monozygotic twins. One investigator made numerous photographs of the eye grounds of twenty-three pairs of twins. He found a most remarkable and consistent resemblance in the number, distribution and even the branching of the retinal blood vessels.

From the standpoint of growth career, the noteworthy and instructive feature about Olga and Orma is their thorogoing psychobiological resemblances. As the tables show, these resemblances extend from the patterns of the friction ridges of the skin to patterns of behavior. Chance, not even when weighted by similar external environment, could scarcely account for the marked similarities in size and form of the teeth, color, and texture of eyes and hair, and identity of success and failure in 15 out of 18 intelligence tests.

Such resemblances must be based on a fundamental similarity of genetic constitution, which came to most striking expression in almost identical pathologic changes in the eyes. Recall that the colobomas traced back to a very early stage when the embryo was less than a half-inch in length. Normally the margins of the optic cup are even and regular. In this instance the optic cup of each eye in some way became notched and a blemish resulted. How did it happen? If a single "environmental" adversity caused the notching of the optic cup, it must have operated coincidentally within an extremely brief and critical interval on four rapidly organizing structures which simultaneously reached identical levels of maturity. This is an excessively remote possibility. It is still more unlikely that four defects of as many choroids, so similar in size, outline, position, and pigmentation, could have occurred at different times in consequence of four separate moments of infection, of irritation, or of damage neatly directed at each of the four eyes. It is, however, conceivable that the original single zygote or the constitutive factors in the twin embryos, which already held the hereditary determiners of all four eyes, held also the specific factors (or mutations) which delimited the development of the choroid. Similar specific factors would likewise account for the persisting remnant of the left hyaloid artery and for the correspondences in the shape and refraction of the four eyes. These eyes were derived from a single cell with one genetic constitution.

As in the case of hemi-hypertrophy (B.D., page 68), the physiology of twinning gives us a revealing glimpse into the genesis of developmental anomalies. Sometimes these anom-alies, as in the present instance, are so ingrained and funda-mental as to constitute a handicap. In other instances they are mild and negligible even though they sometimes are omi-nously labeled physical *stigmata*. Comparable developmental mechanisms account for many of the normal and healthy fea-tures of the child's makeup. Indeed, his whole physical and psychological individuality must have a constitutional basis. And this basis may even determine in some measure the scope and severity of physical complications which have a defi-nitely external origin.

§ 57. *Twins Jessie R. and Joan R.*
Irregular Development. Appeared Retarded at 28 Weeks,
Low Average at 10 Years
(28 weeks—10 years)

Jessie and Joan were identical or monozygotic twins, born after a gestation period of 8.5 months. Jessie weighed 5 pounds 3 ounces; Joan, 5 pounds 6 ounces. Their parents were Italian of low socio-economic level. Their father was a truck-driver, reliable, diligent, and a generally respected citizen. The mother, a primipara, died a few days after the twins were born. The infants were hospitalized for five weeks after birth and were then placed in a child-caring institution until their father remarried and re-established the home. We examined the twins at frequent intervals during their infancy and at least semi-annually through their tenth year. When infants, their behavior was so retarded that the ratio between behavior age and chronological age was approximately 75. As they grew older, their behavior caught up with their age and today there is no question that their mental develop-ment is quite average. In Table XX we have listed the three examination ratings which correspond to the examination ages of twins Laura T. and Lewis T. (§ 58) with whom twins Jessie R. and Joan R. will later be compared.

TABLE XX

JESSIE R.

Behavior level

Chronological age	Motor	Lan- guage	Adap- tive	D.Q.
28 weeks or 6.5 months......	20 wks.		20 wks.	About 75
44 weeks or 10.5 months.....	40 wks.	32 wks.	32 wks.	About 75
6 years...........	Stanford-Binet mental age, 6 years			I.Q. 100

TABLE XXI

JOAN R.

Behavior level

Chronological age	Motor	Lan- guage	Adap- tive	D.Q.
28 weeks or 6.5 months......	20 wks.		20 wks.	About 75
44 weeks or 10.5 months.....	40 wks.	32 wks.	32 wks.	About 75
6 years...........	Stanford-Binet mental age, 6 years			I.Q. 100

Comment:

It has been our experience that twins are more likely to be slow in their development in infancy than children of single births. Prematurity is frequently, but not always, a compli-cating factor. In this instance, according to the history, the twins' birth was not more than two weeks premature. This slight prematurity could not account for the eight weeks dis-crepancy between their behavior and their age at the 28-week examination. One might attribute the behavior lag of these particular children to the poverty of their institutional environment, if the same lag were not also seen in children residing at home. Perhaps the very process of twinning itself may alter the biochemical mechanisms of growth in such a way that the early rate of growth is relatively retarded. In the present instance these apparently intrinsic retardative factors gradually ameliorated, and mental growth then pro-ceeded at an average rate.

§ 58. Twins Laura T. and Lewis T.
Borderline Inferior, Consistent Development
(6.5 months—6 years)

In contrast to twins Jessie R. and Joan R., whose behavior was retarded in infancy and who later proved to have aver-age mental endowment, it is interesting to present another pair of twins whose growth career has been very consistent. Laura T. and Lewis T., fraternal twins, were the result of their mother's third pregnancy. At the time of the twins' birth she was married to a former saloon-keeper and boot-legger, but he claimed that the twins were illegitimate. Both parents had been married previously and the mother was ad-mittedly immoral. Both parents were Italian.

The twins were born at a hospital. Laura, weight 2,575 grams, length 19 inches; Lewis, weight 3,400 grams, length 20 inches. Six weeks after birth they were returned to the hospital because of malnutrition. There they both had pneu-

TABLE XXII
LAURA T.
Behavior level

Chronological age	Motor	Lan-guage	Adap-tive	Personal-social	D.Q.
6.5 months.....	5 mos.	?	−5 mos.	−5 mos.	75–80
10.5 months....	9 mos.	−9 mos.	8 mos.	8 mos.	75–80
5 years, 11 months....	Yale scale. General level about 52 months				About 75

TABLE XXIII
LEWIS T.
Behavior level

Chronological age	Motor	Lan-guage	Adap-tive	Personal-social	D.Q.
6.5 months....	−5 mos.	?	5 mos.	−5 mos.	75–80
10.5 months....	9 mos.	8 mos.	−8 mos.	8 mos.	70–75
5 years, 11 months...	Yale Scale. General level about 48 months				About 70

monia. At the age of 5 months they were sent to a children's home for convalescent care. Our first examination of the twins was made at the institution when they were 6.5 months old. Re-examinations were made at 10.5 months and at 5 years and 11 months. The accompanying tables chart the course of their development.

Comment:

The development of these twins has been remarkably consistent. Their behavior at the age of 6.5 months was an accurate indication of their capacities for growth, in spite of the fact that they had been subjected to the hazards of twinning, to illness, and to an institutional environment during infancy.

Why should these twins follow a consistent course of development while the R. twins improved in their performance relative to age as they grew older? Both pairs of twins were of Italian parentage, of low socio-economic level, and both were institutionalized during infancy. The R. twins were monozygotic, while the T. twins were fraternal. After infancy the R.'s were in a favorable home environment, while the T.'s were less fortunate. Are either or both of these factors responsible for the differences in the development of these twins? Do monozygotic twins have a slower earlier development than dizygotic twins? It is not inconceivable that such is the case. We should also like to know within what limits behavior development depends on the preschool environment.

§ 59. General Statement

Normal development presupposes a normal physical and mental endowment, to which must be added a favorable physical, social, and experiential environment. Conversely, deviations and abnormalities in endowment or in environ- mental factors produce departures from normal development. These terms are used in a broad sense, and include the child with primary retardation, complicated or uncomplicated by physical factors, the potentially normal child born with physi- cal or sensory defects, and the normal or potentially normal child who suffers from an environmental catastrophe, whether toxic, infectious, or traumatic. Endowment and environment thus become inextricably intertwined, and the whole ques- tion of diagnosis and prediction is exceedingly complex.

Visual, auditory, prehensory, locomotor, and social experi- ence all play important roles in normal development, and any interference in their functioning, as blindness, deafness, paralysis, etc., will have distorting or retarding effects. The question is, how severe and how permanent will the effects be in a given case? Prolonged illness brings with it a reduc- tion and conservation of energy. The child is confined to bed, often isolated; he does not "feel like playing" and play is the exercise of function. Usually, on recovery, development quickly rebounds to a normal level. It is quite possible, how- ever, to imagine conditions of prolonged prostration and de- bility, particularly during the critical years of development, severe enough to destroy much of the elasticity of the re- bound.

Injuries to the developing brain are among the commonest causes of developmental deviations due to physical complications. The extent of the deviation will depend upon the extent, severity, and location of the damage, as well as on the vulnerability of the organism. The fetus and the newborn infant are particularly susceptible to injury.

It is impracticable to list all the causes of cerebral injury, but a few illustrative examples may be cited. Severe neonatal jaundice, asphyxia, lead poisoning, cerebral hemorrhage, massive or minute, and infections such as syphilis, meningitis, and encephalitis, all can result in destruction of cerebral tissue. The destruction may be gross, microscopic, or even ultramicroscopic. These conditions are usually considered broadly as "injuries" causing secondary retardation. They may, of course, also be imposed upon a primary or congenital retardation, or there may be inherent predisposing factors in the native endowment which lead to their occurrence in an apparently normal child.

Congenital abnormalities are also physical complications in a very real sense. There may be an actual aplasia of the brain or a congenital absence of any of its parts. Tumor and hydrocephalus can encroach upon normal brain substance, and the various degenerative diseases, as amaurotic family idiocy, cerebral sclerosis, etc., result in deterioration. These conditions are usually considered as primary even though they may not be immediately manifest, because the *anlage* is presumably inherent in the genetic constitution of the individual. Probably mongolism should also be placed in the group of primary retardation, as there is no definite evidence at present that it belongs elsewhere. Thyroid deficiency may be congenital or acquired, and results in a metabolic disturbance producing defective development.

There are very few conditions in which the mental development can be predicted with surety, solely on the basis of the physical complications. Mongolism is one of the few, and there are pitfalls even here (Ernest N.). In all cases before a prognosis is formulated, one must determine the tendency of the condition to progress, to remain static, or to improve, either spontaneously or under treatment. This re-quires comparative re-examinations.

Barring progressive disease, the capacity of the organism to revert toward the normal is enormous even in the presence of a permanent disability. Children differ too, by their en-dowment, in their ability to surmount handicaps imposed on them. Two birth-injured children with equal motor and speech disabilities may show wide differences in their poten-tialities. In estimating the developmental caliber of a child suffering from a recent cerebral insult, it is important to remember that the early reaction to injury usually exagger-ates the actual damage and a certain amount of recovery often takes place. Harold P. and Paul V. are excellent examples showing profound injury with later marked im-provement, completely unforetold by the raw scores made on their first examinations. Errors in the opposite direction may easily be made by the sympathetic examiner who tends to excuse poor performance on the grounds of physical handi-caps (Celia R.).

It requires keen clinical judgment to evaluate the impor-tance of physical handicaps in an individual case. If the brain is spared, development can, under proper conditions, proceed remarkably normally, in spite of severe sensory and motor handicaps. The brain can even retain considerable capacity for growth and function, after what might appear to be devastating injury. Handicapped children should be given every opportunity for optimal development, and should be repeatedly observed before a final judgment affecting their future care is pronounced. The effect of the specific handi-cap on performance itself and on the ability of the child to meet the demands of the examination must be carefully evaluated before an accurate diagnosis can be made.

§ 60. *Edwin R.*
Birth Trauma. Strikingly Normal Development
(6 weeks—52 weeks)

The parents of Edwin R. had three normal children aged 14, 12, and 6 years. Edwin was the fourth child. His birth was extremely difficult; forceps delivery was unsuccessful and he was finally delivered by version and extraction. He was a large baby, weighing 9.5 pounds and showed evidence of severe trauma to the head. Scalp and face were badly contused and lacerated. Fully 45 minutes elapsed after birth before respiration was well established. The fontanelle was tense and full; there was unilateral facial weakness and his cry was weak. During the first three days of life he had frequent twitching of the face, arms, and legs. The extrem-ities were spastic and the fontanelle full. The spinal fluid was xanthrochromic.

A serious cerebral trauma was at first suspected, but when the presence of tetany of the newborn was revealed by Chvostek's sign and by a low blood calcium value (7.3 mgms. %) the significance of the twitchings was altered and it was considered possible that the damage to the brain was not severe. He improved slowly and by the tenth day, although he was very sluggish and inactive, he was no longer spastic. He remained in the hospital six weeks, improving steadily and was seen by us in consultation just before he was discharged to his home. Edwin's parents were naturally worried about the outlook for normal development and wanted whatever reassurance we could give them.

A description of his behavior at 6 weeks and a summary of his progress during the first year of life is given in the following paragraph and table:

At 6 weeks of age, although Edwin was active, his pos-tural responses and head control were below the 4-week level. He was alert and attentive, but social responses were very questionable and vocalizations were also below the 4-week level. On the other hand, his visual following of a moving object (dangling ring) was competent and complete, and he gave brief but definite regard to the rattle; both of these items are normal adaptive responses for his age.

TABLE XXIV

Age wks.	Developmental level wks.	D.Q.	Comment
6	3–6	Unassigned	Prognosis guarded
21	16	Unassigned	Development satisfactory; outlook good
32	32+	100+	Normal infant
52	52+	100+	Normal infant

This case is cited as a remarkable instance of normal development in spite of an extremely adverse birth and neonatal history. At the time of his first examination it was impossible to foretell with any certainty this favorable outcome. The following evidence, however, had a favorable import, pointing to this happy prognosis: Edwin's almost complete physical recovery in six weeks; the normal character of his adaptive responses, his alertness, the quality of his attention. The deficient social and vocal responses might be attributable to the lack of normal experience that hospitalization implies. On the other hand, the history of trauma at birth and the physical signs of cerebral injury were indisputable. While it was possible, as has been mentioned, that many of Edwin's symptoms could be ascribed to neonatal tetany, not all of them could be explained away on this basis; moreover it was also possible that the tetany was only latent. His behavior showed retardation in the motor, language, and social fields, and he was at an age when performance can have a quite fictitious appearance of normality. In short, the evidence was conflicting and while we could be hopeful we could not be sure. Judgment was reserved.

In such a case, no harm is done by waiting until the outlook is clear. An erroneous adverse prognosis causes much needless unhappiness; a favorable prognosis which has to be retracted builds up hopes that must be destroyed again. The faith that patients or those responsible for them have in their doctor and his word is not something that should be re-warded with guesswork.

Edwin now has no physical or mental residuals of his early difficulties and we have no reservations about the future. He is a healthy, normal outgoing infant. A favorable prognosis can now be safely given on the cumulative evidence of repeated observations during his first year.

§ 61. *Charlotte S.*
Birth Injury—Spastic Quadriplegia. Irregular and Retarded Development
(18 months—6 years)

Charlotte was born at full term by a difficult breech and forceps delivery. The birth weight was 7 pounds and 13 ounces. Nothing abnormal was noticed until she was 6 months old, when the family doctor noticed the poor pos-ture and strabismus and informed the family the child was "birth-injured."

She was first examined at the age of 18 months. She had a mask-like face, spastic arms and legs, with the legs in wide abduction; the left arm and hand were not used at all. Her performance showed much scattering between the 24- and 36-week levels, tending to center near 30 weeks, or about 7 months (D.Q. 40). Even when ample allowance was made for her physical disabilities, a serious degree of retardation remained and we were none too sanguine about Charlotte's future. In fact, we were compelled to consider her definitely feeble-minded, perhaps at an imbecile level, and more or less incapable of training. She was able to grasp a toy but her exploitation was feeble and brief and consisted chiefly in mouthing and banging. She ignored details and demonstra-tions. (It would appear from subsequent examinations that the full significance of some of her behavior was not sufficiently appreciated. The record stated: "Indeed, in all her performances the attitude and approach are in advance of actual performance.")

We were surprised when Charlotte returned at 2 years of age to find a decided alteration in the clinical picture. Comprehension and language had advanced markedly and were between the 15- and 18-month levels. Some of her play was of a highly social and imitative nature, such as "talking" on the telephone. We sensed insight and a real attempt in tower building and scribbling, but her true ability was obscured by her difficulties in coördination. The outlook was certainly much improved but we wisely refrained from committing ourselves any further than that. Muscle-training was, however, advocated and has been intermittently given since that time.

Her further course has been very uneven. At 2.5 years her level was approximately 18 months (D.Q. 60); at 3 years, still approximately 18 months with very meager discernible gains (D.Q. 50); at 4 years, 27+ months (D.Q. 60); at 5 years, approximately 3.5 years (D.Q. 70); and at 6 years again only about 3.5 years (D.Q. 60).

Her attention is fair; she occasionally over-responds with a foolish emotional display, occasionally "leaves the field" entirely. She has become very demanding and dependent; she insists that her mother lie down with her when she goes to bed and wakens almost hourly during the night to be turned. The mother cannot leave the house during the daytime and has gradually enslaved herself to the child. Charlotte is only too ready to pass any difficult task on to her mother, rather than attempt it herself. None of these traits are advantageous, of course, but are cited to show how dominating she is in her helplessness.

The question whether this child is mentally defective or not remains as yet unanswered. Perhaps the fairest estimate, if one must make an estimate, is that of borderline deficiency. This is, however, a far cry from the judgment passed on her at 18 months of age. This and other similar instances have led us to be cautious in interpreting tests given to birth-injured children within the 18- to 24-month age range particularly. This age can almost be characterized as a period when the formal test situations may be very deceptive when applied to the birth-injured. In many cases they do not tap the child's real abilities, whereas in infancy, and from 3 years of age on, these same test situations are much more revealing. Charlotte has shown an unusual amount of variability, but she is certainly capable of learning much more than she has; her disabilities, the over-sympathetic attitude of her family, and the child's own personality, are probably all operating to depress optimum development.

§ 62. Hugh B.
Birth Injury. Slight Motor Handicap
(39 weeks—6 years 1 month)

Hugh B. was an illegitimate child whose mother had completed two years of high school and whose natural father was a college graduate with postgraduate professional training. Hugh was born after a full gestation term and weighed 7 pounds 12 ounces at birth. He was well until the age of 21 weeks when he was hospitalized with parenteral diarrhea, upper respiratory infection, and dehydration. After four weeks in the hospital he was discharged to a child-caring institution for convalescent care.

At the age of 39 weeks, while still residing in the institution, Hugh was referred to us for routine examination. He was found to be an eager, responsive infant whose behavior maturity was between the 30- and 34-week level. He was beginning to pivot when prone. He raked at the pellet; he waved the bell, hitting it on the table with vocalization; and he regarded the ring but not the string, in the ring and string situation. He remained in the institution, where from time to time we observed his development. At 47 weeks of age he could sit unsupported for as long as 15 minutes, but he was reported to lack drive. He had no desire to sit and passively accepted placement in the supine position, which is rarely tolerated at this age.

When he was 55 weeks old we made another full examination. It was reported that he would lie all day in his crib. Unless taken up, he made no attempts to lift his head, or to sit, or to roll over. Placed sitting, he would sit alone for as long as 25 minutes. When supine he would kick and grab his feet. We found his fine motor coördination similarly retarded. He was not able to pick up a pellet; in attempting to do so he flexed his finger and thumb only at their distal joints. His combination of objects resembled behavior of normal 44-week maturity level. In this respect his behavior was consistent with the findings of our first examination. Since he played for prolonged periods with considerable animation and vigor—behavior which was quite inconsistent with his tolerance of the supine position and with his gross motor inactivity—we considered his motor behavior to be more than merely symptomatic of mental retardation. We therefore recommended a thorough orthopedic examination.

The orthopedist found a ligamentous hypermobility and a slight spasticity of the muscles which resulted in incoördination of the movements of hands and feet. The neuromuscular condition was probably based on an obscure prenatal or birth injury. Muscle-training was recommended for the legs. Hugh was placed in a foster-home and exercises were begun.

We have seen this child three times since his condition was diagnosed. Table XXV records his test scorings on each occasion. There has been a gradual improvement in his performance. At his last clinic examination, he scored an average intellgence quotient on the Revised Stanford-Binet scale. When last examined he showed some motor disability. He had difficulty in folding a piece of paper to make a triangle.

TABLE XXV

HUGH B.

Chronological age	Behavior level					Comment
	Postural	Prehensory	Language	Adaptive	Personal-social	
39 weeks	32 wks.	−32 wks.	32 wks.	−32 wks.	32 wks.	Very stimulated by test materials—attention, responsiveness and eagerness not in accord with assigned level
55 weeks	−40 wks.	−32 wks.	?	44 wks.	44 wks.	Pursues activity for prolonged periods with considerable vigor and animation. Motor behavior defective
37 months	?	33 mos.	27 mos.	+33 mos.	27 mos.	Took first step at 22 months of age. Now runs about room. Sturdy appearing
49 months	36 mos.	48 mos.	?36 mos.	+42 mos.	−42 mos.	Hand grip weak. Performance relatively better than at 37 months
6 years, 1 month	Stanford-Binet mental age rating: 6 years, 0 months. I.Q.: 100.					Considerable scattering of performance. Failed man completion test at 4 years and repeating 4 digits at 4.5 years, but he copied the diamond, discovered the absurdities, and scored the comprehension test at year 7

No other motor disability was noticed. It was significant, however, that he made three adequate copies of the diamond, a test placed at 7 years. He is now an attractive, robust child.

Infant tests which do not separate motor items for independent estimate may lead to serious error in the appraisal of a child suffering from a delimited motor handicap.

§ 63. Harold P.
Accidental Asphyxia. Deviation of Normal Development
(23 weeks—27 months)

Harold was born precipitately, twenty-two days prematurely after an eight-hour labor. His birth weight was seven pounds and he breathed and cried spontaneously. The neonatal period was normal and, according to the mother, his development to the age of 21 weeks was also entirely normal. The baby was considered bright; he laughed and cooed and made some effort to sit up. He always slept in the prone position and one morning a few moments after he had taken his bottle and been placed prone in his carriage to sleep, his mother found him "smothered," limp, breathless and blue. Artificial respiration was administered for five to ten minutes before he gasped. He was rushed to the hospital, where he vomited intermittently for about an hour, and then convulsed for about a week. Following the convulsions he was either irritable or semi-stuporous for several days, then gradually recovered, though he seemed seriously retarded.

The history raised several interesting questions. Had this baby actually suffocated and was his condition due to asphyxia? Or had he had a convulsion that fateful morning similar to the convulsions that were observed afterwards, and if so, what caused the convulsions? Was this an episode occurring in a mentally deficient or an epileptic child? Or was this a non-exudative encephalitis?

We examined Harold at the age of 23 weeks, and found

him greatly retarded, his behavior near the 8-week level. His expression was stupid and vacuous, his attention almost impossible to elicit. Five weeks later, his behavior had risen to a 16-week level. Hand and arm movements showed some incoördination and attention patterns were defective. Still, a certain amount of recovery was evident.

At 37 weeks his general developmental level was approximately 32 weeks. The facies was normally alert and responsive, the attention well sustained and essentially normal in quality. A slight incoördination in the use of the eyes and hands remained. If allowance for the alleged prematurity was made, Harold's recovery was practically complete, all in sixteen weeks. If he was not premature, and the normal birth weight might well be considered evidence against it, his development was still within the normal range (D.Q. about 85).

Re-examinations have shown the latter surmise to be more plausible. There has been no further relative improvement. At 16 months his development was approximately 13 months; at 27 months, near 21 months (D.Q. about 80). The gait and use of the hands were slightly awkward, the attention consistent with the level. He is a dull-normal child who gives evidence of having suffered a mild impairment in development.

Perhaps we should now attempt to answer some of the questions previously posed. Certainly we can say with assurance that his attack was not an episode in a mentally defective child. It is also unlikely that he is an epileptic, as such a severe attack, lasting over a week, so early in life would ordinarily be but the forerunner of a series of subsequent attacks, and they have not occurred. The encephalitis question must remain moot, though there was no real evidence that he suffered an infection. In view of the prone sleeping posture, suffocation is probably the most tenable explanation.

§ 64. *Ellen R.*
Polio-encephalitis. Deviation of Normal Development
(40 weeks—3 years)

Ellen was the youngest of ten children who had been removed from their home because of degrading home conditions. Both parents were alcoholic. All the children were
examined at this Clinic shortly after their transfer to the
care of a social agency; seven were average in intelligence
(including Ellen), two were superior, and one was dull-
normal. All made a favorable clinical impression from the
standpoint of both development and personality.

Ellen was first seen at 40 weeks and gave a perfectly
normal performance for her age. She was described as a
vigorous, outgoing infant who exploited toys lustily. At 18
months her general developmental level was slightly above 18
months. She was considered a favorable adoption candidate,
although the agency did not plan to separate her from her
brothers and sisters.

At 19 months she had polio-encephalitis, with convulsions,
coma, and paralysis of the right arm and leg. She was ill
about six weeks, but apparently made a good recovery. Two
months later, the arm was declared normal in power and
function and a month after that full power had returned
to the leg. She was, however, exceedingly active, and in
fact over-active. About this time her foster mother died suddenly and Ellen was transferred to a new home.

She returned for re-examination at 25 months, just three
weeks after her new placement. She had made a poor gain
since her last examination, and her general level was approximately 21 months. Whereas she had had about three words
and a well-developed jargon at 18 months, she had no words
or jargon at 25 months, though her comprehension of language was consistent with her general level. At 18 months
she built a tower of five cubes; at 25 months a tower of two.

In view of her illness and recent change in placement, it remained possible that her relatively poor showing on this examination should not be taken too seriously.

At 30 months, however, the retardation persisted, and her score was 24-27 months. She showed a few peculiarities of behavior, the most outstanding of which was her persistence in trying to find a door knob on the right-hand side of the door, when the knob was plainly to be seen at the left; it finally had to be shown to her. Articulation was poor, though she had about four single words; toilet habits had not yet been established. She had shown no distinct hand preference before her illness, but was definitely left-handed at this examination.

At 3 years the level was slightly above 30 months; she had several successes at the 3-year level but language, particularly, remained retarded. A favorite remark, "duba-dubadub," seemed grotesque from a child who was able to imitate the three-cube gate, match four color forms and identify seven pictures.

Obviously the normal course of this child's development has been skewed. Her examinations before her attack of encephalitis revealed her to be a normal, stable, average-or-slightly-better child, cut from the same cloth as her siblings. Now she is restless, slightly perservative, and a little retarded. The alterations in the personality field are probably the most serious as far as her future is concerned.

§ 65. Paul V.
*Streptococcus Meningitis. Marked Apparent Deterioration
with Rapid Return toward Normal
(42 months—7 years 9 months)*

Between the ages of 42 months and 53 months Paul was in attendance at the Guidance Nursery because of problems of feeding and general over-dependence. At the beginning and end of this period, developmental examinations were made. These indicated that he was at least of average intelligence, and the impression was suggested that his immaturity, overactivity, and distractibility might be concealing a relatively higher level of ability. He preferred the left hand.

The guidance worker's summary of his behavior at the end of the period was as follows:

Paul was very unsettled emotionally, and expressed his feelings very vociferously. The first day with the group he had an exaggerated tantrum at rest period, when he kicked, tore a sheet, threw the cot, scratched, threw himself down, etc. When none of this behavior accomplished his ends, he controlled himself. It took more than a week for him to get used to his mother's departure. He often wept or whined to get his own way. He seemed unable to adapt to emergencies quickly. He has gradually been helped to better techniques for controlling his emotions in these social situations, and has become a much happier child. He has a nice sense of humor, can take a joke, and likes to tell funny stories.

After some difficulties, he learned to fit into a small organized group, to take suggestions from other children, and to give his ideas in play. In conflict situations with other children he does not defend himself vigorously from older ones, but does very well with those of his own age. He is apt to appeal to the adult for help, but accepts suggestions for solving his own problems in most instances.

Birth had been normal. There was a history of digestive disturbances practically from birth, and at 42 months he had a very irregular appetite, which led to his being referred for guidance.

The case was closed on our records at the age of 4½ years, and we did not see him again until he was 7 years 2 months of age. At 6 years 10 months he was taken to the hospital with streptococcus meningitis, following which he was referred for examination because of apparent mental deterioration.

At 7 years 2 months the picture was perfectly characteristic of a mentally defective child with a developmental level of about 18 months. Facial appearance, emotional ex-

pression, and vocalization were all consistent with the examination results. He had a round, smooth, bland face with an
extremely immature play of emotion. Vocalization during
our observation did not include any spontaneous words, and
his nurse reported that his only non-imitative word was
"no," although when he had entered the hospital he had
used such constructions as asking, "Is that tooth-brush sterilized?" He repeated single words and some two-syllable
phrases. There was no lack of coöperation; attention span
was short, but he could always be brought back to a task.
There was definite evidence of satisfactory hearing.

The left hand was used exclusively at this time, the right
side being paralyzed. He scribbled vigorously and spontaneously, laughing approvingly, and called attention to his
performance. No imitative drawing was elicited. Cubes were
spontaneously laid out in a straight line. He constructed a
tower of seven cubes, but had to be specifically directed to
place nearly every cube. The pile was somewhat unsteady,
and, when asked to place another, he held his hand in a
protective position against them and looked up, vocalizing
in a way that suggested concern lest the tower fall over.

His invariable response to the question "What is this?"
was "Two." Asked to point to specific pictures, he scored
only one doubtful success, which he did not repeat.

Throughout the examination, the quality of his responses
did not suggest in any way that the lowered performance was
the result of temporary attentional or emotional disturbance,
nor was there any indication that a potentially higher level
of ability was being concealed. The picture was consistent in
every way with that seen in definitely defective children of
the developmental level indicated.

Paul was re-examined four months later, following reported improvement. At this time he appeared a different
child altogether. On the Stanford scale he passed all tests in
Group IV, three out of four in Group V, four out of five at
VI, and one test (repeating digits) at VII. Success was also

closely approached on several other tests within this range. The mental age score was 5 years 8 months, and the intelligence quotient 75.

He was friendly and talkative, somewhat euphoric, and his emotional attitudes and general demeanor were more like those of a four-year-old than a child of either his true age or the mental age shown. The right side was still paralyzed; he was unable to walk alone or to use his right hand effectively.

The most recent examination was made three months later, at the age of 7 years 9 months. He was getting about, with great difficulty, on crutches. Again he was entirely coöperative, euphoric, and very good natured. He kept up a stream of conversation in a loud voice, frequently showing signs of the enjoyment of jokes and plays on words that had been noticed during his earlier Guidance Nursery visits. After identifying a dime correctly, he added, "Ten cents— that's ten pennies, and [tapping his head] sense in your head, that's different." Use of language was excellent, although his vocabulary score was not above his general level.

His mental age score at this time was 6 years 4 months, with an intelligence quotient of 81—a rise of six points, representing a gain of eight months, over a three-month period. Scattering was reduced; the only test failed below Group VII was V-3, involving esthetic comparison, and one test— definitions superior to use—was passed at VIII.

There is no indication that he has yet reached his limit on the return toward full normality of intelligence. His rate of gain, which was extremely rapid between the first two examinations following his illness, has slowed down considerably, but is definitely continuing. He is still handicapped by his right hemiparesis. We cannot predict what lasting personality complications may have been brought about through his experiences, but those so far observed have a relatively benign aspect; his hyper-excitability and his euphoric attitude toward his illness have served to stimulate his coöperation in the program of physiotherapy that is being carried out.

The case illustrates dramatically the hazards of attempting a certain diagnosis of deterioration too soon after the illness or accident that has raised the question. It would have been particularly easy to have been misled on the first examination in the present case because of the remarkable consistency of the clinical picture in suggesting a specific developmental stage. The avoidance of a definite prediction at this time and the request for re-examination have been completely justified.

§ 66. Celia R.
Congenital Cataracts and Myopia
Normal Development in Spite of Severe Visual Defect
(41 weeks—25 months)

Celia was an illegitimate child under the care of a social agency. Her mother had congenital cataracts with "20-percent vision" and had spent nine years in a school for the blind. At the age of 18 she could read Braille and had reached the seventh grade. Her baby also had bilateral congenital cataracts. At 2 months, Celia was placed in a foster home where she remained until the age of 22 months, when she was transferred to a second foster home.

She was first seen at 41 weeks. Her expression was normally alert, the cataracts obvious. She had some vision, but a high degree of myopia was revealed by ophthalmoscopic examination. She reached for a toy if it was held close to her eyes and exploited it by transferring it from hand to hand over the bridge of her nose. She fumbled for a dropped toy, apparently guided by sound, and she was reported to discriminate voices. Her interest and drive were normal, and she fussed in the absence of toys. Her general level was approximately 32-36 weeks and the developmental outlook was considered good.

At 52 weeks, she showed real progress. The development of precise grasp in the absence of precise vision was particularly noteworthy. She crept, pulled to her feet, and cruised about her bed, imitated sounds, and could play pat-a-cake. Her general level was close to 40 weeks and her progress was considered satisfactory in view of her visual handicap.

At 18 months the comment was made, "Tests requiring visual discrimination are failed, but in general succeeds nicely at the 18-month level. Very busy with investigatory activities. Shows more interest in lights than usual (for age), less than usual social rapport. She perhaps misses the cues the normal child gains through changes in facial expression." She walked well and was remarkably sure-footed, seeming always ready to catch her balance if she should stumble.

Two weeks after this examination the eyes were operated on and the cataracts were needled. Two weeks later we made a re-examination. There was definite evidence of the depressing influence of her recent hospital experience, and also definite evidence of slightly improved vision. She no longer played with an object over the bridge of her nose and she reached directly for objects six to eight inches away. She reacted much more to visual cues, ignoring tactile and auditory cues to a large extent; this change actually made some of her performances seem poorer than before. For example, she showed much less caution in walking and fell more frequently.

At 25 months her development was slightly above the average. She saw well enough to identify a large outline picture, if she peered at it very closely. She is a most attractive little girl and her outlook is far from dark, in spite of her serious handicap.

Since watching Celia's development, we are much less lenient about attributing serious retardation in infancy to visual defect.

§ 67. Henry 2.
Hydrocephalus and Spina Bifida
(17 months—4 years 6 months)

This unfortunate boy was born two weeks prematurely, by breech delivery after a fifteen-hour labor. His birth weight was 7¼ pounds and he had a spina bifida which was repaired twenty-four hours after birth. There was also a hydrocephalus which continued to increase gradually but steadily. The lower extremities were paralyzed, as were the bladder and rectum. He had good orthopedic care from the very beginning, but in spite of this fact he developed a severe scoliosis of the spine with deformity of the chest, due to the weight of the head. The head was enormous, and even at 4½ years of age he was unable to hold it erect without some support.

He was first examined at the age of 16½ months. He was an appealing and friendly child with a greatly enlarged head (circumference 63.4 cm.) and a small, pinched face; the legs were paralyzed. He sat with support, using the hands to help maintain posture; the mother helped support the head. Fine motor and adaptive behavior were near the 12-month level but it was felt that he was handicapped in the use of his hands by the constant necessity to use them as props. In the fields of language and personal-social behavior his development was even slightly precocious. He had about twenty words and was beginning to use words in combination. His favorite amusement at that time was picture books, and he could identify pictures of babies, cars and dogs.

Examination at three years showed the head still increasing in size (circumference 68.8 cm.); scoliosis with deformity of the chest and contractures of the hands had appeared and in addition to all his other afflictions he was reported to have had a mild convulsion. His responses were practically confined to the language field and in this field they were entirely normal for his age. He engaged chiefly in imaginative play and, "in his mind does everything, goes to fires, bakes cakes, helps with the housework," all by the magic of verbalization.

At 4½ years the picture was virtually unchanged, though the head size had continued to increase (circumference 70 cm.). His experience and achievement had been necessarily confined to the verbal-perceptual fields, but his use and comprehension of language was quite up to the average for his age. His favorite occupation was listening to the radio, and he had a wide knowledge of the programs, the performers, the location of the stations on the dial; he could even identify the advertising with the program.

Henry is remarkable in many ways; he incites sympathy rather than pity, and his company is enjoyable rather than depressing. It is amazing that intellectual and personality development could proceed so normally in spite of the crippling of the entire body and the limited life he is forced to lead. Most remarkable is the normal mental development in a child with such a severe hydrocephalus. We assume this to be a communicating hydrocephalus, the type commonly associated with spina bifida and having common cause with it, a serious defect in the development and cleavage of the nervous and meningeal tissues. In these instances the ventricles are enormously dilated and the cortex reduced to only a very thin layer of tissue. Nevertheless, in some instances, a considerable degree of normal development may be realized.

§ 68. *Ernest M.*
Mongolism. Prediction of Consistent Development
at Moron Level Not Sustained
(20 weeks—5 years 6 months)

Ernest is presented to show the dangers of too exact prediction in the condition known as mongolism. He was first examined at 20 weeks of age and his facies and habitus were typically mongolian. His developmental level was approximately 10 weeks. A note on the record reads, "In regard to the future the mother was told that he would probably pro-ceed something like a normal child of half his age, and that he would be a contented, good-natured, affectionate child who would eventually walk and talk to a certain extent, but that he would never be able to keep up in regular school though he might be able to attend kindergarten." Re-examination at 36 weeks of age tended to confirm this prognosis. "He has maintained his rate of development very satisfactorily, and at the present time responds in most respects at a high 4-month level."

At 5 years and 6 months, when, on the basis of the early prediction, his development should have been at or above the 30-month level, we found that Ernest had failed dismally to live up to expectations. Motor, language, and personal-social behavior were at approximately the 36-*week* level; adaptive and prehensory behavior approximately 28 weeks. Interest-ingly enough, the examiner's mental set was such that the examination was begun with the 2-year level in mind. He was offered the picture-book, the multiple cubes, and the cup and cubes; while perfectly affable, he made no approach on the test materials. At that point the examiner suddenly realized the situation, and shifted to the infant scale. A single cube was presented, promptly secured, and the remaining situa-tions were exploited unhesitatingly. At the end of the ex-amination Ernest was offered the paper and crayon, a situa-tion usually well exploited from the age of 44 weeks on; Ernest promptly dropped the crayon on the floor. In other words, in his choice of test materials and situations he almost unerringly indicated his maturity level.

To return to the question of the early prediction, it was well qualified with probablys and mays, but the meaning to the parent was plain enough and we must accept responsibil-ity for it. Time proved it to be in error. The error, however, lay not in the interpretation of the behavior, or in the admin-istering of the tests, but in the failure of the examiner to evaluate the results in terms of mongolian infants. In our experience the vast majority of mongolian infants do relatively well in infancy, and a surprisingly large number are classified as morons. When they become 3, 4, 5 years old, however, many of these same children must be reclassified, most of them as imbeciles, a few as idiots; only a few 'maintain their early rate of development. Prediction in the mongolian infant should be made with this tendency to progressive retardation in mind.

§69. *Eunice L., Florence S., Eva R.*
Cretinism. Poor, Moderate, and Excellent Response
to Thyroid Therapy[1]

Eunice L. (15 weeks—48 months)

Eunice was the eighth child of an Italian family. The birth history was negative except for pre-eclampsia in the mother. Eunice was first seen at the age of 15 weeks, because serious mental retardation was suspected. One by one the classical signs of cretinism appeared while she was under observation. Treatment with the dried gland (thyroid) was begun at 36 weeks of age. Table XXVI summarizes the course of her development.

Her response to treatment was obviously poor. She is still dwarfed and still defective, despite intensive and long-continued treatment. The case is instructive because therapy was begun at a relatively early age and was still relatively unavailing. The improvement from D.Q. 40 to D.Q. 60 will make some difference in amenability to training, but it is not enough to make her a self-sustaining individual. And, as time goes on, it becomes increasingly apparent that D.Q. 60 does not represent her status as well as D.Q. 50, though she

[1] These three children are reported more fully in: Gesell, A., Amatruda, C.S., and Culotta, C.S.: *The Effect of Thyroid Therapy on the Mental and Physical Growth of Cretinous Infants. Am. J. Dis. Child.*, 52: No. 5, 1117-1138, 1936. Eunice as 36 A, Florence as 21 F, and Eva as 46 S.

TABLE XXVI

EUNICE L.

Examination	Age	Developmental level	D.Q.	Duration of treatment	Height index (i)	Comment
I	15 wks.	6 wks.	40	0	25	? cretinous appearance
II	20 wks.	8 wks.	40	0	—	appearance more suggestive
III	32 wks.	12 wks.	35	0	25	definite cretinous
IV	40 wks.	14 wks.	35	4 wks.	—	more active
V	44 wks.	16 wks.	35	8 wks.	35	altered appearance
VI	52 wks.	20 wks.	35	16 wks.	45	defective behavior persists
VII	15 mos.	30 wks.	45	29 wks.	55	more normal quality
VIII	18 mos.	40 wks.	45	42 wks.	60	some social sensitivity
IX	24 mos.	60 wks.	60	16 mos.	60	irritable
X	30 mos.	18– mos.	60	22 mos.	60	attention and persistence poor
XI	36 mos.	18 mos.	50	28 mos.	65	behavior stereotyped
XII	48 mos.	24 mos.	50	40 mos.	55	compliant

(i) The height index is the ratio between height age and chronological age, in accordance with the Engelbach norms.

will probably continue to fluctuate in the 50-60 zone. Her future care remains a social rather than a medical problem.

The hopes for improvement that were entertained when cretinism was diagnosed were sadly disappointed. Eunice serves to remind us that there are many cretinous infants who, from a practical standpoint, do not respond to prompt, efficient treatment.

Florence S. (21 weeks—36 months)

Florence was the ninth child of an Italian family. The birth history was normal, the birth weight 12 pounds; examination showed a malformation of the left nostril, a coloboma of the left iris and a dermoid cyst in the lower nasal quadrant of the left sclera. The child was brought to the hospital at 21 weeks of age because of the deformity of the nose and eye, and because of enlargement of the abdomen. Cretinism was diagnosed and treatment instituted at once. Her progress under treatment is summarized in Table XXVII.

This child made an intermediate response to treatment and succeeded in breaking into the dull-normal zone, only to fluctuate (probably) between a borderline and a dull-normal classification. Florence rose definitely above the defective

TABLE XXVII

FLORENCE S.

Examination	Age	Developmental level	D.Q.	Duration of treatment	Height index (i)	Comment
I	21 wks.	9–10 wks.	45	0	45	congenital malformations
II	28 wks.	12 – wks.	45	7 wks.	64	very little change
III	36 wks.	18 wks.	50	15 wks.	72	
IV	44 wks.	20 wks.	45	23 wks.	72	behavior more normal in quality
V	52 wks.	28 wks.	50	31 wks.	80	appearance more normal
VI	15 mos.	44 wks.	65	43 wks.	82	repetitive quality
VII	18 mos.	60 wks.	75	59 wks.	85	stereotyped patterns
VIII	24 mos.	18 mos.	75	19 mos.	80	poor quality
IX	36 mos.	24 mos.	65	31 mos.	75	? fluctuation

(i) The height index is the ratio between height age and chronological age, in accordance with the Engelbach norms.

level, but has not attained an average development, and will probably not show any further rise in D.Q. (65-75) as time goes on. She is still somewhat dwarfed.

Actually Florence did better than was expected, and we can only confess that we were misled by the presence of con' genital malformations, and considered her to have a primary retardation in addition to a thyroid deficiency. The response, however, even at best cannot be called entirely satisfactory.

Eva R. (46 weeks—5 years)

Eva was the fourth child of a family of Irish descent. The birth history was negative, the birth weight 10 pounds 11 ounces. At 6 months the family became concerned because Eva was slow to develop, was very constipated, and had a large abdomen and a protruding tongue. A photograph taken at the time showed the typical signs of cretinism. The diag' nosis was not made, however, until she was 40 weeks old, and treatment with dried thyroid was begun at the age of 46 weeks. Table XXVIII summarizes her career.

Obviously Eva has responded well to treatment. Her stature at 5 years is above normal for her age, whereas in infancy she was very dwarfed. Her mental status is now normal, whereas her development was defective before treatment was given. She is now a normal child in every

TABLE XXVIII

Eva R.

Examination	Age	Developmental level	D.Q.	Duration of treatment	Height index (i)	Comment
I	48 wks.	24 wks.	50	0	50	sluggish
II	49 wks.	24+ wks.	50	3 wks.	—	more active
III	52 wks.	28 wks.	50	6 wks.	62	
IV	60 wks.	40 wks.	65	14 wks.	—	appearance entirely altered
V	16 mos.	46 wks.	68	22 wks.	82	acceleration of physical growth
VI	20 mos.	18— mos.	85	9 mos.	90	slightly shy
VII	24 mos.	21+ mos.	88	13 mos.	97	eager, demanding
VIII	36 mos.	33 mos.	92	25 mos.	108	normal emotional reactions
IX	47 mos.	45 mos.	95	36 mos.	114	good control of attention
X	5 yrs.	58 mos.	97	49 mos.	115	normal 5-year-old child

(i) The height index is the ratio between height age and chronological age in accordance with the Engelbach norms.

respect, as long as thyroid treatment is maintained. She is in kindergarten and holds her own well with the other children her own age. The outlook for continued normal development is excellent.

This happy outcome could not be foretold when Eva was first seen. Most cretins do not respond so completely. Her prompt response to treatment, however, constituted a favorable sign. After only 14 weeks of therapy there was a perceptible acceleration in developmental rate, and before a year of treatment was completed Eva was within the normal range. Physical growth responded equally promptly.

Discussion:

These three cases were selected to illustrate the diversity of response to thyroid treatment in cretinism. All these children were typical cretins with the thick, dry skin, myxoedematous infiltrations, fatty pads, large protruding tongue, protuberant abdomen, umbilical hernia, delay in osseous development, in closure of the fontanelles, in dentition, and with the dwarfing and mental retardation. All were sluggish, inactive, slept excessively, ate poorly, and were very constipated; all had a low body temperature and slow heart rate. Eunice was retarded to D.Q. 35-40 and began treatment at

8 months of age; Florence was retarded to D.Q. 45-50 and began treatment at 5 months; Eva was retarded to D.Q. 50 and began treatment at 10 months. In Eunice the response was so small as to be almost negligible and she remains defective; Florence shows a modest degree of improvement and is now in the borderline-dull zone; while in Eva, who is now normal, we are certainly very close to a complete cure (as long as treatment is continued).

Eunice took 16 months to show any significant rise in D.Q., Florence took 10 months, while Eva took only 3 months. It is our experience that the prompter the response the greater the response. It is not an "all-or-none" phenomenon. Probably most common is the intermediate response which entails improvement but is far from satisfactory. In general, the prediction of normal development in cretinism, therefore, should be guarded.

These various types of response to therapy are related to the degree of developmental injury caused by the original endocrine deficiency. The degree of injury, in turn, probably depends more on the organism suffering the insult than on the severity of the insult itself. Factors of resistance, immunity, thresholds, timing, balance, etc., are all involved and the infant has many protections against irrevocable damage. These protections may fail in varying degrees because the infant is vulnerable. Only rarely, by a happy combination of circumstances, can normality be completely restored. Only slightly less rarely, on the other hand, by an unhappy combination of circumstances, does the protection fail completely.

§ 70. Cora M.
Multiple Congenital Deformities. Prolonged Hospitalization in Infancy. Depression and Recovery of Development (54 weeks—43 months)

Cora was first seen at the age of 54 weeks. She was the first child of a young Polish couple. Although her birth was normal, she had multiple congenital deformities, involving all the extremities. Arms and legs were extended, the joints immobile, hands and feet clubbed. She was able to move the head, jaw, and spine freely, but was otherwise quite helpless.

She was sent to the hospital at the age of 7 weeks and spent her whole first year there. She had a room to herself and was cut off from the fairly social and stimulating life in the ward with the other children. She had frequent febrile episodes associated with a generalized skin eruption and spent considerable time under a light tent, further narrowing her outlook. The hands and feet were consistently splinted and bandaged, so that although toys were tied to her bed, she had never touched a toy. The high spot of her day was the massaging and exercising of her crippled limbs.

When first seen (age 54 weeks) she had an alert and normal facies. Her physical handicaps made it impossible to apply the usual tests, but she was able to roll to the side, to lift her head, and she showed mild pleasure and some adaptability in an improvised game with the examiner. She was, however, very passive and institutionalized. She tolerated all manipulations with docile equanimity, accepted the ministrations of the nurse, and the nurse's leaving the room, without obvious response. Vocalizations were spontaneous rather than responsive and included laughing, squealing, and single syllables.

It was felt that the loss of use of her hands constituted a serious deprivation and that special training would be needed to develop her latent abilities. Her life in the hospital needed enriching and her experience, widening. Normal or near normal potentialities were suspected in spite of the fairly serious apathy.

Cora was moved into the ward, she was dressed and placed outside the covers of her bed, the head of the bed was raised, and the splints were worn only at night. Daily play periods were instituted; she was taken into the sun-room, and was given sitting experience, motor exercise, and opportunities for play with toys. Special, daily periods for sustained intimate social play with the other children and with the examiner were arranged. The nurses were advised to play and talk with Cora. This program continued for five months, and definite improvement in sitting, in imitative and expressive behavior, in vocalization and comprehension occurred. There was also a modest improvement in the manipulation and enjoyment of toys.

At the conclusion of this period, when Cora was about 17 months old, she could sit for brief intervals, had two "words" and understood simple phrases as "want to walk," "is your milk good?" She enjoyed play and shouted with joy when the examiner opened the toy-box. She seemed unhappy whenever it became necessary to replace her in the light tent or to reapply splints or casts, and these episodes definitely retarded her progress. Nothing in her behavior, however, approached what would be expected of a normal child of her age, or even a handicapped child whose opportunities for full development had been favorable. In other words, although Cora was no longer passive and inert, and although she had developed an interest in her surroundings, a capacity for play, and a modest vocabulary, the results were in no way startling or revolutionary, and the question of her normality remained far from settled.

The most serious deficit in Cora was the generally poor quality and variability of her attention. Early in the course of her training she seemed to fatigue very readily and to withhold responses as a matter of economy. It suggested a frailty in makeup that was not borne out by the robustness of her demands and the activity that developed later. Interestingly enough, she always preferred play with the other children to play with the examiner, and motor play to play with toys.

The special program was discontinued at 17 months, but Cora continued to participate in the ward life. At 2 years of age she was moved to a crippled children's hospital and we did not see her again until she was 3 years 7 months old. She

had had no orthopedic treatment, though consecutive ortho-
plasties were planned.

At 43 months of age Cora was an attractive, happy,
friendly child, beautifully adjusted, and the pet of the institution. Her vocabulary was excellent and she talked volubly
and enjoyed the examination thoroughly. She was able to sit
unassisted and to get about on the floor by hitching. She was
able to pick up a cube and had learned to use her crippled
hands very cleverly. Her responses were all above the 3 year
level and in spite of her handicaps and institutional life, her
development was very close to normal.

Her future will, of course, depend a great deal on how
much the orthopedic surgeons can do for her, but in any
event Cora has a mind which she can use, even if she is never
able to use her legs. In her present protected environment
where deformity and disability are commonplace, Cora has
not yet felt herself to be different or at any disadvantage. She
has flourished and thrived and has developed a hardy and
attractive personality, her emotional development is healthy,
and mental development has kept pace. The world may not
be Cora's oyster, but it is entirely possible that she may
become a useful and contented person.

We present this case because Cora seems to us almost a
brand snatched from the burning. The poverty of her early
environment and experience had a seriously depressing and
deadening effect which could well have permanently injured
her development. Her arms and legs were very conscientiously
treated, but the child herself was in effect badly neglected.
Every crippled children's institution knows that the children
must have developmental opportunities as well as orthopedic
treatment, and every orthopedist knows that for all his skill
in restoring function to a disabled child, the child must have
a certain degree of intelligence to learn to use that function.
In the case of infants, these principles are sometimes forgotten
or overlooked; they remain true, however. Babies do not "just
grow." They need developmental opportunities as much, or

even more, than older children do, and given these opportunities they can do miracles in surmounting handicaps.

§ 71. Edna A.
Multiple Congenital Deformities with Mental Defect
(21 months)

In contrast to Cora A. we present Edna M., another Polish child with essentially the same physical condition. The disability, however, affects only the legs; the arms and hands are entirely normal. Edna has four older brothers and sisters and has always lived at home. She has received a great deal of attention and affection from her family, and has had all the opportunities that Cora so sadly lacked.

Her development at 21 months is only describable in terms of 20 weeks. She coos and laughs, and discriminates strangers. She makes a very crude and inaccurate prehensory approach upon a toy and can only grasp an object if it is very favorably placed. Exploitation is confined to grasping and lifting; there is no transfer or mouthing and only fleeting pursuit of a lost object. She does not hold two objects, exploit details, or imitate.

Edna is very seriously retarded and has not the capacity to avail herself of the favorable influences of normal family life. She has normal arms and hands, but can barely pick up an object. The orthopedist may be able to transform her surgically, but is doubtful that she will ever walk, even if treatment is carried on for years.

Comparing the two children, Cora's physical and environmental handicaps are more severe, yet Edna is the more crippled child. Physical and mental handicaps do not always run parallel and may, under favorable circumstances, be more or less completely dissociated. In Cora's case the physician treating her was not concerned with (or did not perceive) her early lack of development because "the mentality is not affected in this condition." He was in fact honestly astounded to learn that she was over a year old; he thought she was (at 54 weeks) about 6 months old. The days and weeks tend to slip by with prolonged hospitalization, not uncharted, but unreckoned. The doctor actually had noticed her development, but he had not calculated it in terms of the child's age. Edna's retardation, on the other hand, was recog- nized at once because she was first seen at the relatively ad- vanced and known age of 21 months. She was saved months or years of useless treatment and her family were spared the pain of shattered false hopes by prompt developmental diag- nosis.

O. Foster Care and Child Adoption

Catherine S. Amatruda

§ 72. *General Statement*

All of the children described in this section were essentially normal. Most of them came from families from the
lower walks of life. Some had no homes of their own; others,
very bad homes. Each child became dependent on a social
agency for care and supervision. We must assume that the
social agencies made thoughtful plans and deliberate placements with the well-being of the child in mind. We must
remember too that social agencies are not infallible, and that
they are often handicapped by limited funds, facilities, and
personnel, sometimes even by prejudices. Imperfections in
child placement which appear in the case reports are not to
be construed as an indictment of social agencies. We have
found the agencies quite open to suggestion and ready to
improve their plans when so advised. The indictment is rather
of a society whose defects injure the small and helpless.

Normal social experience is essential to normal psychological development. In our present culture, the most favorable environment for the adequate development of a child's
potential abilities is provided by a single family home, with
a relatively stable family situation, normal family emotional
relationships, and a fairly consistent program of child care.

Such a situation gives a child a sense of importance, a
feeling of security which includes confidence in the goodness
of the world and in his own power. He needs all these things
to be free to develop and integrate his maturing abilities.
Eventually he may have to learn that he is not very important
to anyone but himself, that his powers are limited, and that
the world is not altogether good. But the child who has built

up proper attitudes of confidence can meet reality when he must. He is at least not defeated before he starts.

The feelings of insecurity and lack of confidence that result from conflicting authority, inconsistent treatment, lack of respect and consideration for the child's individuality, antagonistic parental attitudes, or being shifted from home to home, place a disabling handicap upon a young child. He becomes timid, fearful, and withdrawn, and refuses to accept and assimilate new experiences; or he may become dependent and clinging, and in his anxiety demand frequent reassurances. He is thus emotionally held back or thrown back into babyhood, and the normal process of growing up which implies in part an increasing realization of self as an independent individuality is retarded and blocked.

When an adult's means of livelihood are removed, his sense of security is seriously threatened. The anxiety states that result, and the tendency of such persons to demand governmental help and protection, and to shift their responsibility onto government, constitute an interesting parallel. Although the reaction is not so simple as it sounds, the same regressive tendency is there, the same loss in emotional maturity and independence. Small wonder that disharmonies and upheavals in a child's world should disturb wholesome growth and integration.

The cases related in the following pages tell their own stories. Martha and Gerald are included to show that in certain robust personalities, environmental deficiencies may be relatively unimportant. In all the other cases reported, faulty environmental factors are assumed to play a major part in causing developmental fluctuations and emotional disturbances.

When a child comes under the care of a social agency, and his own home cannot be restored or established, or when he cannot be placed with suitable relatives, the agency must place him in a boarding-home, an institution, or in an adoption home. Since the family situation differs in each case, the solution of how to care for the child must also differ. Place-ment in adoption would seem to be the ideal answer, as indeed it is, but it is not always the practical answer. Many dependent children are unsuited by physical defects, limited mental endowment, or serious personality difficulties for adoption placement. Many are too old to appeal to adopting parents. Many have "hereditary taints" which appall the prospective parents or even the agencies. In other cases the unmarried mother is unwilling to relinquish her child even though she can never offer him a home. In all such cases the agency must make the best of a bad situation.

A boarding-home is the next answer. Too much praise cannot be given to the splendid women who open their homes to dependent children. It has been our experience that the considerations of "board money" are small indeed, though it is true that many could not afford to care for these children without it. The main considerations are the love of children, lonely homes, and a desire to help. Admirable motives, how-ever, do not always make for admirable deeds, and there are some foster mothers who are unsuited to their task chiefly by reason of their own personality difficulties or of their ig-norance. It is the responsibility of the agency to choose their boarding-homes wisely and to select the individual home for the individual child with a great deal of insight.

Boarding-homes should be selected with an idea of at least relatively permanent placement in mind. Shifting a child from home to home means poor social work. Foster-home placement does not mean simply placing a child under a roof, but giving him a substitute home and incorporating him into it.

A few children need institutional care, for diagnostic or treatment purposes. In other cases, if the child is to return to his own home within a period of only a very few weeks, there can be no great objection to temporary institutional placement. The institution on the whole is not, however, a favorable environment for normal development. Normal personal relationships are lacking, experience is limited, individuality is of necessity suppressed in favor of group living. Happily, the old "orphan asylum" is on its way out; first the name was replaced by some more euphonious and less stigmatizing term, then environmental conditions were improved. But clearly no matter how innocuous the title or how attractive the buildings, or how well-meaning the persons in authority, an institution is still an inadequate substitute for a family home, and therefore an improper place for a normal child.

Adoption remains the best solution, if it is feasible in a particular case. If the home is well chosen, it gives the child not a substitute home, but a home and a family of his own. Adopting parents need not be wealthy, cultured, or ambitious to provide a fine home for a child. Indeed, they are often very simple, kindly persons. The spirit and feeling in the home are far more important than its social or economic status; the motive in taking a child far more important than what the home can "give" the child. Adoptions should, however, be protected and regulated. The first consideration should always be the child. That is why amateur placements by inexperienced persons are dangerous, though there are factors of safety even in human relationships, and many such placements work out very well. The doctor, however, places a child as a favor to his patients; the lawyer, to accommodate his clients; the family, to relieve the family situation. The social agency, on the other hand, is in name and fact *agent* for the child.

To be a suitable candidate for adoption, a child should be physically and mentally normal; or to put it more realistically, he should have no serious physical or mental abnormalities. The ideally normal child is a fiction, just as the ideal parent is a romance, and we are dealing with real children and real parents. There must be an element of faith and even of chance in every adoption, as there is in every marriage or in every birth. The element of chance can be materially reduced, however, by proper preparations.

The adopting parents must be realistic; they should be completely informed about the child who is to come to them. If they are mature enough to be fit persons to adopt a child, they are mature enough to evaluate this information in terms of their requirements and emotional responses. They should realize that, although we say adoption gives a child a home of his own, it is always an adoption home, the child always an adopted child. They must accept this, and be ready to tactfully teach the child to accept it from the very beginning. Only on such firm, honest ground can adoption be successful.

The adoptive candidate should be "groomed" for his adoption: physical defects remedied, and the best possible conditions for development provided until the adoption placement is made. Supervision of development is essential and should be continued during the probationary period in the home.

The probationary period is a very important element in any adoption situation. Apart from the original investigation into the adoptive home, and the early supervision of the child, it is the greatest insurance factor we have. This period should never, except under extraordinary circumstances, be less than a year, and is often wisely extended beyond that time. It should be a two-way arrangement: the adopting parents are at liberty to return the child at any time during that period if he does not fit into the home; and the child, through the medium of the agency, should be permitted to reject the home as unsuited to his needs. Proper pre-adoption work will reduce these rejections to a minimum; as a matter of fact, they are extremely rare, and probably should occur oftener than they do. The probationary period corresponds to the engagement period preceding marriage and has much the same value. Hasty adoptions are as risky as hasty marriages. Child placement is no field for bargain-counter tactics; it is a serious responsibility, only to be intrusted to skillful persons with a real understanding of the hazards of child development.

§ 73. James W.
Irregular Development Associated with Illness and Unfortunate Home Care
(5 months—41½ months)

Mr. and Mrs. W. had had three children. The oldest child was rated average, the other two dull-normal. Mr. W. was a mattress-worker and also a pianist. James was born in the hospital at full term; he weighed 8 pounds, 8 ounces. Mrs. W. died when James was born and at the age of 7 weeks James was placed in an institution for dependent children. Four days later he was sent to the hospital with diarrhea and an upper respiratory infection. The diarrhea persisted and when 5 months old he was referred to us because no satisfactory diagnosis had been arrived at and the doctors wished to cover all possible aspects of the case.

The examination was made in the hospital ward. His behavior, as far as it could be tested in this setting, appeared to be at a full 4-month rather than 5-month level. However, the examiner considered the outlook for future development was somewhat better than this rating indicated and diagnosed him as potentially approximately average.

This diagnosis was confirmed when James was re-examined. He had been discharged from the hospital three weeks after our first examination and placed in a foster home where he was surrounded by affection and attention. At 18 months, although he did not yet walk alone, he said at least five words, he filled and refilled the cup with cubes, he indicated his toilet needs by pulling at his pants and making a fretting noise, and he shook his head "no-no" when touching a forbidden object. His reactions were slow. The examination was less complete than usual because the child was obviously tired. We rated his behavior as we have indicated in Table XXIX. James's own home was then re-established. Mr. W. married a widow with three children of her own, all with above-average intelli-

TABLE XXIX

JAMES W.

Chrono-logical age	Behavior level					Comments
	Pos-tural	Prehen-sory	Lan-guage	Adap-tive	Personal-social	
5 months	General behavior level about 4 months					Very interested in people—watches them and smiles with vocalizations
18 months	−15 mos.	+15 mos.	−18 mos.	+15 mos.	18 mos.	Slow and deliberate. Late in *p.m.*, child obviously tired. Postural behavior retarded; does not yet walk alone
21 months	18 mos. Language: "bye-bye," "daddy," "see," "wow-wow," "kitty," "ma-ma," "hey-dad," and jargon	+18 mos.	−21 mos.	+18 mos.	+18 mos.	Still has chronic diarrhea. Gait unsteady. Behavior in examination secured only with great patience. Ratings based largely on reported behavior
33.5 months	(30 mos.) Built tower of 9 blocks Reported to say only three words: "yah," "no," "namie" for Ernie					Unresponsive—withdrawn. Brightened up when stepmother withdrew. Sullen when she returned
41.5 months	−36 mos.	+30 mos.	?	36 mos.	36 mos.	Excellent adjustment

gence. When James was 2 years old he was taken home into this newly established family.

Mrs. W. brought him to us at the age of 33.5 months, saying that he was a great problem in the home. He would wake up eight to ten times a night, sobbing, sometimes screaming and clawing the air. He was reported to tear his blanket and his sleeping-suit every night. He would not play with his toys, but instead just sat motionless for hours. He coöperated not at all with dressing, undressing, or toilet needs; he was unresponsive to the other children in the home; and he cried a great deal, especially after his former foster mother had visited him. Examination revealed a markedly withdrawn child who cried and retreated both actually and psychologically whenever approached. Out of his stepmother's presence, and permitted freedom of activity, he gradually pursued his own interests, pulling paper from the wastebasket and patting a doll, but he still appeared suspicious of any interference with his own pursuits. It was rather obvious from interview with his stepmother that he was in an unsympathetic if not antagonistic home. For a child of his disposition this was very unfortunate and had produced a regression of his behavior to a very immature level. Language was almost completely suppressed and his actual performance was not as mature as it had been when he was a year younger.

Two months later Mrs. W. deserted the home and James was placed in more favorable surroundings. In a foster home his behavior problem disappeared, his physical condition showed marked improvement, and his general adaptation became normal. We re-examined him when he was 41.5 months old. He could go up and down stairs, he imitated the vertical and horizontal stroke, he matched three color shapes and in his foster home he helped with the dishes, never breaking them, brushed his hair, put on his stockings, and tried to put on his shoes. His language expression was very meager but he was reported to put two words together; his comprehension was at an adequate 3-year level.

The deleterious effect of an unsympathetic environment on a sensitive and social child is repeatedly observed. In addition, this child was physically weak. In this particular case it was the child's own home which distorted his development, but similar situations arise in foster-home placements.

§ 74. Jason N.
Irregularity Associated with Unfavorable Environment
(23 weeks—6 years)

Jason N. was the tenth child of Italian parents. His mother was reported to have an I.Q. of between 48 and 55. She was also "a somewhat nervous or hysterical individual." His father drank and was reported to be cruel to Mrs. N. The family of twelve individuals lived in five rooms in "a run-down, foreign section of the city."

Jason was born at full term. His birth weight was 8 pounds. When 2.5 months old he was hospitalized with diarrhea, vomiting, fever, dehydration, and bilateral otitis media. When convalescent from this illness he was transferred to a child-caring institution. There he was examined by us at the age of 23 weeks. He was an alert, rather tense infant, very sensitive to slight sounds. In general his behavior while not quite up to 23 weeks maturity, was very near average particularly when we gave weight to his most mature responses.

Seated in the supportive chair at the crib table top, he reached for objects, usually hitting them from reach. His perceptive behavior was the most immature aspect of his development; he disregarded the pellet on the table and, instead, followed the examiner's hand; also he gave no heed to dropped objects. But his general apparent alertness gave an impression of normality.

The next examination, almost nine months later, when Jason was 14.5 months old, revealed behavior very consistent with our previous observations. He failed to measure completely up to his age level, but he was definitely within average limits. He cruised about, practically stood alone, although he was somewhat timid about standing, gave the examiner objects saying "ta-ta," and was reported to feed himself. His unwillingness to release objects in his play was interpreted as conditioned by his environment rather than as inability.

When 16 months old Jason walked alone for the first time. When 18 months old he became a rather serious feeding problem; he refused to eat unless a certain nursemaid were present. Forcible feeding, of course, aggravated his resistance. After the problem had been corrected, he was returned to his parents. The home conditions, as we have indicated, were very poor. Within a few months after his return home, the visiting nurse reported that he cried a great deal, would not eat unless fed, and screamed when put on the toilet. The physician at the Visiting Nurses Conference, where Jason was taken by his mother, considered him physically and mentally retarded. His mother failed to keep the appointment with us.

Jason was again referred to us at the age of 32 months, when the Board of Education considered him "much too subnormal" to be allowed to remain in their nursery school group. We found his behavior to be below the 27-month, but above the 24-month, level, and we classified him as dull-normal or possibly borderline unstable. He had a silly laugh but adjusted fairly well to the examination. Frequent temper-tantrums were reported.

Mrs. N. again became pregnant, and four of the children were removed from the home. Jason was placed in a second child-caring institution. They referred him to us for examination and advice at 46 months. Then, with only one exception, his behavior scored at the 30-month level; he built a bridge, a 3-year-old test. Although his adjustment to examination was in certain respects very good, we noticed that his hands trembled when building with blocks, so that his structures were likely to fall. He would respond correctly to a test and yet be unable to repeat his performance. He persisted

TABLE XXX
JASON N.

Chronological age	Behavior level					Comments
	Motor	Prehensory	Language	Adaptive	Personal-social	
23 weeks	24 wks.	20 wks.	20 wks.	20 wks.	20 wks.	Alert; rather tense infant. Sensitive to slight sounds. Cries more than usual
14.5 months	13 mos.	12 mos.	13 mos.	?	14 mos.	Good adjustment after initial inhibition. Reported to cry frequently
32 months	Behavior not up to 27-month level. Adapted blocks to formboard and imitatively put blocks in row without chimney, pushing them and saying "choo-choo"—full 24-month behavior					Silly laugh but good adjustment. Temper tantrums. Reported by Board of Education as "much too subnormal for nursery-school group." Reported by physician as mentally and physically retarded
46 months	?30 mos.	?30 mos.	?30 mos.	?36 mos.	?30 mos. Consider retardation due to personality—environmental conflict. Expect improvement in rating to follow more favorable placement	Good adjustment after initial crying. Has been in institution for a few months. But hands trembled and he was frequently unable to repeat correct responses. Foster-home placement strongly advised
6 years	Stanford-Binet mental age score: 5 yrs. 6 mos. I.Q.: about 90. Performance even and consistent					Came willingly and quietly to examination room. Started drawing at once. Considerable improvement in behavior reported by foster parent. Appeared dull at first

to an extraordinary degree in his errors but the very fact that he did persist was significant. We reviewed his record thoroughly and concluded that his present behavior had undoubtedly been distorted by his environment. We quote the recommendations:

> Every effort should be made to place the child in a more fortunate environment, otherwise we may expect him to develop into an unstable child of borderline mentality. He may well become a delinquent. Foster-home placement where he will have personal care and attention and where a process of re-education will be begun is indicated. In a favorable environment future behavior difficulties may be avoided and his potentialities for normal mental growth realized.

Our predictions, which were contrary to the psychometric indications, were borne out. He was finally placed in a boarding-home. When retested at the age of 6 years, his I.Q. was fully 90.

We report this case because it is so easy to err, as we did at his 32-month-old examination. We then classified him as dull-normal or possibly borderline. We were influenced by the facts of his heredity (and by the opinions of those with whom he came into contact), and we failed to consider the effect of an unfavorable environment on the behavior growth of a child with his particular personality characteristics.

§75. Anthony R.
Long Institutional Experience Followed by Foster Home Placement
(5 years 10 months—6 years 5 months)

Family history:

Anthony R. is the illegitimate child of a young woman of Italian parentage who has been employed as a domestic. The maternal grandmother has been at a state hospital for mental diseases for the past seven years, and the maternal grandfather at one time was committed to the same institution for several months. Because of this history, Anthony has not been considered by the agency a suitable prospect for adoption.

Social history:

The boy remained in the institution where he was born until three months before our first examination, when at the age of 5 years 7 months he was placed in a boarding-home. The foster mother has felt that he was difficult to manage. She reports him as "very mischievous" and says that he takes pleasure in teasing younger children, especially a younger child placed in the same boarding-home. He started kinder-garten two months ago, and occasionally does not return home when school is out; at times he has been as much as two hours late in returning home. When this happens it is impossible to get an explanation from him; when questioned, he will simply stand and look at the foster mother, without answering.

History of psychometric examinations:

I. Age 5 years 10 months: mental age 4 years 6 months, range IV-VI, intelligence quotient 77.

II. Age 6 years 5 months: mental age 5 years 10 months, range V-VII, intelligence quotient 90.

At the time of the first examination, Anthony appeared as an active, talkative, distractible boy; good-natured, but diffi-cult to keep on the task in hand. Articulation was mildly defective, the outstanding characteristics being a lisp and the substitution of "w" for the "r" sound. The examination record showed only a slight scattering, with all 4-year tests being passed, three out of six at 5 years, and one success (counting thirteen pennies) at 6 years. He preferred the right hand for drawing and throwing and was left-eyed on ten trials with the V-scope. Because of the lack of a normal home background during the first five and a half years of life, and the relatively short time he had been in the foster home, definite classification on the basis of this examination was not reported. The factor of attention was likewise given weight in deciding to defer such action. The report to the referring agency merely stated his mental age as "within normal limits" and a re-examination after a few months longer in the home was requested.

The second examination, made seven months after the first one, justified the caution, showing a rise of thirteen points in the intelligence quotient. At this time, all the 5 year tests were passed, together with four out of six at 6 years, and one at 7 years. Speech had improved considerably, with only a slight lisp remaining of the original defect. Span of attention and general motor coördination, including the fine manual control required for drawing, were much better than at the previous visit. He had spent the entire year in kindergarten; he enjoyed this, and the teacher had no complaints.

The impression of the foster mother's attitude received at this time was not too favorable. She did not feel that there had been any improvement to speak of since she first took the boy, and had not even thought that there had been any gain in speech. She had many trivial problems to discuss, most of which involved merely the normal situations familiar to most parents, especially in the case of rather excitable, active children. Certainly the tendency to tease the younger child in the home, for whom she showed a definite emotional preference, indicates no alarming defect of personality in a child who has been deprived of a normal home life for his first five and one half years. Nor can we feel surprise or con-cern when a kindergarten child fails to hurry home from school every day, even though he has no ready explanation for the delay when crossly questioned. It was felt that her patience was not very great, and that she lacked insight into the normal problems of child care and training. While it is not desirable to advise a change of home without excellent reasons, it was advised that serious thought be given to the possibility of finding a more appropriate foster home for Anthony.

While the rise of 13 points in intelligence quotient after a period of only 7 months is impressive, raising the score as it does from the borderline-dull range to a low average, the special significance of the case lies in the fact that the gain was made under what would hardly be described as particularly favorable circumstances. The case of Anthony goes far to confirm our belief that, from the standpoint of providing the best opportunity for bringing out potential abilities, even a mediocre family home is superior to an institution.

§ 76. *Eleanor B.*
Abnormal and Retarded Behavior in Infancy.
Normal Development in New Foster Home. Adoption
(40 weeks—33 months)

Eleanor was the illegitimate child of a 40-year-old woman of the working class. The putative father was the black sheep of what was described by the social agency as a fairly good family. The birth was entirely normal; some feeding difficulties were encountered during the first two months of life, but the health record since that time has been excellent. Eleanor was placed in foster home A at the age of 2 months, where she stayed until she was 14 months old. She was then moved into foster home B and was later adopted by this second family.

The accompanying table summarizes the results of her developmental examinations during the time she was under observation.

It is convenient to divide our discussion of this child's development into two periods: the time when she was in foster home A, and the time when she was in her adopting home B. During the first period, although she was consistently rated at

TABLE XXXI

Exam.	Age	Developmental level	Classification	Remarks
I	40 wks.	32–34 wks.	Dull-normal	? language
II	52 wks.	36–38 wks.	Dull-normal, borderline	Unstable
III	56 wks.	40–48 wks.	Dull-normal	Unstable
IV	24 mos.	24 mos.	Average	Improved—needs guidance
V	33 mos.	30–36 mos.	Average—high average	Permit adoption

the dull-normal level there were several significant features in her behavior that caused us to question whether this rating was really representative of her potentialities.

At 40 weeks her adjustment was entirely undiscriminating; she indulged in frequent hand play at a very immature level; attention was of poor quality and her exploitation of toys was almost entirely confined to mouthing and transfer; her interest in the examiner was excessive. On the other hand, this child had one "word" and her comprehension of simple phrases was entirely normal for her age.

Her performance was equally poor and about equally retarded during the entire first period, but *language* continued to be well developed. At 56 weeks Eleanor had ten words. Temper tantrums with breath-holding appeared, and even during her clinic visits it was noted that she was overemotional and that her emotional tone was unstable, with frenzied activity one moment, fussing the next. She showed signs of fatigue before fifteen minutes of examination time had elapsed. We described her as inferior, unstable, and not a suitable candidate for adoption, although improvement was expected.

Eleanor was transferred to foster home B at about 14 months of age, and after about ten months this second foster mother asked for permission to adopt her. Her performance at two years was normal for her age. She was docile, coöperative, and persistent and showed only slight evidences of negativism. A tendency to sinistrality was noted at this age for the first time. The foster mother's management was not altogether good and she described Eleanor as "hard to manage—she has a terrible temper—at times so obstinate." Guidance was given and an extended probationary period was advised.

At 33 months the picture was even better. The foster mother's methods of management had improved and she reported very few tantrums. Eleanor's coöperation and interest in the examination were of good quality and the only traces of her former difficulties that were noticed were the slight scattering, and some tendency to perseverate in her responses. As in the past, language performance was best (her comment on the picture in the Dutch Scene was, "light, Jack and Jill crying, kitty like my kitty, bread to eat"), but her responses in other fields of behavior were fully normal for her age. The inhibitions previously placed on adoption were removed. Reports since that time (Eleanor is now 4½ years old) indicate that she is doing nicely and that the adopting parents are extremely happy with her.

Discussion:

While it is entirely possible for a child to be inferior and unstable, it is wise to be cautious in describing an obviously unstable child as inferior, particularly in infancy. The normal language development was considered significant and proved to be the best indicator of potential normality. The factor that did not receive sufficient weight was the environmental factor. Eleanor's foster home was described by the social agency as "an excellent baby-home; the foster mother gives good physical care and takes pains not to spoil the baby." If one underlines the word—*physical* in that last sentence, and realizes that it is possible to try too hard not to "spoil" a baby, a truer picture of Eleanor's early life is seen. Its effect on a sensitive child can be imagined and is probably actually observed in this case. Later contacts with

foster mother A caring for other children have served to emphasize the impression that her charges were well fed, well
cared for, and their lives well regulated, but that her attitude
was cold and unloving. The fact that Eleanor blossomed into
normality when placed in more friendly surroundings, even
though management was poor in the beginning, adds weight
to this hypothesis.

Several questions remain unanswered in our study of this
child. One of the most important is, what was in the past,
and what will be in the future, the role of the instability in
her personality makeup? The history of feeding difficulties
in the first two months of life may indicate that this is a very
deep-seated and innate part of her being. On the other hand
we have no information about the details of her feeding history at that time, and a perfectly valid reason for feeding
difficulties may have existed. The fact that evidences of instability are marked in one environment, but fade almost
completely under a more suitable environment, tends to indicate that the personality deviations are not too serious in
character.

§ 77. Dinah D.
*Pseudo-defective Behavior in Infancy. Normal Development
in New Foster Home
(40 weeks—2 years)*

Dinah was an illegitimate child, born precipitately at full
term; her birth weight was 6 pounds. She required resuscita-
tion immediately after birth, but her subsequent neonatal
course was uneventful. She was moved from the hospital to
institution A, but at 10 weeks "feeding difficulties" required
hospital care again for a week. At 13 weeks of age she was
placed in foster home B; at 1 year in foster home C.

The mother was 24 years old at the time of Dinah's birth.
She had completed two years of high school, had some busi-
ness-school training, and had worked irregularly as a typist.
There was some evidence of instability in the mother's family;

a brother was "no good," her mother deserted her family, her grandfather was a rigid, fanatical person. The investigating agency considered the mother promiscuous, impractical, and unreliable, but in spite of her family's condemnation she refused to give up her child and finally established a home for her. The baby's father was also in his early twenties; he had an equivalent amount of high-school education and had a good work record as a clerk.

Dinah was first seen when she was 40 weeks old, after six months in foster home B. She was an attractive infant, alert and friendly, and normal in appearance except for an inconstant internal strabismus of the right eye. Her behavior showed considerable scattering; motor behavior 32 weeks, language behavior 36 weeks, prehensory, adaptive, and personal-social behavior 20 weeks. The foster mother described frequent sudden outbursts of temper for no apparent reason, "she will cry and scream for over an hour; nothing will stop her until she stops herself." The clinical impression was that Dinah was defective, though the relatively normal language development was admittedly a warning signal that further study was needed to establish her status more definitely.

At 2 years of age Dinah was seen again. She had been in foster home C for a full year. She gave an entirely normal performance at the 2-year level, even though her adjustment to the examination was endangered by her foster mother's failure to accompany her to the Clinic. No problems of any kind were reported, though Dinah was described as "sensitive."

The social worker reported that Dinah began to "unfold and blossom" as soon as she was removed from foster home B and placed in foster home C. One is tempted to look into foster home B. By the time this brief analysis was made we had had some further experience with this home. We have now studied 3 infants from this home (Dinah was the second), all of whom showed various degrees of retardation and behavior deviation, all of whom were tremendously improved after placement elsewhere. While this is not proof of any malfeasance, it is a serious indictment against the home as a foster home. Other factors, if they exist, have not been eliminated; there is a fairly plausible history that might lead one to suspect a mild birth injury, for example, with compensatory changes with increasing age. Because Dinah's response to change in placement was so prompt and com- plete, however, one is inclined to regard it virtually as proof of a therapeutic test.

§ 78. George V.
Moderate Retardation Associated with Repeated Placements
(28 weeks—30 months)

George was the illegitimate son of a Polish girl in her early twenties. The mother was also illegitimate. She finished the primary grades and was employed as a houseworker. Noth- ing was known of the father. George's birth and neonatal history are entirely normal. He lived in institution A with his mother from 10 days to 5 months of age, in foster home B for 1 week, in foster home C for 3 weeks, in institution D from 6-9 months, in foster home E from 9-20 months, and then in foster home F.

TABLE XXXII

SUMMARY OF DEVELOPMENTAL COURSE

Exam.	Age	D.L.	D.Q.	Approximate rating
1	28 wks.	28 wks.	100	Average
2	40 wks.	36 wks.	90	Low average
3	52 wks.	44 wks.	85	Dull-normal—low average
4	15 mos.	52–56 wks.	80–85	Dull-normal
5	21 mos.	15 mos.	70	Borderline-dull
6	30 mos.	27 mos.	90	Low average

Discussion:

The course of development is of interest in view of the downward trend, now reverting toward the original normal status in spite of repeated placements, none of them ideal.

Some of these changes in placement were unavoidable, others cannot be so readily excused. A great many of the advantages of foster-home care are lost under such circumstances. In children who are at all sensitive, normal development is affected to a greater or less extent by feelings of insecurity, which often manifest themselves in over-dependence on the foster mother.

His first examination was made at 28 weeks, shortly after his placement in foster home C. His development was normal for his age and he was considered to be emotionally well constituted. His next three examinations showed a steady downward trend, until at 15 months he was in the dull-normal zone (I.Q. 80-85). He also showed signs of emotional dependence on the foster mother, while she seemed to enjoy and to foster this attitude. His poorest showing was on his fifth examination, made, however, only 1 month after the change from foster home E to foster home F. He was timid and dependent, and his performance, taken at its face value, would indicate a retardation to the borderline zone.

Re-examination at 30 months showed a return to the low average level. If foster home F were superior in any way to foster home E it would be easy to ascribe the improvement to this superiority. It was, however, certainly no better. He was still very dependent; a description of the foster mother's tactics when she was permitted to use her own judgment in bringing about an adjustment to the examination illustrates her methods of management fairly graphically:

He is carried into the room; his face puckers and he cries. The foster mother hugs him and he stops. She then places him in the chair before the table and he immediately cries again. She says, "Let him cry a few minutes, he'll stop." Wipes his eyes roughly, holds handkerchief forcibly over his mouth, saying "No-no! Now stop it! The man will come after you. Do you want to go bye-bye? See the kitty. Do you want candy? Then stop crying—the lady will scold you!"

At this point the examiner intervened. He finally responded

well to praise and reassurance and made a good positive adjustment. His performance was well within the normal range.

It would seem that this boy is essentially stable (our impression throughout), but that during a certain phase in his development he was more susceptible to depressing or retarding factors than when either younger or older. Now perhaps he is making his own adjustment to the difficulties that beset him, and development is progressing normally in spite of those factors. It is a good adjustment, made from within, without correction of the environmental influences.

Under these conditions, we might postulate, a more stable child might not have shown any developmental fluctuations; a less stable child, however, might have shown more apparent retardation and would probably not recover until his circumstances were very much more favorable.

§ 79. Martha F.
Normal Development in Spite of Poor Environmental Conditions
(53 months—6 years 4 months)

Martha F., colored, referred at 53 months, for examination to aid in making plans for placement. Re-examined at 6 years 4 months, prior to court hearing for commitment to the County Home.

Family history:

The family home was located in a tenement block with a bad reputation from a social and moral standpoint. The father, a general laborer, had been working with the same company for many years. He was reported as a steady workman, but "of simple mind." It is reported that he was at one time in a state hospital for mental disorders, but this could not be confirmed.

The mother "gives a general impression of being of subnormal intelligence." For ten or twelve years the courts, the Board of Charities, and the Humane Society, have had constant reports of her neglect of her children, her drunkenness, and her immorality.

Martha is the seventh of eight children, the oldest being 25 years old when Martha was first seen, and the youngest being 2½ years younger than herself. Several of the children have been examined at the Clinic, prior to or during commitment to state care. All have earned dull-normal ratings, with intelligence quotients between 80 and 90.

Social and personal history:

Early development. Dentition at 1 year; sat up alone at 5 months; walked at 14 months; used single words at 11 months. Toilet habits are reported to have been irregular. Because of extreme neglect, the child was removed from the home two days before our first examination; at this time the mother was sentenced to jail for six months for neglect of her children.

Examination I—age 4 years, 5 months. A cheerful, responsive child, spontaneously conversational and quite coöperative. Some difficulty was experienced in following her conversation because of faulty enunciation, but comprehension and use of language appeared to be fully up to average. Attention and persistence were weak on tests which she considered hard for herself, but she responded well to encouragement. Her rating in terms of the developmental schedules was between 4 and 4½ years, her best performances being her copying of a square, counting four pennies, and drawing a recognizable "man." Motor control appeared generally good. The general quality of her performance was taken to indicate probably average intelligence.

Examination II—age 6 years 4 months. Stanford mental age score 5 years 10 months, range from V through VII, intelligence quotient 92. Following her first examination,

Martha was placed in what is considered to be an excellent colored foster home with two of her siblings. She had made good adjustment both at home and at school. The relation-ships between the children in the home, and between the children and the foster mother, are reported as particularly good. In the psychometric examination she was again coöper-ative and friendly, with a great deal of spontaneous conversa-tion. There was no trace of the earlier speech difficulty. Drawing was again of good average quality. There was no irregularity or inconsistency in her examination record; only one test (giving differences) was passed at 7 years, while all the 5-year tests were passed.

The history of extreme neglect in the child's own home, where she had lived up to two days previous to the first examination, might reasonably have been taken as casting doubt upon the representativeness of her performance·at that time. The defective speech likewise might have been thought of as possibly lowering her score. In addition to this, her use and comprehension of language has given an impression of brightness beyond what she has actually shown in her general development. Yet, if her performance at 6 years 4 months is taken as a criterion, her psychometric record at 53 months was fully representative of her basic ability. She was, of course, unusually coöperative and responsive, with good at-tention control for her age; and she showed good ability to overcome her timidity in the face of difficult tasks. The basic stability of temperament that allowed these traits to emerge so conspicuously despite unfavorable environmental condi-tions, has also prevented the intellectual development from being adversely affected.

§ 80. Gerald F.
Series of Traumatic Events; Normal Developmental Progress
(48 weeks—24 months)

Gerald was the illegitimate son of a Polish girl in her late twenties. His birth and neonatal history are normal. The mother finished the eighth grade, had a good record as a domestic, and was considered by the agency caring for her child to be of normal intelligence. One of her brothers was in an institution for the feeble-minded. Nothing was known of the child's father.

Gerald lived with his mother in her employer's home from 2 weeks of age until he was 4 months old, when he was placed in foster home A. His first examination took place at the age of 48 weeks, seven months after placement. He was very shy and his adjustment to the examination was only fair. His developmental level was approximately 40-44 weeks, but it was felt that his performance probably did not fully represent his true ability.

When Gerald was 13 months old his foster father suddenly died. To relieve the foster mother during the trying period of her husband's funeral, Gerald was sent to the hospital to be circumcised. He returned to the home after 2 weeks, ill with whooping cough. The foster mother was greatly disturbed by her husband's death and by Gerald's illness, and by her own account held the baby on her lap for hours each day, rocking and weeping; he would appear greatly distressed, pat her cheek and plead, "No-no " These emotional scenes were continuing unabated when Gerald appeared for his second examination at 15 months. He was only mildly inhibited and gave a normal performance for his age. Because the foster mother was so dependent on the child for emotional satisfaction, a change in placement was advised. It was then discovered that the foster mother herself had a serious heart condition, and the doctor feared that Gerald's removal might have fatal consequences. A woman came into the home to help care for Gerald, until the foster mother died six months later. He was then, at 21 months of age, moved to foster home B, where a healthy atmosphere prevailed.

His third examination took place at 24 months, just three months after placement in his new home. He made a mature adjustment to the examination and his development was slightly above the average.

Discussion:

Gerald's career has had its dramatic and tragic episodes, and the series of events which culminated in his change of homes might well be expected to have left their mark. Development has, however, proceeded normally and there is remarkably little evidence at present of any serious effects. Personality traits and emotional responses seem normal and wholesome. What, then, is the difference between this child who suffered so much with such fortitude, and another child whose development is seriously distorted by a few months of institution life or by a period in an unsympathetic foster home? Improper as we felt his first foster home to be, Gerald certainly did not lack love and affection. It was overdone, it was sentimental, possessive, pernicious, and dangerous, but perhaps it was also good in that it enabled him to develop feelings of security strong enough to withstand the successive blows which followed.

§ *81. Christine E.*
Improvement in Development with Improvement in
Placement. Adoption
(24 weeks—42 months)

Christine was the illegitimate child of an Italian mother and a Jewish father. The baby was placed in institution A, where she remained to the age of 17 months; she was then placed in foster home B; at 29 months she was placed in adoptive-home C.

Her career can be briefly told. As she progressed from less favorable to more favorable environments she improved in her showing on examination in almost exact proportion, and so promptly as to make the relationship most convincing.

Three examinations were made during her institutional period; on each occasion she was considered dull-normal. After six months of foster home experience, she earned a dull-

TABLE XXXIII

Christine E.

Placement	Examination	Age	Developmental level	Classification	Comment
Institution A	1	24 wks.	20 wks.	Dull-normal	Prominent hand regard and finger-sucking
	2	35 wks.	30-33 wks.	Dull-normal—Low average	Hand regard, shuddering, rocking—scattering
	3	18 mos.	13-15 mos.	Dull-normal	Inferior performance
Foster home B	4	24 mos.	21 mos.	Dull-normal—Low average	Active—animated—chatterbox
	5	28 mos.	24 mos.+	Low average	Eager and talkative
Adoptive home C	6	36 mos.	36 mos.	Average	Attractive—friendly
	7	42 mos.	42 mos.+	High average	Placement seems ideal

normal to low average rating. Four months later a low average development was indicated. Placement in adoption in a simple home without exacting academic requirements and with a full year's probation period was recommended.

At 3 years 7 months after she had entered her adoptive home her development was clearly average. At 42 months her performance was slightly above her age level. Christine has progressed step by step from a dull normal to a high average rating. Her adoptive placement seems ideal.

CHAPTER VI

THE INDIVIDUALITY OF GROWTH CAREERS

LIFE and growth are almost interchangeable terms. Growth is a fundamental function of life, common to plants, animals, infants, children. When thought of in its most general aspects, growth is a chemical phenomenon, a method of assimilating and retransforming energy. When thought of in its individual, human, and psychic manifestations, growth (while still remaining chemical!) is a highly distinctive phenomenon bound up with personality itself. No two children grow up in precisely the same way. Even very "identical" twins may be just different enough (and alike enough) to make excellent exceptions for proving the rule. The rule is: Every mental growth career has its own individuality.

The individual differences in growth characteristics considered in the foregoing chapters are due to differences (a) in original capacity to grow, (b) in general rate or tempo of growth, (c) in patterns of developmental organization. In this volume we were not directly concerned with the average child or the usual child, but largely with children who are exceptional in various ways. In attempting to interpret why a child failed to follow the usual course of development, or why he presented unusual patterns of organization, we repeatedly referred to basic personality factors. The defect in such interpretation is the lack of specific knowledge about these factors. Lack of knowledge does not, however, imply lack of importance or validity. Careful study of the case reports suggests that a recognition of basic personality factors increases our understanding of a child career. Conversely a study of the developmental progress of a child furthers under-

303

standing of his personality. Every child has distinctive patterns and modes of growth, which are the most fundamental
and complete expression of his constitutional characteristics.
Objective study of development in terms of process as well
as the products of growth constitutes a sound approach to
the elusive problem of personality.

Personality may be regarded as a pervasive superpattern
which expresses the unity and the behavioral characteristicness of the individual. Personality has also been defined as
"the dynamic organization within the individual of those
psycho-physical systems that determine his unique adjustments to the environment." When Allport elaborates the
doctrine of functional autonomy, he states that "the course
of individuality is one of greater and greater divergence
from the relatively standard pattern of infancy."

Our data do not lend support to the concept of a relatively
standard pattern of infancy. Nor are the findings of embryology in harmony with such a concept. From the standpoint
of embryology the infant is already far advanced in the cycle
of life. He is already stamped with individuality rather than
with a standard pattern. As an organism he already has
biochemical idiosyncrasies and constellations, methods of respiration, of food intake and food utilization, of postural
tensions, of sleep, of neuro-glandular regulation which constitute his "essence," which *are* his constitutional characteristicness to date, and also tomorrow. For the morrow is inevitably
influenced by the already realized constitutional makeup. This
perpetuation of characteristicness is not incompatible with
morphogenesis and maturing. It is, however, inconsistent
with the idea that individual differences at birth are slight
and increase with age, or that the period of infancy is in any
sense neutral or generic when compared with later periods of
the life cycle. Infants are individuals, almost infinitely removed from a zero point of homogeneity. They differ as
adults differ, and if we had an adequate biometry we should

probably find that in a mathematical sense they differ as greatly and diversely as do adults.

It is sometimes said that infancy is a period of instability subject to wide fluctuations, and that the child finally settles down to a normal course of development in response to environment and education. Such statements are true only in a partial and often misleading sense. The organism always fluctuates; the swings may narrow with age (in some functions), but the modes of fluctuations, the methods of making adjustments, are highly idiosyncratic—i.e., individual. They are likely to persist as part of the characteristicness which we call individuality. They come into evidence when an infant is placed upon a rigid feeding schedule. They come into even clearer evidence when the infant is permitted self-regulation by self-demand schedules of feeding and sleep as shown in day-by-day behavior charts which graph the distribution of hunger, feeding, sleep, and waking behavior.[1] Such characteristic methods of self-regulation set limits to the modifiability of the organism. They determine the limits of growth and to some extent the very profiles of growth. They insure a certain stability to the organism as well. Mental growth is both labile and stabile but nature sets metes and bounds to the lability, and a constitutional core of characteristicness determines the way in which the individual will meet new situations and incorporate them. Throughout life the manner in which the child profits by experience is influenced by inherent factors. It is impossible to resolve completely the antithesis of nature and nurture. It is artificial to press unduly a distinction between intrinsic and extrinsic factors, but it must be emphasized that environment as such cannot impart growth. Environmental factors support, inflect, and modify, but do not generate the progressions of development.

[1] Gesell, Arnold, and Ilg, Frances L.: *Feeding Behavior of Infants, A Pediatric Approach to the Mental Hygiene of Early Life.* Phila., Lippincott, 1937, pp. ix + 201.

Biographic studies of twins and experimental studies by the method of co-twin control furnish significant illustrations of the stability of growth careers. The biographic sketches in the present volume point in the same direction. We may also cite in brief summary the results of an experimental study in prediction which concerns the individuality of growth ca- reers. We attempted in the most objective manner possible to determine whether the behavior and growth characteristics of the first year of life foreshadow those of the fifth year. The study was based upon an analysis of the cinema records of five different infants. The children were photographed under homelike conditions at lunar month intervals through- out the first year of life. These extensive cinema records em- braced the major events of the infant's day, namely sleeping, waking, bath, dressing and undressing, feeding, play, and social behavior at advancing age levels. Additional cinema records and psychological observations of the same children were made at the age of 5 years.

A trained and unbiased observer (L.B.A.) *who had never seen the infants,* made a detailed analysis of the cinema rec- ords covering the first year of life. On the basis of the objec- tive evidence of the films alone, an estimate of fifteen behavior traits was made and the children were arranged in rank order for each trait.

The same children were again studied at the age of 5 years, and were again rated with respect to the 15 behavior traits which they had displayed in infancy. The two appraisals were made independently.

Is the strength of a behavior trait in the first year of life predictive of a similar strength in the fifth year? The 15 traits of behavior individuality which were considered fol- low: 1. energy output; 2. motor demeanor; 3. self depend- ence; 4. social responsiveness; 5. family attachment; 6. communicativeness; 7. adaptivity; 8. exploitation of envi- ronment; 9. "humor" sense; 10. emotional maladjustment; 11. emotional expressiveness; 12. reaction to success; 13. reaction to restriction; 14. readiness of smiling; 15. readiness of crying.

For each child and for each trait at 1 year and again at 5 years a comparative judgment was made. Out of the 75 com-parative judgments, 48 rank assignments coincided; 21 showed a displacement to the extent of 1 rank order only; 5, a displacement of 2; and 1 a displacement of 3 orders.

Our periodic cinema records clearly show prophetic char-acteristics in the behavior traits displayed in the first year of life. We compared five personalities in the making. None of these personalities is finished; but each is already distinc-tive. One child is agile, another almost awkward; one is so-cially outgoing, another restrained; one is very perceptive of the feelings of others; one restlessly inquisitive, one self-con-tained; one is gay, another sober; one quick, another slow; one is given to lasting moods, another passes blithely from mood to mood. We have demonstrated (to our own satis-faction at least) a significant degree of internal consistency in the behavior features of these children at one year and at five years of age. This consistency seems to rest upon a bio-logical characteristicness which lies at the core of human individuality. Because of this characteristicness, the first year of life does indeed foreshadow the fifth year of life.

Perhaps there is such foreshadowing even in the early growth career of the artist. We turn to a juvenile chapter in the biography of Walt Disney. Now that he has been adorned with an honorary degree by Yale and Harvard, the sobriety of our concluding chapter will not be unduly dis-turbed by a reference to him. For that matter, there was a dash of the sober and solemn in a certain event which took place in his childhood, thirty years ago on a Missouri farm.

One sleepy afternoon an owl was drowsing on this farm. Seven-year-old Walt crept up on the owl and, boy-like, he encircled the owl's neck with his fingers. The owl instinc-tively fluttered his huge wings; instinctively little Walt was possessed of fear. He seized the owl, hurled it to the ground, stamped on it instinctively—and, perhaps unwittingly, killed it!

That experience has lingered with Walt Disney and, in a way, that owl has continued to flap its wings in the nether regions of his subconscious. It is tempting to attribute some of Disney's gift of fantasy to this dramatic experience of childhood, because this experience certainly helped to direct his special attention to birds and beasts and mice and men (owls being rather fond of mice!). There may be a deep and dark connection here, to which some would give great weight. But must one "explain" Walt Disney himself on the basis of this traumatic boyhood event? Rather, must we not assume that he had a sensitively attuned individuality which made him incorporate and transform this experience in a unique way—an individuality which doubtless had certain decisive growth characteristics even in infancy, long before the episode of the drowsing owl?

So utterly unforeseen are the vicissitudes of life that our common sense will deter us from attempting to forecast too precisely the developmental career even of a mediocre child. "However closely psychical changes may conform to law, it is safe to say that individual histories and biographies will never be written in advance."

In the intervening half-century since William James expressed this view, psychology has indeed become more evolved and more quantitative. It is steadily increasing the areas of prediction. The boundaries of certain areas of approximate and general predictability our biographies of child development have attempted to indicate.

With scientific progress the possibilities of developmental prediction will be enlarged. The social and medical demands for such prediction will inevitably intensify as part of an effort to bring the hygiene of early child development under improved control. Meanwhile we shall do no disservice to the child if we interpret him in terms of the processes of growth. The degree, the tempo, and the style of his mental growth denote his individuality.

We pay vastly too much attention to mere training and instruction. Our central task, particularly in the first five years of life, is to discover and to respect individuality. If we focus upon this difficult but fascinating problem of under'standing individuality, a new atmosphere will seep into home and school. There will be more tolerance, more kindness, and much more humor. More humor, because we cannot get a true estimate of ourselves or of others without that sense of proportion which is the sense of humor. More kindness, be'cause we shall appreciate the needs of individuality even in the very young. More tolerance, because we shall see many of the "faults" of children as symptoms of immaturity. For such reasons, growth is a key concept for a humane philos'ophy of infant care and of child guidance.

ADDENDUM

For the benefit of readers and students who are not familiar with the methods of diagnosis used in the developmental examination of infants and young children, reference
is here made to the basic manuals and source books.

The system of developmental diagnosis used in the early
examinations was first described in a volume entitled, *The
Mental Growth of the Preschool Child: A psychological outline of normal development from birth to the sixth year, including a system of developmental diagnosis* (Macmillan).
This volume was published in 1925 and is now out of print.
The system of diagnosis outlined, although it remains unchanged in principle, has undergone revisions and elabora-
tions which are described in later publications. The reader
may gain a concrete impression of the materials and procedures used by inspecting the numerous photographic illustrations which appear in the various publications. The
procedures are also illustrated in the *Yale Films of Child
Development* which are included in the subjoined bibliography.

The system of developmental diagnosis which we have
used is not directed toward the measurement of intelligence
as such but is an instrument for the analytic appraisal of
maturity in diverse fields of behavior as follows: a. Postural
behavior; b. Prehensory behavior; c. Perceptual behavior; d.
Adaptive behavior; e. Language and social behavior. In an
earlier version, the categories Motor behavior and Personal-
social behavior were also used.

The examination procedures are designed to elicit characteristic behavior in all of these fields, so that the examiner
may in the end be in a position to specify the maturity in

310

individual fields of behavior as well as the general level of maturity. The category called *Adaptive behavior* corresponds most closely to intelligence in its conventional sense. In developmental diagnosis, however, pains are taken not to identify intelligence too uncritically with other forms of ability.

The examination devices and materials which are used in the conduct of a developmental examination are relatively simple. They consist of a clinical crib which is adjustable and permits us to observe the child in supine, prone, standing or sitting positions. As early as the age of 16 weeks the child is placed for a brief period of observation in a specially adapted Morris chair. Test objects like cubes, bell, ring and string, pellet, formboard, paper and crayon, etc. are presented. The patterns of behavior which the child displays in these standardized situations are appraised on the basis of normative criteria which have been tabulated in detail. These criteria are based on systematic cinema studies and stenographically recorded observations of a large number of normal children.

The basic publications are listed below in chronological order:

1925. *The mental growth of the preschool child. A psychological outline of normal development from birth to the sixth year, including a system of developmental diagnosis.* (Gesell, A.) N. Y., Macmillan, pp. 447.
This book discusses norms of development, comparative studies of ten levels of development including the fetal and neonatal levels, principles of developmental diagnosis and supervision.

1929. *Infancy and human growth.* (Gesell, A.) N. Y., Macmillan, pp. xvii + 418.
Outlines monthly increments of development in infancy, and an infant development recording schedule for sixteen age levels. Assembles genetic studies of infant behavior which illustrate developmental trends, defects and deviations.

1930. *The guidance of mental growth in infant and child.* (Gesell, A.) N. Y., Macmillan, pp. xi + 322.
Part I: Progress of guidance concepts. Part II: Problems and methods of child guidance. Part III: Science and the protection of child growth. Special chapters on the early recognition of developmental defects and on infant adoption.

1934. *Infant behavior: Its genesis and growth.* (Gesell, A., Thompson, H., Amatruda, C. S.) N. Y., McGraw-Hill, pp. viii + 333.

A detailed account of the normative characteristics of infant behavior based upon a study of 107 infants examined at lunar month intervals from 4 through 56 weeks. Summarizing accounts of behavior trends and sequences in various behavior fields and situations.

1934. *An Atlas of infant behavior: a systematic delineation of the forms and early growth of human behavior patterns,* illustrated by 3,200 action photographs, in two volumes. (Gesell, A. et al.) New Haven, Yale Univ. Press, pp. 922.

The action photographs and associated text serve as normative standards of reference for diagnostic purposes and for the study of genetic sequences.

1937. *Feeding behavior of infants. A pediatric approach to the mental hygiene of early life.* (Gesell, A., Ilg, F. L.) Phila., Lippincott, pp. ix + 201.

The psychological aspects of feeding behavior and methods of regulation from a psychological standpoint. An outline of the developmental neurology of feeding behavior patterns.

1938. *The psychology of early growth including norms of infant behavior and a method of genetic analysis.* (Gesell, A., Thompson, H., Amatruda, C. S.) N. Y., Macmillan, pp. ix + 290.

Tabulates in lunar month intervals the incidence and frequencies of 1108 behavior items in 25 behavior situations. A definitive summary of methods and procedures used in the normative investigation with detailed instructions for the analytic appraisal of growth status.

The Yale Films of Child Development. A series of twelve sound films published and distributed by Erpi Classroom Films, Inc., Long Island City, N. Y.

These films depict the course of normal mental growth both in normative and naturalistic situations. The films entitled: *The Study of Infant Behavior,* and *Behavior Patterns at One Year* delineate the methods used in developmental examination.

INDEX

Explanatory Note. Names of persons and titles of books in this index are set in SMALL CAPITALS. *Illustrations, growth graphs,* and *tables* are separately listed under the above headings.

A

Imagination, 61

Imaginative: drawings, 122
 play, 124, 261

Imbeciles, 263

Immaturity, 211-223, 255
 of attention control, 183
 confused with prematurity, 221-223
 faults as symptoms of, 309
 importance of age in, 216
 of personality. See Personality, immature.

Inconsistency: of behavior, 46
 of results, normative examinations, 151

Individual: differences, 74, 304
 in growth characteristics, 303
 studies of behavior growth, 113-302
 in twins. See Twins, individual differences in.

Individuality, 21, 25, 303-309. See also Personality.
 of growth careers, 306
 needs of, 309
 respect for, 276, 309
 traits, 106
 understanding of, 309

Infancy: atypical behavior in, 192-195
 pattern of, not standard, 304

INFANCY AND HUMAN GROWTH, 8, 41, 47, 73, 86, 228, 311

Infant: development
 fluctuations in. See Development, irregular.
 immature, 213. See also Immaturity.
 mature, 213
 newborn, maturity of, 213
 normal, 246. See also Development, normal; Normal children.
 normative. See Normative infant.
 premature, 213. See also Prematurity.

INFANT BEHAVIOR: ITS GENESIS AND GROWTH, 312

Injury: birth. See Birth injury.
 cerebral. See Cerebral injury.
 reaction to, 243

Insecurity: feelings of, 276, 295
 felt by institution child, 276

Insight, 125

Instability, 154, 188, 192, 291, 292
 emotional. See Emotional instability.

Institution, child caring, 204, 207, 218, 219, 235, 283, 284. See also Institutional background.

Institutional, background, 179, 181, 186-188, 189, 193, 194, 200, 204, 207, 280, 294, 300
 care, 277
 child, insecurity felt by, 176
 environment, 238, 277
 experience, 286-289
 life, effects of, 176, 268, 300

Insurance factors, 67, 106, 107

Integration: of function
 delayed, 174
 processes of, 175
 slowness of, 175

Intelligence. See also Development.
 average, 195-200
  low, 19
 fluctuating, 43, 44. See also Development, irregular.
 gain in. See Intelligence quotient, gain in.
 of grandparents, 286, 287
 of mother. See Mother, intelligence of.
 normal, 78, 198
 quotient, gain in, 47-49, 51, 114-125, 179, 181-183, 185, 189, 193-200, 203-207, 235, 236, 251-252, 288, 300-302.
 superior. See Development, superior.
 variation in. See Variation in I.Q.

Interpretation: of examinations, need for caution, 177, 182

IRENE R., 114, 125, 126

Irregular development. See Development, irregular.

Irregularities: See also Development, irregular.
 in early mental development, 171-208
 of performance. See Performance, irregularity of.

Paul B. Höeber, Inc., 49 East 33rd St., New York, N. Y.
Medical Book Department of Harper & Brothers

$\mathcal{C}$lassics In

$\mathcal{C}$hild $\mathcal{D}$evelopment

An Arno Press Collection

Baldwin, James Mark. **Thought and Things.** Four vols. in two. 1906-1915

Blatz, W[illiam] E[met], et al. **Collected Studies on the Dionne Quintuplets.** 1937

Bühler, Charlotte. **The First Year of Life.** 1930

Bühler, Karl. **The Mental Development of the Child.** 1930

Claparède, Ed[ouard]. **Experimental Pedagogy and the Psychology of the Child.** 1911

Factors Determining Intellectual Attainment. 1975

First Notes by Observant Parents. 1975

Freud, Anna. **Introduction to the Technic of Child Analysis.** 1928

Gesell, Arnold, et al. **Biographies of Child Development.** 1939

Goodenough, Florence L. **Measurement of Intelligence By Drawings.** 1926

Griffiths, Ruth. **A Study of Imagination in Early Childhood and Its Function in Mental Development.** 1918

Hall, G. Stanley and Some of His Pupils. **Aspects of Child Life and Education.** 1907

Hartshorne, Hugh and Mark May. **Studies in the Nature of Character. Vol. I: Studies in Deceit; Book One, General Methods and Results.** 1928

Hogan, Louise E. **A Study of a Child.** 1898

Hollingworth, Leta S. **Children Above 180 IQ, Stanford Binet:** Origins and Development. 1942

Kluver, Heinrich. **An Experimental Study of the Eidetic Type.** 1926

Lamson, Mary Swift. **Life and Education of Laura Dewey Bridgman, the Deaf, Dumb and Blind Girl.** 1881

Lewis, M[orris] M[ichael]. **Infant Speech:** A Study of the Beginnings of Language. 1936

McGraw, Myrtle B. **Growth: A Study of Johnny and Jimmy.** 1935

Monographs on Infancy. 1975

O'Shea, M. V., editor. **The Child: His Nature and His Needs.** 1925

Perez, Bernard. **The First Three Years of Childhood.** 1888

Romanes, George John. **Mental Evolution in Man:** Origin of Human Faculty. 1889

Shinn, Milicent Washburn. **The Biography of a Baby.** 1900

Stern, William. **Psychology of Early Childhood Up to the Sixth Year of Age.** 1924

Studies of Play. 1975

Terman, Lewis M. **Genius and Stupidity:** A Study of Some of the Intellectual Processes of Seven "Bright" and Seven "Stupid" Boys. 1906

Terman, Lewis M. **The Measurement of Intelligence.** 1916

Thorndike, Edward Lee. **Notes on Child Study.** 1901

Wilson, Louis N., compiler. **Bibliography of Child Study.** 1898-1912

[Witte, Karl Heinrich Gottfried]. **The Education of Karl Witte,** Or the Training of the Child. 1914